阿拉伯国家研究省部共建协同创新中心

MYSTERIOUS ARAB COUNTRIES
神秘的阿拉伯

姜克银 季春燕 编

时事出版社
北京

前　言

　　本书包括十三个单元，内容涉及阿拉伯社会的不同方面。

　　第一单元主要介绍沙特阿拉伯的历史。作为古代著名的贸易中心，沙特阿拉伯的历史最早可追溯到两万年前人类刚刚定居阿拉伯半岛的时候，其历史充分展现了这个民族的灵魂。

　　第二单元主要介绍阿拉伯的地理。阿拉伯半岛的地貌非常多样化，沙漠、山脉、平原、湖泊共存，尤其值得关注的是其较匮乏的水资源和丰富的石油储藏。

　　第三单元主要介绍在阿拉伯世界最为常见的三种媒体形式：报纸、电视和互联网。它们的发展历史、产生基础以及特有价值观能帮助读者更好地了解媒体对于阿拉伯世界所产生的影响。

　　第四单元主要介绍2010年到2012年间每况愈下的埃及经济。虽然发达的旅游业为埃及经济的发展做出巨大的贡献，但是2011年1月和2月爆发的革命将埃及经济推入深渊。

　　第五单元主要介绍埃及现有的教育体制以及政府在推进教育改革方面付出的努力。

　　第六单元主要介绍旅游胜地迪拜。快速发展中的迪拜以其大胆而创新的建筑吸引着全世界的关注，游客们纷至沓来，只为欣赏迪拜那新潮并奢华的美景。

　　第七单元介绍阿拉伯国家的舞蹈。在阿拉伯国家多种多样的舞蹈形式中，肚皮舞因其特有的魅力而在全世界范围内广为流行。

　　第八单元主要介绍阿拉伯音乐。书中对阿拉伯音乐基础知识做了简要的介绍。

　　第九单元主要介绍阿拉伯国家悠久而灿烂的服饰文化，包括早期的服饰材料、衣物制作、衣着风尚等。

　　第十单元主要介绍阿拉伯国家的烹饪。阿拉伯国家保持着大家庭成员之间分享食物的习惯。因此，阿拉伯半岛的烹调中凝聚着阿拉伯人民的热情和慷慨。

  第十一单元主要介绍埃及的婚礼习俗。在古埃及，婚姻既是一种法律关系，也是一种宗教约束。夫妇双方都有着自己要承担的义务和责任。然而，现代埃及的婚礼在传承传统的基础上又有其自身独有的特点。

  第十二单元主要介绍巴解组织的领导人——阿拉法特。他用毕生的精力来实现建立独立的巴勒斯坦的梦想，但最终未能实现。因此，关于阿拉法特是"恐怖分子"还是革命者，仍存在争议。

  第十三单元主要介绍具有代表性的女作家——格拉迪斯·马塔尔。幼年的生长环境培养了她的艺术和文学才能。格拉迪斯·马塔尔作品中的史诗风格和讽刺手法深受广大文学爱好者的喜爱。

  这本书表面看起来是一项英文文献的编纂工作，但是真正坐下来细细品读后会发现，其内容涉及历史、地理、媒体、经济、教育、婚俗、舞蹈、音乐、服饰、烹饪等多方面。书中有些内容需要从宏观上把握，有些需要从微观上设计，驾驭的难度较大，加之目前国内此类研究成果比较少，可供参考的书目也不多，书中难免出现不足之处，欢迎学界同仁及广大读者批评指正。

姜克银
2019 年 3 月 29 日

Contents

Unit 1	History of Saudi Arabia	(1)
Unit 2	Arabia Geography	(18)
Unit 3	Media in Arab World	(35)
Unit 4	Economic Crisis in Egypt	(55)
Unit 5	Education in Egypt	(71)
Unit 6	Travel in Dubai	(90)
Unit 7	Belly Dance	(108)
Unit 8	Arabia Music	(125)
Unit 9	Egyptian Clothing	(141)
Unit 10	Cuisine in Arabia	(158)
Unit 11	Arabia Marriage	(175)
Unit 12	Yasser Arafat	(190)
Unit 13	Women Writers in Arabia	(208)
Appendix I		(223)
Appendix II		(254)
Appendix III		(265)

Unit 1
History of Saudi Arabia

Warm-Up Questions

1. Which Arab country do you like to go to travel or study or live in? Do you know anything about its history?
2. What do you know about the history of Saudi Arabia?
3. Do you know the location of the Kingdom Center? What do you know about its history?

Text

History is the soul of a nation, to know something about a nation, know its history first. The history of Saudi Arabia, the largest country in the Middle East in terms of area, an ancient trade center, as a state, begins with its foundation in 1932 by Abdul Aziz al-Saud, although the history of what was to become Saudi Arabia goes back to the beginnings of human habitation in Arabia up to 20,000 years ago.

Brief History of Saudi Arabia[①]

Saudi Arabia traces its roots back to the earliest civilizations of the Arabian Peninsula. Over the centuries, the peninsula has played an important role in history as an ancient trade center.

Since King Abdul Aziz al-Saud established the modern Kingdom of Saudi Arabia in 1932, its transformation has been astonishing. In a few short decades, the Kingdom has turned itself from a desert nation to a modern, sophisticated state and a major player on the international stage.

Early History

The first concrete evidence of human presence in the Arabian Peninsula dates back 15,000 to 20,000 years. Bands of hunter-gatherers roamed the land, living off wild animals and plants.

As the European ice cap melted during the last Ice Age, some 15,000 years ago, the climate in the peninsula became dry. Vast plains once covered with lush grasslands gave way to scrubland and deserts, and wild animals vanished. River systems also disappeared. This climate change forced humans to move into the lush mountain valleys and oases. No longer able to survive as hunter-gatherers, they had to develop another means of survival. As a result, agriculture developed—first in Mesopotamia, then the Nile River Valley and eventually spreading across the Middle East.

The development of agriculture brought other advances. Pottery allowed farmers to store food. Animals, including goats, cattle, sheep, horses and camels, were domesticated, and people abandoned hunting altogether. These advances made intensive farming possible. In turn, settlements became more permanent, leading to the foundations of what we call civilization-language, writing, political systems, art and architecture.

---

① http://www.saudiembassy.net/about/country-information/history/.

Unit 1 History of Saudi Arabia

An Ancient Trade Center

Located between the two great centers of civilization, the Nile River Valley and Mesopotamia, the Arabian Peninsula was the crossroads of the ancient world. Trade was crucial to the area's development. Caravan routes became trade arteries that made life possible in the sparsely populated peninsula. The people of the peninsula developed a complex network of trade routes to transport agricultural goods highly sought after in Mesopotamia, the Nile Valley and the Mediterranean Basin. These items included almonds from Taif, dates from the oases, and aromatics such as frankincense and myrrh from the Tihama plain.

Spices were also important trade items. They were shipped across the Arabian Sea from India and then transported by caravan. The huge caravans traveled from what is now Oman and Yemen, along the great trade routes running through Saudi Arabia's Asir Province and then through Makkah and Madinah, eventually arriving at the urban centers of the north and west.

The people of the Arabian Peninsula remained largely untouched by the political turmoil in Mesopotamia, the Nile Valley and the eastern Mediterranean. Their goods and services were in great demand regardless of which power was dominant at that moment—Babylon, Egypt, Persia, Greece or Rome. In addition, the peninsula's great expanse of desert formed a natural barrier that protected it from invasion by powerful neighbors.

The First Saudi State

In the early 18th century, Shaikh Muhammad bin Abdul Wahhab, a scholar and reformer who believes in Islam, began advocating a return to the original form of Islam. Abdul Wahhab was initially persecuted by local religious scholars and leaders who viewed his teachings as a threat to their power bases. He sought protection in the town of Diriyah, which was ruled by Muhammad bin Saud.

Muhammad bin Abdul Wahhab and Muhammad bin Saud formed an agreement to dedicate themselves to restoring the pure teachings of Islam to the Muslim community. In that spirit, bin Saud established the First Saudi State, which prospered under the spiritual guidance of bin Abdul Wahhab, known simply as the Sheikh.

By 1788, the Saudi State ruled over the entire central plateau known as the Najd. By the early 19th century, its rule extended to most of the Arabian Peninsula, including Makkah and Madinah. The popularity and success of the Al-Saud rulers aroused the suspicion of the Ottoman Empire, the dominant power in the Middle East and North Africa at the time. In 1818, the Ottomans dispatched a large expeditionary force armed with modern artillery to the western region of Arabia. The Ottoman army besieged Diriyah, which by now had grown into one of the largest cities in the peninsula. Ottoman forces leveled the city with field guns and made it permanently uninhabitable by ruining the wells and uprooting date palms.

Modern Kingdom of Saudi Arabia and Its Economy

The young Abdul-Aziz was determined to regain his patrimony from the Al-Rashid family, which had taken over Riyadh and established a governor and garrison there. In 1902, Abdul-Aziz, — accompanied by only 40 followers — staged a daring night march into Riyadh to retake the city garrison known as the Masmak Fortress. This legendary event marks the beginning of the formation of the modern Saudi state. After establishing Riyadh as his headquarters, Abdul-Aziz captured all of the Hijaz, including Makkah and Madinah, in 1924 to 1925. In the process, he united warring tribes into one nation.

On September 23, 1932, the country was named as the Kingdom of Saudi Arabia, an Islamic state with Arabic as its national language and the Holy *Qur'an* as its constitution.

When the modern Kingdom was established, the Arabian Peninsula was an agricultural society depending on farming and commerce-especially date exports and tradegenerated by pilgrims coming to Makkah and Madinah. The discovery of oil in commercial quantities in 1938 changed that. Soon after World War II, steady oil exports provided the funds to build a basic infrastructure of roads, airports, seaports, schools and hospitals. While the economy largely depended on oil revenues, Saudi leaders resolved to bring about basic improvements in the country's economic structure with the objective to diversify the economy away from oil into other fields.

Achievement of such an economic transformation required deliberate planning and careful implementation of a development program with clearly defined objectives. The quest for economic development and growth began in earnest with the introduction of the First Development Plan in 1970 by MOEP, Ministry of Economy and Planning in Saudi Arabia. This triggered a series of ongoing five-year development plans to build a modern economy capable of producing consumer and industrial goods that previously had been imported. The first phase of this process was to establish an infrastructure that could support a modern economic base and allow industry and commerce to flourish. The next was to develop the human resources necessary to help bring about the planned economic transformation. Finally, the focus could shift to economic diversification, including expansion of the industrial, agricultural and other sectors, an expansion that is now well advanced.

The establishment of the physical infrastructure was accomplished in stages during the first three development plans. As the infrastructure was taking shape, the government launched a major effort to expand the industrial base. This was done along two separate, but parallel, courses. One aimed at the expansion of the country's oil industry and the other at establishing a modern non-oil industrial sector. In addition to optimizing revenues from Saudi oil production, the modern oil industry plays an equally important role in the development of the non-oil industrial sector by providing the raw materials and feedstock that facilitate the growth.

Throughout the course of the development plans, Saudi Arabia's steady but dramatic industrial and economic transformation has been accomplished through the careful guidance and active support of the government. Today, Saudi Arabia is one of the fastest developing countries in the world.

New Words

trace [treɪs] v. to go back over again 追溯（由来）；上溯；回溯
monotheistic [ˌmɔnəuθɪˈɪstɪk] adj. believing that there is only one god 一神论的
sophisticated [səˈfɪstɪkeɪtɪd] adj. ahead in development; complex or intricate

老练的；精密的；世故的

concrete ['kɔːŋkriːt] adj. capable of being perceived by the senses; not abstract or imaginary 实在的；具体的

roam [rəum] v. walk about without any fixed plan or purpose 漫游；闲逛；徜徉

lush [lʌʃ] adj. produced or growing in extreme abundance 繁茂的；茂盛的；丰富的

scrubland ['skrʌblənd] n. an uncultivated region covered with scrub vegetation 灌木丛林地

vanish ['vænɪʃ] v. get lost, especially without warning or explanation; become invisible 消失；突然不见

oases [əu'eɪsiːz] n. a fertile tract in a desert 绿洲；避风港，名词 oasis 的复数形式

pottery ['pɔtəri] n. the craft of making earthenware 陶器

domesticate [də'mestɪkeɪt] v. make fit for cultivation, domestic life, and service to humans 驯服的；驯养的

intensive [ɪn'tensɪv] adj. tending to give force or emphasis 密集的；彻底的；精细的

settlement ['setlmənt] n. a community of people smaller than a town 定居点

caravan ['kærəvæn] n. a procession (of wagons or mules or camels) traveling together in single file （穿越沙漠的）旅行队；商队

artery ['ɑːtəri] n. a major thoroughfare that bears important traffic 动脉

sparsely [spɑːsli] adv. in a sparse manner 稀少地；贫乏地

aromatic [ˌærə'mætɪk] n. 芳族植物；芳香剂

frankincense ['fræŋkɪnsens] n. 乳香

myrrh [mə:(r)] n. 没药（一种树胶树脂）

spice [spaɪs] n. 调味品；香料

ship [ʃɪp] v. transport commercially; go on board 装运；（用船）运送

turmoil ['təːmɔɪl] n. a violent disturbance 混乱；骚动

invasion [ɪn'veɪʒn] n. any entry into an area not previously occupied 侵略；侵入

sheikh [ʃeɪk] n. 族长；酋长

advocate ['ædvəkeɪt] v. push for something 提倡；主张 n. a person who pleads for a cause or propounds an idea 拥护者；提倡者

persecute [ˈpɜːsɪkjuːt] v. cause to suffer （尤指宗教或政治信仰的）迫害
suspicion [səˈspɪʃn] n. doubt about someone's honesty 猜疑；怀疑
dispatch [disˈpætʃ] v. send away towards a designated goal 派遣；调度
expeditionary [ˌekspɪˈdɪʃənerɪ] adj. (used of military forces) designed for military operations abroad 探险的；出征的（尤指军事上）
artillery [ɑːˈtɪlərɪ] n. 炮，大炮；炮兵部队
besiege [bɪˈsiːdʒ] v. surround so as to force to give up 围困；包围
uninhabitable [ʌnɪnˈhæbɪtəbl] adj. not fit for people to live 不适宜居住的
patrimony [ˈpætrɪmənɪ] n. 遗产；教会财产
garrison [ˈɡærɪsn] n. 守备队；驻地；要塞
legendary [ˈledʒəndrɪ] adj. celebrated in fable or legend 传说的；传奇的；著名的
headquarter [ˈhedˈkwɔːtə] n. 总部；司令部
generate [ˈdʒenəreɪt] v. produce; bring into existence 产生；生成
pilgrim [ˈpɪlɡrɪm] n. someone who journeys to a sacred place as an act of religious devotion 朝圣者
infrastructure [ˈɪnfrəstrʌktʃə] n. the basic physical and organizational structures and facilities needed for the operation of a society or enterprise (e.g. buildings, roads, power supplies) 基础设施
revenue [ˈrevənjuː] n. a state's annual income from which public expenses are met （国家的）岁入；税收
diversify [daɪˈvɜːsɪtɪ] n. the state of being diverse 差异；多样性
deliberate [dɪˈlɪb(ə)rət] adj. marked by careful consideration or reflection; with care and dignity 深思熟虑的
implementation [ɪmplɪmenˈteɪʃ(ə)n] n. the act of accomplishing some aim or executing some order 实施；执行
flourish [ˈflʌrɪʃ] v. grow vigorously; gain in wealth 茂盛；繁荣；活跃
parallel [ˈpærəlel] adj. being everywhere equidistant and not intersecting 平行的
optimize [ˈɔptɪmaɪz] v. to improve the way that something is done or used so that it is as effective as possible 优化
feedstock [ˈfiːdstɔk] n. the raw material that is required for some industrial process 原料；给料（送入机器或加工厂的原料）

Mysterious Arab Countries
神秘的阿拉伯

Phrases & Expressions

play an important role in	在…中起重要作用
live off	依赖…生活
give way to	让步
be crucial to	对…是至关重要的
in turn	反之；反过来；依次；轮流
seek after	寻求；追求
the great expanse of	一望无垠的
dedicate oneself to doing	专心致力于；献身于
take over	接管；被接手
with the support of	在…支持下；有了…的支持
made a concerted effort to	齐心协力；做出巨大努力
be determined to	下决心；决心做
in earnest	认真地；坚定不移地
take shape	成型；形成

Proper Names

Saudi Arabia [ˈsɔːdɪ əˈreɪbɪə]	沙特阿拉伯
Arabian Peninsula [əˈreɪbɪən pɪˈnɪnsjulə]	阿拉伯半岛
Abdul-Aziz al-Saud [ˌaːbdulaˈziːz æl saːˈuːd]	阿卜杜勒·阿齐兹（1876—1953年）
Mesopotamia [mesəpəˈteɪmɪə]	美索不达米亚（亚洲西南部）
the Nile [naɪl] river	尼罗河
Mediterranean Basin [medɪtəˈrenɪən ˈbeɪsn]	地中海盆地
Taif [taːɪf]	塔伊夫（沙特阿拉伯西部城市）
Oman [əuˈmaːn]	阿曼（西南亚国家）
Yemen [ˈjemən]	也门（西南亚国家）
Asir [æˈsɪə]	阿西尔（沙特阿拉伯省份）

Makkah ['mækə] 麦加（Mecca 阿拉伯语名称）
Madinah ['medɪnə] 麦地那（阿拉伯语名称）
Babylon ['bæbɪlən] 巴比伦（古代巴比伦王国 Babylonia 的首都）
Persia ['pə:ʃə] 波斯（西南亚国家，现称伊朗）
Riyadh [ri:'ja:d] 利雅得（沙特阿拉伯首都）
Hijaz ['hi:'dʒæz] 汉志（沙特阿拉伯省名）
Ottoman ['ɔtəmən] 土耳其人
Turki ['tə:kɪ] 突厥语；突厥人

Background Information

1. Abdul-Aziz al-Saud (1876 - 1953)

The legendary King Abdul-Aziz (also known as Ibn Saud) was the first founder of Saudi Arabia and the father of the present-day king. He began conquering today's Saudi Arabia in 1902, by restoring his family as emirs of Riyadh. He then proceeded to first conquer the Nejd (1922) and then the Hejaz (1925). He progressed from Sultan of Nejd, to King of Hejaz and Nejd, and finally to King of Saudi Arabia in 1932. His reign ended in 1953.

(Note①: In Arabic names, prefix "al-" is the definite article in Arabic—the equivalent of "the" in English. Surnames that begin with "al" often refer to the place where someone's ancestors were born. "Ibn" ("son of") seems to be spelled "ibn" when used at the beginning of a name, and "bin" when preceded by another bit of the name (Joe bin Bob, or just Ibn Bob). Or it's "Ibn" in the Middle east and "Bin" in north Africa.)

2. MOEP (Ministry of Economy and Planning)

MOEP, the Ministry of Economy and Planning, (formerly Ministry of

---

① http://en.wikipedia.org/wiki/Wikipedia: Arabic_ names.

Planning until its mandate was revised and broadened in 2003 to take over numerous macro-economic concerns from the Ministry of Finance) has developed a set of economic models in devising quantitative targets for its five-year plans:

a. The Century Model: as its name implies, the CM provides long term projections to analyze trends of prices of oil, water and human resources. b. The Selection Model: this is a general equilibrium model to arrive at medium-term forecast and therefore recommend policies with respect to development priorities. c. The Implementation Model: this will be used to explore sectoral trends and the necessary policies as a follow-up to implementation of the plan. d. Oil Model: this is used to develop projections of oil revenues under alternative scenarios on the world oil market. The models are extensively applied in setting the macroeconomic framework of each plan.

3. The Ottoman Empire

The Ottoman Empire (1299 – 1923), sometimes referred to as the Turkish Empire or simply Turkey, was a contiguous transcontinental empire founded by Turkish tribes under Osman Bey in north-western Anatolia in 1299. In 1453, the Ottoman state was transformed into an empire. During the 16th and 17th centuries, in particular at the height of its power under the reign of Suleiman the Magnificent, the Ottoman Empire was one of the most powerful states in the world—a multinational, multilingual empire, controlling much of Southeast Europe, Western Asia, North Africa and the Horn of Africa.

Study & Practice

I. Read Aloud and Memorize

Read the following paragraph aloud until you have learned them by heart.

Unit 1 History of Saudi Arabia

Saudi Arabia traces its roots back to the earliest civilizations of the Arabian Peninsula. Over the centuries, the peninsula has played an important role in history as an ancient trade center.

Since King Abdul-Aziz al-Saud established the modern Kingdom of Saudi Arabia in 1932, its transformation has been astonishing. In a few short decades, the Kingdom has turned itself from a desert nation to a modern, sophisticated state and a major player on the international stage.

II. Answer the Following Questions

1. Why was it said that Arabian Peninsula has played an important role in history?
2. Why did humans move into the places where Arabian Peninsula was located?
3. Where is the Arabian Peninsula located in?
4. Why was Arabian Peninsula untouched by the political turmoil?
5. Who advocates a return to the original form of Islam?
6. What marks the formation of modern Saudi Arabia?
7. What role does oil industry play in economic development in Saudi Arabia?
8. What are the objectives and phases of ongoing five-year development plans mentioned?

III. Cloze

Complete the following passages according to your own understanding, and change the forms where necessary.

Mysterious Arab Countries
神秘的阿拉伯

Passage 1 Oil[①]

Saudi Arabia is the world's largest _____ (1) and exporter of oil, and has one quarter of the world's known oil _____ (2) — more than 260 billion barrels. Most are _____ (3) in the Eastern Province, including the largest onshore field（陆地油田）in Ghawar and the largest offshore field（近海油田）at Safaniya in the Arabian Gulf.

Saudi refineries produce around 8 million barrels of oil per day, and there are plans to increase _____ (4) to around 12 million barrels per day.

Saudi Arabia plays a unique _____ (5) in the global energy industry. Its policies on the production and export of oil, natural gas and petroleum products have a major _____ (6) on the energy market, as well as the global economy. Mindful of this responsibility, Saudi Arabia is _____ (7) to ensuring stability of supplies and prices.

The Kingdom has repeatedly acted in times of _____ (8) — such as the Gulf Crisis of 1990 – 1991, the 2003 Iraq war and market _____ (9) of the late 1990s — and covered any drop in oil supplies by increasing its output. In this way, Saudi Arabia has prevented major shocks to the global economy from a loss of supply or sharp price _____ (10).

Passage 2 Saudi Arabia[②]

On March 15, 1938, oil was _____ (1) in Saudi Arabia, by the Aramco Company, which Standard Oil, Texaco and Mobil were a _____ (2) Oil transformed a _____ (3) dust bowl into a _____ (4) so wealthy that when King Faisal assumed power, his primary problem was _____ (5) to do with too much _____ (6).

Fortune-hunting, corruption and inexperience _____ (7) special problems, so Faisal aspired to modernize the nation through _____ (8) public expenditures on housing, schooling, transportation and medicine. For a country that _____ (9) floats on oil, transformation of a once nomadic desert _____ (10) a flowering modernized state is very real. It is an

---

① http: //www. saudiembassy. net/about/country-information/energy/oil. aspx.
② http: //www. hjenglish. com/new/p99391/.

Unit 1　History of Saudi Arabia

ironic destiny for a land that also protects the Holy Islamic city of Mecca.

IV. Spot Dictation

In this part, you will hear a passage three times. When the passage is read for the first time, you should listen carefully for its general idea. When the passage is read for the second time, you are required to fill in the blanks numbered from 1 to 10 with the exact words you have heard. Finally, when the passage is read for the third time, you should check what you have written.

Agriculture in Saudi Arabia[①]

At its founding, the country _____ (1) the simple, tribal economy of Arabia. Many of the people were nomads, engaged in _____ (2) camels, sheep, and goats. Agricultural production was _____ (3) and subsistent. Two major _____ (4) on cultivation are poor water supply and poor soil. Less than 2 percent of the total land area is used for crops. Of the cultivated land, about half consists of rain-fed dry farming, two-fifths is in tree crops, and the remainder is irrigated. The kingdom's development plans have given _____ (5) food production special attention, and the government has made subsidies and generous _____ (6) available to the agriculture sector. _____ (7) and earth-filled dams have been built, primarily in the southwest, to store water for irrigation and as a means of flood control. Agricultural _____ (8) has been great in irrigated areas, while the amount of land given to rain-fed farming has decreased. _____ (9) resources of subterranean water have been discovered in the central and eastern parts of the country and exploited for agriculture.

The kingdom has achieved _____ (10) in the production of wheat, eggs, and milk, among other commodities, though it still imports the bulk of its food needs.

---

① https://www.britannica.com/place/Saudi-Arabia/Economy#ref45210.

V. Translation

Turn the following sentences into English, using as many words and phrases you have learned from the text as possible.

1. 该公司是一家致力于现代化办公家具经营的专业性公司。

2. 严重的缺碘症主要发生在居住在偏远、与世隔绝地区的人们身上。（Deficiency of iodine）

3. 总统得出结论：他必须让位于更年轻、更有决断力的候选人。

4. 包括奥巴马总统及前美国总统在内的很多美国人认为，美国必须停止依赖外国石油进口，这对美国国家安全来说是至关重要的。

5. 阿卜杜拉王子保证沙特将尽其所能维护石油市场的平衡，保持石油价格的稳定。（Prince Abdullah）

6. 警方提醒群众警惕涉嫌的恐怖分子。

7. 经过一个月的战斗，殖民者占领了阿拉伯国家的一些重要军事阵地。

8. 据说伊拉克的智慧宫建成于数百年以前。

Unit 1 History of Saudi Arabia

VI. Oral Practice

Find a partner or partners, and discuss with them about the following questions.

1. Do you know anything about The Arab Spring?
2. In your mind, is Saddam Hussein an hero or not?
3. Describe the following picture first, show your opinion, and then offer your suggestion.

图片来源：https: //bedroomfurniture. club/search/cartoon-afghanistan-obama. html.

VII. Broaden Your Horizon

Brief Introduction of the Arab World[①]

The Arab homeland stretches some 5,000 miles —from the Atlantic coast of northern Africa in the west to the Arabian Sea in the east, and from the Mediterranean Sea in the north to Central Africa in the south. It covers an area of 5.25 million square miles. With seventy-two percent of its territory (领土) in Africa and twenty-eight percent in Asia, the Arab world straddles two continents, a position that has made it one of the world's most strategic regions. Long coastlines give it access to vital waterways: the Atlantic Ocean, the Mediterranean Sea, the Arabian Gulf, the Arabian Sea, the Gulf of Aden, the Red Sea and the Indian Ocean.

---

① http: //www. alhewar. org/ArabCivilization. htm.

Mysterious Arab Countries
神秘的阿拉伯

The population of the Arab nation—approximately 422 million—is a youthful one. Over half of the population is under the age of twenty five. Any person who adopts the Arabic language is typically called an Arab. The concept of average population density has little meaning when applied to the Arab world. Since significant human settlement is found only where water supplies are adequate, the overwhelming majority of Arabs live in relatively high concentrations along coastal areas and major river valleys. The most striking example of this phenomenon is in Egypt where more than ninety percent of the population lives on less than five percent of the land.

Agriculture is the primary economic activity in the Arab homeland. The most important food crops are wheat, barley, rice, maize, dates and millet. These are largely consumed within the region, while cotton, sugarcane, sugar beets and sesame are exported as cash crops. Contrary to popular belief, relatively few Arab countries possess petroleum and natural gas resources.

It was in the Arab land that man first organized into a settled form of society, cultivating grain and raising livestock, establishing cities and promoting diverse skills and occupations. In such a setting, rich and complex cultures were nourished: ancient Egypt, Sumer, Assyria, Babylonia and Phoenicia were great civilizations, legends even in their own day, whose traces continue to be uncovered in archeological sites throughout the region.

It was in this same area that the three great monotheistic religions—Judaism, Christianity and Islam—originated, in time spreading to all corners of the world. The followers of those faiths lived in harmony throughout the centuries in the Arab homeland, since all considered themselves the people of one God.

The Arab people are further united through their membership and participation in the League of Arab States. One of the oldest regional organizations in the world, the Arab League was founded on March 22, 1945, even before the formal establishment of the United Nations. The primary objective of the Arab League, as it is commonly called, is to facilitate maximum integration among the Arab countries through coordination of their activities in the political sphere as well as in the fields of economics, social services, education, communications, development, technology and industrialization.

The headquarters of the Arab League are in Cairo, Egypt, which also hosts some of the League's specialized agencies. Additional agencies are based in the capitals of other Arab countries. The twenty-two member states of the League, in alphabetical order, are: Algeria, Bahrain, Comoro Islands, Djibouti, Egypt, Iraq, Jordan, Kuwait, Lebanon, Libya, Mauritania, Morocco, Oman, Palestine, Qatar, Saudi Arabia, Somalia, Sudan, Syria, Tunisia, United Arab Emirates, and Yemen.

The Arab nation in the twentieth century is a region in transition— developing, modernizing, and building the foundation for its own renaissance. Its great and ancient cities—Cairo, Damascus and Baghdad— with populations well into the millions, are rapidly expanding their municipal services, communications systems and other facilities. New construction is evident everywhere as high-rise buildings replace the covered bazaars of former times.

In spite of all of this development and modernization, the Arab nation is also dedicated to preserving its traditions and values which are largely rooted in Islam. Its people are reaching out for progress while endeavoring to avoid the confusion that so often accompanies rapid change.

Mysterious Arab Countries
神秘的阿拉伯

Unit 2
Arabia Geography

Warm-Up Questions

1. Do you know anything about the Arabia? What kind of things are you interested in?
2. What do you think is the most important thing in Arabia? Give your reasons.
3. Ecology, a significant theme, arouses people's increasing concern. What's your opinion on keeping ecological balance?

Text

The standard definition of the Arab world comprises the 23 countries and territories, with 22 of which constitute the Arab League. It stretches from the Atlantic Ocean in the west to the Arabian Sea in the east, and from the Mediterranean Sea in the north to the Horn of Africa and the Indian Ocean in the southeast. And this article is an introduction of the geography of Arabia.

The Geography of Arabia[1]

It is a convention of historians to begin the history of a region with its geography. They do so partly because the drama of history is played out in the "theater" of its geographical backdrop; and partly because of the factor known in geopolitics as the "determinism of geography." It has been said that not only institutions but geography, climate, and many other conditions unite to form the influences which acting through successive generations, shape up the character of individuals and nations, and character plays a vital role in shaping up their history.

In the Arabian Peninsula, Islam emerged and developed and then came out of it. It was in the Arabian cities of Makkah and Medina that the classic Islamic identity was evolved, and Islam actually "jelled". A grasp of the geography of Arabia, therefore, is necessary for the understanding of the drift of its history.

Arabia, like any other region, has the kind of terrain that molds and modifies those who live in it and move through it. It's a stern, grim and inhospitable land, and is or was, until the obtrusion of oil, a constant challenge for survival to the wits of man. His survival in it depended upon his ability to come to terms with it.

Contrary to popularnotions, despite the fascinating sand, Arabia has considerable variety in the configuration of its surface, the salient features of which are broiling sand, mauve mountains, jagged gulches, friable rocks, flinty plains, constantly shifting sand dunes and oases, and mirages of lakes, streams and gardens.

Arabia has many parts which are highly photogenic. They possess a peculiar and haunting beauty — the beauty of textured sand, which likes the waves of the sea, is forever in motion. The ripples of sand extend as far as the horizons and beyond, in a world of silence and emptiness. The sun makes bright scales on the sand, and the wind makes strange, surrealistic patterns in it only to obliterate them a few moments later. Thus the wind is constantly

---

[1] http://www.al-islam.org/restatement/2.htm.

creating, destroying and recreating beauty. Sand can be piled up into massive dunes which can rise more than 150 meters above bedrock. Depending on the direction and force of the wind, the dunes assume a variety of shapes like the spectacular crescent moon or long parallel ridges or great pyramidal massifs which may be called sand mountains.

If the desert has many faces, it also has many moods, and most of them are unpredictable. One moment it may be deceptively benign and tranquil but the very next moment, it may become vicious, temperamental and treacherous like a turbulent ocean. Whole caravans of men, camels and horses, are said to have disappeared in it, devoured, as if, by the cruel and hungry sands. In a sandstorm which can last for several days, the sun, the moon, the stars, the contours of the landscape and the horizons are all obliterated, and towering columns of dust spin crazily, flashing surreal shadows over the surface of the roiling desert.

But through it all and forever, the desert remains remote, silent, savage, forbidding and formidable; and it remains overwhelming in its vast and awesome loneliness. Some people believe that the desert has its own "mystique" which profoundly affects men. It is against this backdrop that the Arab—the son of the desert—played out his life.

The most important component of the ecology of the Arabian Peninsula is water. Its presence or absence has shaped its history to a great extent. Although the Tropic of Cancer passes through the center of the Arabian Peninsula, the land is not tropical. Its summers are long and extremely hot, with temperatures rising as high as 130 degrees Fahrenheit in many places. Winters are short and cold. Rainfall is scanty, averaging four inches a year. The south-west corner, however, gets relatively heavy rainfall, as much as twenty inches. However, the vegetation is generally very sparse due to lack of rain and due to the high salt content of the soil. True trees are rare, and shrubs are common. All plants have had to adapt themselves to the conditions of desert existence.

Settlers were attracted to the site of Makkah by the presence of the spring discovered by Hajra, the wife of Ibrahim and the mother of Ismail, and was named by her as Zamzam. Assured by the availability of its waters in all seasons, they built the city of Makkah around it. The hydrosphere of the region consists of wells, torrents and flash-floods. The whole area is devoid of rivers and streams with the exception of the sixty-mile long Hajar in the Republic of Yemen. But even this is not a perennial stream, since it becomes a stream only when torrential rains fall in its basin. Thus, water is precious and has an indispensable impact on the life in Arabia.

A new and complex factor of tremendous geopolitical significance is the presence of vast reservoirs of oil in the Arabian Peninsula. In 1900 the whole peninsula was thinly populated, and was desolate, poverty-stricken and isolated. It was one of the few regions in the world almost untouched by western influence. Then came oil and everything changed. Saudi Arabia sold her first concession in 1923, and the first producing well was drilled in 1938. Within a few years, annual revenues from petroleum exceeded $1 million. The kingdom passed the $1 billion mark in 1970, and the $100 billion mark in 1980. Life in Saudi Arabia and in the other oil producing sheikdoms in the Persian Gulf was transformed by the effects of the new wealth — spectacular fortunes, rapid economic development, the arrival of foreign labor, international clout — perhaps more radically than life has been transformed anywhere else at any time in human experience.

The oil wealth is changing the face of the land in numerous parts of Saudi Arabia and the Gulf sheikdoms. It has made it possible to enlist modern technology to draw water from great depths or to convert sea water through desalination, and to bring barren lands under cultivation by using it for irrigation. Reclamation of land for farming is also changing the demographic character of the peninsula. Nomadic tribes are striking roots in permanent settlements wherever availability of water is assured. Most sophisticated techniques are being applied in an attempt to control sand movement and to tame a hostile environment.

The most important animal in Arabia was the camel. The Arabian camel is the single-humped variety, ordromedary, as against the two-humped camel of Central Asia, the Bactrian. The dromedary has flat, broad, thick-soled cloven hoofs that do not sink into the sand, and it can travel long distances in the desert. The milk of the camel formed an important part of the diet of the desert Arabs, and camel hair was used by them to make their tents. The camel, therefore, was indispensable for survival in the desert.

But amazingly and incredibly, the camel has almost disappeared from

Mysterious Arab Countries
神秘的阿拉伯

Saudi Arabia and all the sheikdoms of the Persian Gulf. William J. Polk writes in his book, *Passing Brave*, published by Alfred A. Knopf, New York, in 1973:

"Shortly before his death in 1960, the great English desert explorer, St. John Philby, prophesied that within thirty years Arabia would have no camels. He was laughed at then but today it seems that his prophecy may have been overly generous. The camel and its parasite, the nomad, have almost disappeared from Arabia. Thus the era which began about 3000 years ago with the domestication of the camel, is ending. The camel has played a major role in the rise of civilization."

Diesel trucks, trains, and jet airplanes have taken the place of camels and camel caravans. Most Arabs now travel by automobile or by air. The camels and the camel caravans have become "obsolete" in Arabia.

New Words

convention [kən'venʃn] n. something regarded as a normative example 惯例；习俗；规矩
backdrop ['bækdrɔp] n. background 背景
geopolitics [ˌdʒi:əu'pɔlətɪks] n. 地缘政治学
determinism [dɪ'tə:mɪnɪzm] n.（philosophy）a philosophical theory holding that all events are inevitable consequences fate 宿命论；决定性要素
institution [ˌɪnstɪ'tju:ʃn] n. a custom that for a long time has been an important feature of some group or society 习俗；制度
an organization founded and united for a specific purpose 机构
successive [sək'sesɪv] adj. in regular succession without gaps 连续的；相继的
cradle [kreɪdl] n. 摇篮；发源地
evolve [ɪ'vɔlv] v. gradually change and develop 发展；使进化
drift [drɪft] n. a general tendency to change（as of opinion）趋势；动向
terrain [te'reɪn] n. a piece of ground having specific characteristics or military potential 地形；地势；领域
stern [stə:n] adj. severe 严厉的；严峻的

Unit 2 Arabia Geography

inhospitable [ˌɪnhɔ'spɪtəbl] adj. unfavorable to life or growth 不适于居住的
obtrusion [əb'tru:ʒən] n. 闯入；闯入的东西
notion ['nəuʃən] n. an idea or belief about something 概念；观念
wilderness ['wɪldənəs] n. a wild and uninhabited area 荒野；荒漠
considerable [cɔn'sɪdərəbl] adj. large or relatively large in number or amount or extent or degree 相当多（大）的
configuration [kənˌfɪgə'reɪʃn] n. an arrangement of a group of things 结构
salient ['seɪlɪənt] adj. the most important or outstanding 最突出的
broiling ['brɔɪlɪŋ] adj. very hot 炙热的
mauve [məuv] adj. 淡紫色的
gulch [gʌltʃ] n. 峡谷
friable [fraɪbl] adj. easily broken 易碎的
flinty ['flɪntɪ] adj. harsh and without emotion 坚硬的；冷峻的
dune [dju:n] n. （由风吹积成的）沙丘
mirages ['mɪra:ʒ] n. 海市蜃楼
desolate ['desələt] adj. empty and lacking in comfort 荒凉的；无人烟的
photogenic [ˌfəutəu'dʒenɪk] adj. 易上镜的
haunting ['hɔ:ntɪŋ] adj. remaining in one's mind 萦绕心头的；难以忘怀的
textured ['tekstʃəd] adj. 有织纹的
surrealistic [səˌrɪə'lɪstɪk] adj. 超现实主义的
assume [ə'sju:m] v. take on a certain form or show 呈现
crescent ['kresənt] adj. 新月形的
pyramidal ['pɪrəmɪdəl] adj. 金字塔形的；锥形的
massifs [mæ'si:f] n. 山丘
unpredictable [ˌʌn'prɪdɪktəbl] adj. impossible to foretell or unknown in advance 无法预言的；不可预测的
deceptively [dɪ'septɪvlɪ] adv. in a misleading way 迷惑地；欺诈地
benign [bɪ'naɪn] adj. kind, gentle and harmless 温和的；善良的
tranquil ['træŋkwɪl] adj. calm and peaceful 安静的；宁静的
vicious ['vɪʃəs] adj. violent and cruel 凶猛的；残暴的
treacherous ['tretʃərəs] adj. dangerous and unpredictable 变化无常的；危险的
turbulent ['tɜ:bjələnt] adj. characterized by unrest or disorder 汹涌的；湍急的

Mysterious Arab Countries
神秘的阿拉伯

caravan ['kærəvæn] n. （穿过沙漠地带的）旅行队（如商队）；拖车
devour [dɪ'vauə(r)] v. destroy completely or eat eagerly 吞没；毁灭
obliterate [ə'blɪtəreɪt] v. destroy completely 毁掉；抹除
roiling ['rɔɪlɪŋ] adj. rough and confused 不安的；混乱的
savage ['sævɪdʒ] adj. extremely cruel, violent, and uncontrolled 野蛮的；凶猛的
formidable ['fɔ:mɪdəbl] adj. very great or impressive 强大的；令人生畏的
overwhelming [,əuvə'welmɪŋ] adj. so strong as to be irresistible and very intense 强大的；势不可挡的
awesome ['ɔ:səm] adj. very impressive and often frightening 令人敬畏的；可怕的
mystique [mi:'stɪk] n. 神秘性；奥秘
component [kəm'pəunənt] n. an abstract part of something 成分；组件
presence ['prezəns] n. the state of being present, current existence 存在；出席
tropical ['trɔpɪkl] adj. 热带的
Fahrenheit ['færən,hait] n. 华氏的（冰点为32度，沸点为212度）
scanty ['skæntɪ] adj. lacking in quantity 不足的；勉强够的
sparse [spa:s] adj. small in number or amount, not dense 稀疏的；稀少的
settler ['setlə] n. a person who settles in a new place or moves into new country 移居者；定居者
hydrosphere ['haɪdrəusfɪə] n. [地物] 水界；水圈、水气
torrent ['tɔrənt] n. a heavy rain or a fast stream of water 奔流；急流
devoid [dɪ'vɔɪd] adj. completely lacking 缺乏
perennial [pə'renɪəl] adj. lasting three seasons or more 常年的；四季不断的
tremendous [trɪ'mendəs] adj. extraordinarily large in size or extent or amount or power or degree 极大的；巨大的；惊人的
significance [sɪg'nɪfɪkəns] n. the quality of being significant 意义；重要性
reservoir ['rezəvwa:] n. a large or extra supply of something 水库；蓄水池
concession [kən'seʃən] n. 特许（权）
annual ['ænjuəl] adj. yearly or once every year 每年的；一年的
exceed [ɪk'si:d] v. go beyond 超过；超越
sheikdom ['ʃeɪkdəm] n. （阿拉伯）酋长统辖的领土；酋长国

spectacular [spek'tækjulə] adj. sensational in appearance or thrilling in effect 壮观的；惊人的
fortune ['fɔ:tʃu:n] n. a large amount of wealth; luck 财富；命运；运气
radically ['rædɪkəlɪ] adv. very important and great in degree 根本地；彻底地
numerous ['nju:mərəs] adj. amounting to do a large indefinite number 许多的；很多的
enlist [ɪn'lɪst] v. hire for work or help or support in doing something 取得（帮助）；支持
desalination [di:ˌsælɪ'neɪʃən] n. the removal of salt (especially from sea water) 脱盐作用；减少盐分
barren ['bærən] adj. dry and bare 贫瘠的；荒芜的；空的
demographic [ˌdemə'græfɪk] adj. of or relating to demography 人口统计学的
dromedary ['drɒmədərɪ] n. 单峰驼
indispensable [ˌɪndɪs'pensəbl] adj. not to be dispensed with; essential 不可缺少的；绝对必要的
contour ['kɒntuə] n. a line drawn on a map connecting points of equal height 轮廓
incredibly [ɪn'kredəblɪ] adv. not easy to believe 难以置信地；非常地
prophesy ['prɒfɪsaɪ] v. predict or reveal through; deliver a sermon 预言；预告
parasite ['pærəsaɪt] n. 依赖他人为生；寄生
nomad ['nəʊmæd] n. 游牧民
domestication [dəʊˌmestɪkeɪʃən] n. adaptation to intimate association with human beings 驯养；教化
obsolete ['ɒbsəli:t] adj. old, no longer in use or valid 废弃的；老式的

Phrases & Expressions

shape up	开始形成；顺利发展
depend upon	依赖于
contrary to	与…相反
come to terms with	与…达成协议；忍受
in motion	在开动中；在运转中

adapt one selves to	调整以适应
with the exception of	除了
to a great extent	在很大程度上
be devoid of	缺乏
laugh at	嘲笑
take the place of	代替

Proper Names

Zamzam [ˈzəmzəm]	源泉
Hajra [ˈhɑːdʒrə]	夏甲（先知易卜拉欣的第二任妻子，以实玛利的母亲）
Ibrahim [iːbrəˈhiːm]	易卜拉欣（先知）
Ismail [ˈiːsmel]	以实玛利（先知易卜拉欣的儿子）
The Republic of Yemen [ˈjemən]	也门共和国
Persian Gulf [ˈpəːʃən gʌlf]	波斯湾（简称海湾，在伊朗和阿拉伯半岛之间）
Gulf sheikdoms [ˈʃiːkdəm]	酋长国
William J. Polk [ˈwɪliəm dʒeɪ ˈpɔlk]	威廉·波尔克
Hajar [ˈhɑːdʒə]	哈贾尔山脉（也门共和国）
Tropic of Cancer	北回归线

Background Information

Ibrahim[①]

  Ibrahim (or Abraham) is recognized in Islam as a prophet and apostle (最初的传道者) of God (Arabic: Allāh) and patriarch of many peoples. Ibrahim embodies the type of the perfect Muslim and the *Qur'an* mentions Ibrahim as a model for mankind. Many aspects of Islamic worship, including pilgrimage and prayer, recognize and honor the importance of the life and

---

① http://islam.about.com/od/abraham/p/ibrahim.htm.

teachings of this great prophet. The Islamic holy day Eid al-Adha（古尔邦节）is celebrated in memory of the bravery of Ibrahim.

Many of the rites of Islamic pilgrimage (Hajj) refer back directly to Abraham and his life: Abraham's second wife is Hajar (Hagar), who gave birth to Ismail (Ishmail), who Muslims believe was Abraham's first-born son.

In the Arabian Peninsula, Abraham, Hajar, and their infant son Ismail found themselves in a barren valley with no trees or water. Hajar was desperate to find water for her child, and ran repeatedly between two hillsides in her search. At last, a spring emerged and she was able to quench their thirst. This spring, called Zamzam, still runs today in Makkah, Saudi Arabia. During the Hajj pilgrimage, Muslims reenact Hajar's search for water when they pace several times between the hills of Safa and Marwa.

As Ismail grew up, he was also strong in faith. Allah tested their faith by commanding that Abraham sacrifice his beloved son. Ismail was willing, but before they followed through, Allah announced that the "vision" had been completed and Abraham was allowed to sacrifice a ram instead. This willingness to sacrifice is honored and celebrated during Eid Al-Adha at the end of the Hajj pilgrimage.

Study & Practice

I. Read Aloud and Memorize

Read the following paragraph aloud until you have learned them by heart.

The oil wealth is changing the face of the land in numerous parts of Saudi Arabia and the Gulf sheikdoms. It has made it possible to enlist modern technology to draw water from great depths or to convert sea water through desalination, and to bring barren lands under cultivation by using it for irrigation. Reclamation of land for farming is also changing the demographic character of the peninsula. Nomadic tribes are striking roots in permanent settlements wherever availability of water is assured. Most sophisticated techniques are being applied in an attempt to control sand movement and to tame a hostile environment.

II. Answer the Following Questions

1. What factors influence the shaping up of the character of nations?
2. Why was Arabia called a constant challenge for survival?
3. How did the author describe the desert?
4. What role did water play in the Arabian Peninsula?
5. Why did the settlers choose the site of Makkah to live in?
6. What has been changed since the presence of oil?
7. What examples are listed to support the sentence "techniques are being applied to tame a hostile environment"?
8. Why did the author say it was amazing and incredible that the camel has almost disappeared from Saudi Arabia?

III. Cloze

Complete the following paragraphs according to your own understanding, and change the forms where necessary.

Paragraph 1 ①

The geographical alignment (地理定位) of United Arab Emirates (阿拉伯联合酋长国) _____ (1) the climatic condition of the country. _____ (2) in 24 degree North and 54 degree East, the country enjoys a sub-tropical climate with extremely hot and humid conditions. The demography (人口学) of United Arab Emirates forms an _____ (3) part of the United Arab Emirates Geography. The _____ (4) of UAE is 4,444,011 as established in the year 2005. The United Arab Emirates statistics _____ (5) a detailed insinuation into the administration and the infrastructure of the country. This includes details _____ (6) nutrition, health, diseases, economy and _____ (7) These statistics are particularly _____ (8) in determining the growth _____ (9) of the country. The United Arab Emirates flag is the binding factor among the people of UAE.

---

① http://www.mapsofworld.com.

Unit 2 Arabia Geography

Spotting colors like red, white, black and green, the UAE flag _____ (10) unity, fertility, wealth and history.

Paragraph 2[①]
United Arab Emirates Geology

United Arab Emirates Geology gives a vivid description of the _____ (1) and components of soil, rocks, gemstones and natural resources of the country. _____ (2) the Geology of United Arab Emirates, the country is _____ (3) into two distinct parts. The desert floor, the coastal plains, the aeolian sands (风积沙) and gravel _____ (4) makes first part while the _____ (5) part comprises Oman Mountains. United Arab Emirates Geography _____ (6) land and water as the country is located at the Arabian Gulf. The _____ (7) area of Abu Dhabi in UAE has the salt encrusted flat, _____ (8) is known as coastal sabkhas (盐沼). The soil in the United Arab Emirates is _____ (9) in minerals and salts. The principal _____ (10) are hard limestone of cement and construction sand. These are extremely useful and fulfill the modern needs.

IV. Spot Dictation

In this part, you will hear a passage three times. When the passage is read for the first time, you should listen carefully for its general idea. When the passage is read for the second time, you are required to fill in the blanks numbered from 1 to 10 with the exact words you have heard. Finally, when the passage is read for the third time, you should check what you have written.

Physical Geography[②]

Physical geography is the study of natural features and phenomena on the planet's surface and our _____ (1) with them. These features include _____ (2), climate, the local water cycle, and land formations. As

---

① http://www.mapsofworld.com.
② https://education.seattlepi.com/physical-geography-place-affect-human-life-3619.html.

humans have _____ (3) across the planet, they have had to adjust themselves to all the changing conditions they were _____ (4) to. For an instance, Arctic-dwelling Inuit adapted by storing more body fat and increasing _____ (5) rates, due to the climatic influence, which is the pattern of variation in temperature, _____ (6), and pressure over an area for long periods of time. All humans need water to survive, so people tend to _____ (7) near bodies of water. For example, nearly the entire population of Egypt is _____ (8) around the delta of the Nile River because the rest of the country is an arid desert, making it difficult to sustain plants and prevent _____ (9) loss of life. Soil carries out several functions that _____ (10) impact human activity. Soil recycles nutrients, regulates water quality, sustains life, and provides structural support for buildings. Without healthy soil, a previously fertile area turns into a desert.

V. Translation

Turn the following sentences into English, using as many words and phrases you have learned from the text as possible.

1. 尼罗河谷从阿斯旺到开罗郊区延伸约 800 公里。(Aswan)

_____

_____

2. 尼罗河谷和三角洲，地球上最广泛的绿洲，是由世界上最长的河和该国看似无穷无尽（inexhaustible）的资源形成的。

_____

_____

3. 西部沙漠面积约 70 万平方公里，覆盖了大约 2/3 的埃及总土地面积。

_____

_____

4. 阿瑟用了很长时间才学会如何来对待自己的残疾。

_____

_____

5. 沙特阿拉伯（Saudi Arabia）是由有界的7个国家和3个水域构成的。

6. 现代科技已经找到并增加了大部分地下水的可用性。

7. 应变是自身适应环境变化的能力，是进化的基本需要。

8. 我们不应该被这些外表蒙骗，事实上这些外相之下缺乏真正的智慧的增长。

VI. Oral Practice

Find a partner or partners, and discuss with them about the following questions.

1. What's your opinion on the fact mentioned in the text that camels and caravans are replaced by modern vehicle?
2. Arab countries cover the vast desert, what should we do about the governance of desert?
3. With the development of the society, there are some definitely unavoidable conflicts between modern technology and environment protection, according to you, how can we keep the balance?

VII. Broaden Your Horizon

Facts to Be Known about Arabs[①]

Most people know very little about the Middle East and the people that

---

① www.fas.org/irp/agency/army/arabculture.pdf.

live there. This lack of knowledge hurts our ability to understand, and engage in intelligent discussion about, current events. For example, frighteningly few know the difference between Sunni and Shia Muslims, and most think the words "Arab" and "Muslim" are pretty much interchangeable. They aren't. So here's a very brief introduction aiming at raising the level of knowledge about the region to an absolute minimum.

★ Common Misconceptions about Arabs

1. All Arabs are Muslims, and all Muslims are Arab. Not true!

Arabs are part of an ethnic group, not a religion. Arabs are religiously diverse group-significant numbers of Arab Christians in Egypt, Lebanon, Syria, Palestine, Jordan, and Iraq. Arabs make up between 15%-18% of the Muslim world. Arabs were around long before Islam, and there have been (and still are) Arab Christians and Arab Jews. In general, you're an Arab if you are of Arab descent (blood), or speak the main Arab language (Arabic).

2. The Arab world is backwards and uncivilized. No!

Actually the Arab world represents a highly developed culture and civilization where modern cities mingle with ancient ones.

3. The Arab world is one big desert. No!

Truly the Arab world is geographically complex and diverse.

4. Stereotypes of Arab males:

1) All are "oil-rich Sheiks". Wrong!

As in the West, there are economically diverse segments of the population.

2) Mad dictators. Wrong!

Various types of political systems exist in Arab world.

3) Terrorists. Wrong!

Overwhelming majority are law abiding citizens with families and a wide variety of occupations.

5. Stereotypes of Arab females:

1) All are oppressed by men. Not true!

2) All are veiled. Not necessarily true!

According to Islam, women are supposed to wear veils. In some countries, like Lebanon, Syria and Egypt, it is no imposed upon them and women are free to choose whether to wear veils. However, in other places, all women, even non-Muslims, wear veils out of fear of mistreatment by fanatics or those who pretend to be guardians of Islam.

★ Basic Facts about Arabs

1. Family:

Family is the key social unit to an Arab. This loyalty influences all aspects of an Arab's life. Arabs honor and respect their family. Family honor is always taken as the first priority. It is believed that large families provide for possible economic benefits. Male off-spring are favored, since a son is expected to care for his parents in their advanced age, whereas a daughter becomes part of the son-in-law's family.

2. Hygiene:

Personal hygiene is extremely important to Arabs for both spiritual and practical reasons. Because meals are frequently eaten by hand, it is typical to wash the hands before and after eating. Formal washing of face, hands, and forearm is required before daily prayers or fasting. For them, all flowing water is clean.

3. Eating Etiquette:

Arabs are restricted by Islamic conventions from eating pork and unscaled fish. Alcohol is forbidden. Meat must be butchered in line with *Qur'an* ritual (know as Hallal = "permitted"). The staple of the Arab diet is dark pita bread. Lamb is the most common meat. Always offer snacks to visitors and accept what is offered to you as a guest, but only after modestly refusing the first offer. It is assumed that guests will accept at least a small quantity of drink (tea usually or sometimes Arabic coffee) offered as an expression of friendship or esteem. It is considered rude to decline the offer of drink. When served with a beverage, accept with the RIGHT HAND ONLY! When eating, drinking, offering, or passing use right hand only! When eating with Arabs, especially when taking food from communal dishes, the left hand must never be used because it is considered unclean. Avoid discussions on political issues (national and international), religion, alcohol, and male-female relations over dinner or tea time.

4. Taboo:

Admitting "I don't know" is distasteful to an Arab. Constructive criticism can be taken as an insult. Be careful not to insult.

5. Personal Space:

Most Arabs DO NOT share the American concept of "personal space" in public situations, and in private meetings or conversations. It is considered offensive to step or lean away! Women are an exception to this rule. Do not stand close to, stare at, or touch a woman.

6. Socialization and Trust:

When conducting business, it is customary to first shake the hand of all males present, taking care not to grip too firmly. Allocate plenty of time for refreshment before attempting to engage in business. It is important to first establish respect and trust.

Unit 3
Media in Arab World

Warm-Up Questions

1. Can you list out as many media as possible? Which one is the most popular nowadays?
2. What roles do media play in the society?
3. Do you know the traditional media in China? Share with your classmates.

Text

The term "media" generally refers to "the means of communication". Each medium—from the newspaper to the television to the Internet—arises from distinctive political, economic, and cultural matrices, and holds the potential to influence individuals and society in varying ways. Knowing the major media in Arab world has significant impacts on understanding the role of media in shaping Arab societies and the broader Muslim world.

/ Mysterious Arab Countries
神秘的阿拉伯

Media in Arab World[①]

Prior to the Islamic Era, poetry was regarded as the main means of communication on the Arabian Peninsula. It related the achievements of tribes and defeats of enemies and also served as a tool for propaganda. After the arrival of Islam other forms of communication replaced poetry as the primary form of communication. Imams (preachers) played a role in disseminating information and relating news from the authorities to the people. The marketplace gossip and interpersonal relationships played an important role in the spreading of news, and this form of communication among Arabs continues today. Before the introduction of the printing press Muslims obtained most of their news from the Imams at the Mosque, friends or in the marketplace. Colonial powers and Christian Missionaries in Lebanon were responsible for the introduction of the printing press. It was not until the 19th century that the first newspapers began to appear, mainly in Egypt and Lebanon, which had the most newspapers per capita.

During French rule in Egypt in the time of Napoleon Bonaparte the first newspaper was published in French. There is debate over when the first Arabic language newspaper was published, but the first newspapers were limited to official content and included accounts of relations with other countries and civil trials. In the following decades Arab media blossomed due to journalists mainly from Syria and Lebanon, who were intellectuals and published their newspapers without the intention of making a profit. Because of the restrictions by most governments, these intellectuals were forced to flee their respective countries but had gained a following and because of their popularity in this field of work other intellectuals began to take interest in the field. Intellectuals in the Arab World soon realized the power of the press.

In most Arab countries, newspapers cannot be published without a government-issued license. Most Arab countries also have press laws, which impose boundaries on what can and cannot be said in print. Generally, newspapers in the Arab World can be divided into three categories: government

---

① http://en.wikipedia.org/wiki/Arab_culture.

owned, partisan owned, and independently owned. Yet, profit is not the driving force behind the launching of newspapers, and publishers may establish a newspaper to ensure a platform for their political opinions, although it is claimed that this doesn't necessarily influence the news content.

Another major medium in Arab World is television. Almost all television channels in the Arab world were government owned and strictly controlled prior to the 1990s. In the 1990s the spread of satellite television began changing television in Arab countries. Often noted as a pioneer, al-Jazeera represents a shift towards a more professional approach to news and current affairs. Financed by the Qatar government and established in 1996, al-Jazeera was the first Arabic channel to deliver extensive live news coverage, going so far as to send reporters to "unthinkable" places like Israel. Breaking the mold in more ways than one, al-Jazeera's discussion programs raised subjects that had long been prohibited. However, in 2008, Egypt and Saudi Arabia called for a meeting to approve a charter to regulate satellite broadcasting. The Arab League Satellite Broadcasting Charter (2008) lays out principles for regulating satellite broadcasting in the Arab world.

Technology rather than freedom of speech and money has much to do with why satellite television is sprouting up everywhere. However, the desire for political influence is probably the biggest factor driving television channel growth. The influence of the West is very apparent in Arab Media especially in television. Arab soap operas and the emerging popularity of reality TV shows are evidence of this notion.

Internet access began in the early 1990s in the Arab world with Tunisia being first in 1991 according to Dr. Deborah L. Wheeler. The years of the introduction of the Internet in the various Arab countries are reported differently. Wheeler reports that Kuwait joined in 1992 and in 1993 Turkey, Iraq and the UAE came online. In 1994 Jordan joined the Internet and Saudi Arabia and Syria followed in the late 1990s. In reality the Arab world is not so far behind the rest of the globe with the introduction of the Internet. The people most commonly utilizing the Internet in the Arab world are the youth. The café users in particular tend to be under 30, single and have a variety of levels of education and language proficiency. Despite reports that use of the internet was curtailed by lack of English skills, people were able to search with Arabic.

Mysterious Arab Countries
神秘的阿拉伯

Searching for jobs, the unemployed frequently fill cafes in Egypt and Jordan. They are men and women equally. Most of them chat and they have email. In a survey conducted by Dr. Deborah Wheeler, she found almost all of them to have been taught to use the Internet by a friend or family member. They all felt their lives to have been significantly changed by the use of the Internet.

The use of the Internet in the Arab world is very political in the nature of the posts and of the sites read and visited. The Internet has brought a medium to Arabs that allows for a freedom of expression which is allowed or accepted before. For those who can get online, there are blogs to read and write and access to worldwide outlets of information once unobtainable. With this access, regimes have attempted to curtail what people are able to read, but the Internet is a medium not as easily manipulated as telling a newspaper what it can or cannot publish. The Internet can be reached via proxy server, mirror, and other means. Those who are thwarted with one method will find 12 more methods around the blocked site.

The Internet in the Arab world is a powerful source of expression and information as it is in other places in the world. Freedom that has branched through the introduction of the Internet in Middle East is creating a stir politically, culturally, and socially. It has brought about a snowball effect, now that the snowball is rolling, it can no longer be stopped. Getting bigger and stronger, it is bound to crush down all obstacles. The Internet has created a new arena for discussion and the dissemination of information for the Arab world just as it has in the rest of the world. The youth in particular are accessing and utilizing the tools. There is an increasing division among generations. The Arab World is in conflict internally. People are encouraged and enabled to join in political discussion and critique in a manner that was not previously possible. Those same people are also discouraged and blocked from those debates as the differing regimes try to restrict access based on religious and state objections to certain material. Bloggers have been incarcerated all around in the Middle East for their opinions and views on their regimes, the same consequence which was once given to those who publicly expressed themselves without anonymity. But the power of the Internet has provided also a public shield for these bloggers since they have the ability to engage public sympathy on such a large scale. This is creating a dilemma that shakes the foundation of Arab culture, government, religious interpretation, economic prosperity, and personal integrity.

The Internet is a vast and seemingly endless source of information. Arabs are using it more than perhaps what the world is aware of and it is changing the media.

Whatever the major media mentioned above are, the Arab media values strictly revolve around political news putting the human interest stories to the side. The other value Arab media embraces as important is their global perspective with regard to presentation and production. The global orientation of Arab media integrated with the need to educate their populations, establishes social responsibility as one of the cornerstones of its media values.

Historically, news from various media in the Arab World was used to inform and guide political practitioners with their performance rather than being just a consumer product. Family reputation and personal reputation is a fundamental principle in Arab civilization; exposes of corruption and examples of weak moral fiber in governors and policy makers holds massive consequences especially in the presence of a limited freedom of speech. From a historical perspective, news in the Arab world was not a mass product; rather, its main aim was to provide instruction to the officials and governors, guiding them to improve their performance. The power of news as political tool was discovered in the early 19th century, with the purchase of shares from Le Temps a French newspaper by Ismail the grandson of Muhammad Ali. Doing so allowed Ismail to publicize his policies. Arab Media coming to modernity flourished and with it its responsibilities to the political figures that have governed its role.

Media researchers stress that the moral and social responsibility of media people dictates that they should not agitate public opinion, but rather should keep the status quo. It is also important to preserve national unity by not stirring up ethnic or religious conflict. Saudi journalists stress the importance of enhancing Islam through the media. The developmental role was acknowledged by an overwhelming majority of Saudi journalists, while giving the audience what they want was not regarded as a priority. This view is further endorsed in Kirat's survey where 65 percent of Algerian journalists agreed that the task for the press is to "help achieve the goals and objectives of development plans."

Mysterious Arab Countries
神秘的阿拉伯

New Words

achievement [ə'tʃiːvmənt] n. the action of accomplishing something 成就；成绩

propaganda [ˌprɔpə'gændə] n. information that is spread for the purpose of promoting some cause 宣传；宣传内容

replace [rɪ'pleɪs] v. take the place or move into the position of 取代；代替

disseminate [dɪ'semɪneɪt] v. cause to become widely known 散播；公开；宣传

gossip ['gɔːsɪp] n. light informal conversation for social occasions 留言蜚语；闲话

colonial [kə'ləunɪəl] adj. of or relating to or characteristic of or inhabiting a colony 殖民地的

account [ə'kaunt] n. a record or narrative description of past events 描述；解释

blossom ['blɔzəm] v. develop or come to a promising stage 成长

intellectual [ˌɪntə'lektʃuəl] adj. of or relating to the use of mind; 智力的；有才智的
　　n. a person who uses the mind creatively 知识分子；有极高才智的人

restriction [rɪ'strɪkʃn] n. a principle that limits the extent of something 限制；约束

respective [rɪ'spektɪv] adj. considered individually 分别的；各自的

impose [ɪm'pəuz] v. compel to behave in a certain way 强加；强迫

boundary ['baundrɪ] n. a line determining the limits of an area 边界；分界线

category ['kætəgərɪ] v. a collection of things sharing a common attribute 种类；类别

partisan ['paːtɪzn] adj. devoted to a cause or party 党派的；偏袒的

platform ['plætfɔːm] n. a raised horizontal surface 平台；讲台

satellite ['sætlaɪt] n. man-made equipment that orbits around the earth or the moon 卫星；人造卫星

represent [ˌreprɪ'zent] v. be representative or typical for 变现；表示；代表

professional [prə'feʃnl] adj. engaged in a profession or engaging in as a profession or means of livelihood 职业的；专业的

Unit 3　Media in Arab World

current ['kʌrənt] adj. occurring in or belonging to the present time 现在的；流通的

live [laɪv] adj. in current use or ready for use 现场的；直播的

coverage ['kʌvərɪdʒ] n. the news as presented by reporters for newspapers or radio or television 新闻报道；覆盖范围

mold [məʊld] v. form by pouring (e. g., wax or hot metal) into a cast or mold 形成；制作模具

raise [reɪz] v. cause to be heard or known; express or utter 提出；引起

regulate ['reɡjuleɪt] v. adjust, shape or influence; give direction to 调整；管理；控制

sprout ['spraʊt] v. put forth and grow sprouts or shoots 萌芽；迅速成长

emerge [ɪ'mɜːdʒ] v. come out of, become known or apparent 浮现；显现出来

access ['ækses] v. reach or gain access to 接近；进入

utilize ['juːtəlaɪz] v. put into service; make work or employ for a particular purpose or for its inherent or natural purpose 使用；利用

proficiency [prə'fɪʃnsɪ] n. skillfulness in the command of fundamentals deriving from practice and familiarity 熟练；精通

curtail [kə:'teɪl] v. place restrictions on 削减；缩减

outlet ['aʊtlet] n. an opening that permits escape or release 出路；出口

manipulate [mə'nɪpjuleɪt] v. control (others or oneself) or influence skillfully, usually to one's advantage 操纵；控制

proxy ['prɒksɪ] adj. 代理的

thwart [θwɔːt] v. hinder or prevent (the efforts, plans, or desires) of 反对；阻碍

branch [brɑːntʃ] v. grow and send out branches or branch-like structures 分支；分叉

arena [ə'riːnə] n. place or scene of activity or conflict 活动场所；竞技场

incarcerate [ɪn'kɑːsəreɪt] v. lock up or confine, in or as in a jail 监禁；幽闭

regime [reɪ'ʒiːm] n. a particular system of government 政治制度；政权；政体

anonymity [ænə'mɪnətɪ] n. the state of being anonymous 匿名；笔者不详

engage [ɪn'ɡeɪdʒ] v. take part in; busy oneself with; get the right to use 从事于；忙于；吸引

Mysterious Arab Countries
神秘的阿拉伯

sympathy ['sɪmpəθɪ] n. (capacity for) sharing the feelings of others; feeling of pity and sorrow for sb 同情;同情心

dilemma [dɪ'lemə] n. a situation in which one has to make a difficult choice between two courses of action, both perhaps equally undesirable 困境;进退两难

interpretation [ɪnˌtə:prɪ'teɪʃn] n. explanation 解释;说明;诠释

integrity [ɪn'tegrEtɪ] n. strength and firmness of character or principle; honesty that can be trusted 正直;诚恳;诚实

embrace [ɪm'breɪs] v. include; contain 包括;拥抱

perspective [pə'spectɪv] n. point of view; future 观点;想法;前景

presentation [preznˈteɪʃn] n. a talk, usually to a group of people, in which information is given; outward appearance 报告;外观

orientation [ˌɔ:rɪən'teɪʃn] n. a position or direction 方向;目标

cornerstone ['kɔ:nəstəun] n. 奠基石

expose [ɪk'spəus] n. lay open; uncover; disclose; make known 显露;揭露;暴露

corruption [kə'rʌpʃn] n. lack of integrity or honesty (especially susceptibility to bribery); use of a position of trust for dishonest gain 贪污;堕落

purchase ['pə:tʃəs] v. buy 购买

modernity [mə'də:nətɪ] n. the quality of being current or of the present 现代性;现代作风

dictate [dɪk'teɪt] v. state with the force of authority; command; decree; prescribe 命令;指示

status quo [ˌstətɪs'kwəu] n. the existing state of affairs 现状

agitate ['ædʒɪteɪt] v. argue strongly for sth you want; make sb. feel angry 激烈争论;激怒

enhance [ɪn'ha:ns] v. increase 提高;增强

acknowledge [ək'nɔlɪdʒ] v. accept or admit that sth. exists, is true, or is real 承认

overwhelming [ˌəuvə'welmɪŋ] adj. too great to resist or overcome; very great 势不可挡的;压倒一切的

priority [praɪ'ɔrətɪ] n. thing that is (regarded as) more important than others 优先权;优先考虑的事情

endorse [ɪn'dɔ:s] v. give support or one's approval to 赞同;支持

Unit 3　Media in Arab World

Phrases & Expressions

prior to	早于；优先于
make a profit	赚钱
take interest in	对…感兴趣
lay out	制定；起草
sprout up	突然出现；涌现
in particular	尤其
on a large scale	在很大范围内
be bound to	注定
crush down	压倒；碾碎
revolve around	围绕
put… to the side	把…放在一边
with regard to	关于；至于
in the presence of	当着某人；有某人在场
from a… perspective	从某种角度来讲

Proper Names

Imam [ɪˈmɑːm]	阿訇
Napoleon Bonaparte	拿破仑·波拿巴（法国皇帝）
Deborah L. Wheeler	黛博拉·维勒
Al-Jazeera	半岛电视台
Muhammad Ali	穆哈迈德·阿里

Background Information

1. Imam

An imam is an Islamic leadership position. It is most commonly in the context of a worship leader of a mosque and Muslim community by Sunni

Muslims only. In this context, Imams may lead Islamic worship services, serve as community leaders, and provide religious guidance. It may also be used in the form of a prefix title with scholars of renown.

The Sunnites held the imam to be a man capable of error but deserving obedience provided he maintained the ordinances of Islam. In Shi'ite Islam the imam became a figure of absolute religious authority, possessed of unique insights into the Qur'an and divinely appointed and preserved from sin. The term imam is also given to Muslims who lead prayers in mosques and has been used as an honorary title.

2. Napoleon Bonaparte

Napoleon Bonaparte (15 August 1769 – 5 May 1821) was a French military and political leader who rose to prominence during the latter stages of the French Revolution and its associated wars in Europe.

As Napoleon I, he was Emperor of the French from 1804 to 1815, the first monarch of France bearing the title emperor. He is best remembered for his role in the wars led against France by a series of coalitions, the so-called Napoleonic Wars. He established hegemony over most of continental Europe and sought to spread the ideals of the French Revolution, while consolidating an imperial monarchy which restored aspects of the deposed Ancien Régime. Due to his success in these wars, often against numerically superior enemies, he is generally regarded as one of the greatest military commanders of all time.

3. Al-Jazeera

Al-Jazeera, literally "The Island", abbreviating "The [Arabian] Peninsula", also known as Aljazeera and JSC (Jazeera Satellite Channel), is a broadcaster owned by the Al-Jazeera Media Network and headquartered in Doha, Qatar. Initially launched as an Arabic news and current affairs satellite TV channel, Al-Jazeera has since expanded into a network with several outlets, including the Internet and specialty TV channels in multiple languages. Al-Jazeera is accessible in several world regions. Al-Jazeera is owned by the government of Qatar.

4. Muhammad Ali

Muhammad Ali Pasha al-Mas'ud ibn Agha (4 March 1769 – 2 August 1849) was an Albanian commander in the Ottoman army, who became Wāli, and self-declared Khedive of Egypt and Sudan. Though not a modern nationalist, he is regarded as the founder of modern Egypt because of the dramatic reforms in the military, economic and cultural spheres that he instituted. He also ruled Levantine (黎凡特) territories outside Egypt. The dynasty that he established would rule Egypt and Sudan until the Egyptian Revolution of 1952.

Study & Practice

I. Read Aloud and Memorize

Read the following poem aloud until you have learned them by heart.

The Internet in the Arab world is powerful source of expression and information as it is in other places in the world. Freedoms that have branched through the introduction of the Internet in Middle East are creating a stir politically, culturally, and socially. It has brought about a snowball effect, now that the snowball is rolling, it can no longer be stopped. Getting bigger and stronger, it is bound to crush down all obstacles. The Internet has created a new arena for discussion and the dissemination of information for the Arab world just as it has in the rest of the world. The youth in particular are accessing and utilizing the tools. There is an increasing divide between the generations. The Arab World is in conflict internally. People are encouraged and enabled to join in political discussion and critique in a manner that was not previously possible.

II. Answer the Following Questions

1. What was the major means of communication prior to the Islamic Era?
2. Where did Muslims obtain most of their news?
3. When was the first Arabic language newspaper published?
4. Newspapers in Arab World were under strict regulations, weren't they? What are the regulations?
5. What is the biggest factor that drives the rapid growth of television in Arab World?
6. What is the reaction of regimes towards the growing access to Internet in Arab World?
7. Why did the author compare Internet to a snowball effect?
8. What is the center of Arab media values?
9. When was the political usage of media discovered?
10. According to media researchers, what is the responsibility of media people?

III. Cloze

Complete the following paragraphs according to your own understanding, and change the forms where necessary.

Paragraph 1①

A new Arabic financial website (www. nuqudy. com) reported on Tuesday that the total number of Web users in the Arab world is _____ (1) at about 75 million users by the end of July 2010. However, it said the actual number of Internet surfers in the Arab countries is much higher in the _____ (2) the users of the Web via _____ (3) phones in this region are taken into _____ (4) The report claimed that in some countries the internet penetration rate is low but the cellular penetration rate is close to 100%. Egypt is leading the Arab world in _____ (5) of

---

① http: //www. albawaba. com/main-headlines/report-75-million-internet-users-arab-world.

Unit 3 Media in Arab World

Internet users with 17.5 million. The report _____ (6) the lack of quantity and quality of Arabic content in the Internet. Addressing this _____ (7) will require the introduction of broadband infrastructure, it added. It is _____ (8) mentioning that "Google" is now making strenuous _____ (9) in the field of training in a bid to _____ (10) the amount of Internet content in Arabic.

Paragraph 2[①]

The Arab countries lagged _____ (1) most of the world in _____ (2) the internet. One factor, until the late 1990s, was the technical _____ (3) of using Arabic on the internet (and on computers more generally) which tended to restrict use to those who could work in English or, in some cases, French. Another factor was _____ (4) (including high connection charges). Saudi Arabia and Iraq were the last Arab countries to provide public internet _____ (5), in 1999 and 2000 _____ (6). By the middle of 2008, more than 38 million Arabs were believed to be using the internet at _____ (7) once a month and overall internet penetration had reached 11.1%. This was still only about half the world _____ (8) (21.9%) but all the signs pointed towards continuing rapid _____ (9). Having _____ (10) the inevitability of the internet, the first instinct of Arab regimes was to look for ways to _____ (11) it. This was _____ (12) partly on their fears of political subversion but also on the fears of conservative and religious elements that it would undermine "_____ (13)" values-fears that in both cases were well-founded. The Saudis _____ (14) for an extravagant high-cost, high-tech solution, _____ (15) Iraq under Saddam Hussein surrounded internet use with barely-penetrable bureaucracy.

IV. Spot Dictation

In this part, you will hear a passage three times. When the passage is read for the first time, you should listen carefully for its general idea. When the

---

[①] http://www.al-bab.com/media/internet.htm.

passage is read for the second time, you are required to fill in the blanks numbered from 1 to 10 with the exact words you have heard. Finally, when the passage is read for the third time, you should check what you have written.

Digital Revolution Marks the Beginning of Information Era[①]

The present age is known to be the information era. Another term which refers to this phenomenon is the so-called the third industrial revolution. People begin to realize the power and the importance of information and knowledge. Information is what _____ (1) people to develop and utilize all their talents and abilities to create advanced _____ (2), tools, and instruments. In the information era, technology has been becoming the central axis and speedily _____ (3) globalization. This progress eventually leads to the larger transition of _____ (4) which can build _____ (5) and efficient ways of working and socializing. The third industrial revolution has powerfully transformed the way information _____ (6) across various sectors in a worldwide range such as providing grounds for businesses to move beyond the national markets to the international markets and _____ (7) the interconnectedness of the world. _____ (8), there are people having a negative impression on this great revolution. They see this atmosphere just as a merely _____ (9) progress. They say that it _____ (10) personal privacy, it lessens the professionalism of journalists and it does make people find themselves in difficulty to distinguish between personal and professional life.

V. Translation

Turn the following sentences into English, using as many words and phrases you have learned from the text as possible.

1. 政府关于贸易争端的底线并没有发生变化。

_____

_____

_____

[①] https://medium.com/@BaliWebsitevideos/digital-revolution-marks-the-beginning-of-information-era-463aaf915220.

2. 他们雇佣了一位专家来设计这栋大厦的庭院。

3. 全部安排都应该在我们出发之前完成。

4. 这段路太窄，交通有时不免堵塞。

5. 鸟之将死，其鸣也哀；人之将死，其言也善。

6. 从战略的角度考虑，一个错误的举动就能使你付出极大的代价。

7. 我们正在努力从总体上增强环保意识，特别是提高防治空气污染的意识。

8. 如果我们不得不对这些汽车打折的话，我们就无利可言了。

VI. Oral Practice

Find a partner or partners and discuss with them about Internet with the help of the following questions.

1. How do you look upon the usage of Internet on a very large scale in China? Advantages and disadvantages!
2. Are you used to surfing Internet for information? Why?
3. E-books are getting more and more popular among youngsters, what's your opinion on it?

VII. Language Enhancement

Needless to say, many Arab customs are very different from those in other countries, and you should be aware of what you're expected to do and not to do if you want to know more about the Arab World.

What Are Local Customs Like in Saudi Arabia[①]

Although Arabs are understanding and unlikely to take offence at social blunders, provided they arise from ignorance rather than malice, you will be made far more welcome if you acquaint yourself with local ways of doing things. It's important to remember that you're a foreigner and you must therefore adapt to the customs and social behavior of the region — not the other way round. In addition to actions and behaviour which are regarded as criminal, there are certain unwritten rules that you must observe in order not to offend local sensibilities.

Dress

There are two distinct types of women's clothing in the region: one for locals, the other for expatriates（移居外国者）. Outside the home, most Arab women dress according to religious custom, which means that they must cover most of the body, from head to foot. The traditional black overgarment (*abaya*) is ankle length with long sleeves and a high neckline, and the hair is covered. Some Arab women are totally covered, including their face and hands, especially Saudis and those with strictly religious husbands. This is meant to protect women from unwanted attention, and in Saudi Arabia even foreign women must wear an abaya outside the home; the religious police will stop any woman who has her head uncovered and direct her to cover her hair immediately. In other UAE states, foreign women may wear western clothes but should always dress conservatively.

The region's hot climate and customs call for informal but smart

---

① http://www.justlanded.com/english/Saudi-Arabia/Saudi-Arabia-Guide/Culture.

dressing. Arabs frown on clothes which reveal the shoulders, arms and legs, and any woman dressing provocatively will be regarded as being of 'easy virtue' or perhaps even as a prostitute. In the home, however, when not entertaining close friends or relatives, Arab women often adopt western dress, particularly younger women, and there are no restrictions on the way foreign women may dress in private.

In a business setting, it is appropriate for women to wear conservative suits, in the form of dark-colored trousers or skirts that fall below the knee. The elbows should also be covered at all times with a shirt or vest.

Arab men wear the thobe, a loose, ankle-length robe made from fine white cotton (or heavier woolen material in winter). There are different styles of thobe, both in the cut of the cloth and in the fastenings at the neck and front. Perhaps the most distinctive are those worn by the Omanis, which sport a tassel. The thobe can be worn for all occasions, either social or business. An outer cloak, the bisht, is worn on formal occasions and can be very costly, with border embroidery in gold thread and the material itself of the finest quality.

The traditional, distinctive head covering is the guthra, a white or red and white checkered cloth held in place by the agal, a black 'rope' which was originally a camel tether. There are different types of agal: for example, Qataris normally wear a more African-style headdress, with two long 'tails' reaching down the back. Arab men sometimes wear casual dress on very informal occasions or at the beach, but Saudi men are strongly encouraged to wear national dress at all times.

Obviously, foreign men aren't expected to wear Arab garments, and western dress is the norm. Men should avoid wearing shorts and sleeveless shirts in the street, as is these are regarded as excessively casual, although with the development of tourism, this attitude is softening. However, suits are rarely worn in the Gulf, except for important business meetings and related social events. Standard wear in the office is a shirt (usually long-sleeved), tie and lightweight trousers.

Terms of Address

Arabs generally value civility highly, and it's important that you greet (and part from) local people in the correct way. The use of Arab names can be confusing for newcomers to the region. For example, a man might be called Abdullah bin Abdul Aziz Al-Jishi. Abdullah is his given name and he's the son or grandson of (bin) Abdul Aziz; Al-Jishi is the family or tribal name. To make matters even more complicated, given names are often abbreviated: for example, Mohammed can be shortened to Mohd, Hamad or Hamed. It's important to use the full names, however, particularly on formal occasions and in correspondence. Abdullah bin Abdul Aziz Al-Jishi should never be called Abdullah (let alone the diminutive Abdul), although the patronymic may be omitted and he can be addressed as Abdullah Al-Jishi.

The general formal address is 'Sayyed' ('Sir') for a man or 'Sayeeda' (or 'Sayedity') for a woman, followed by the person's full name. Arab women can be addressed as 'Madame'.

Rulers are usually addressed as 'Your Highness' ('Your Majesty' in the case of the King of Saudi Arabia). Senior members of ruling families are called 'Your Excellency' followed by 'Sheikh' (pronounced 'shake' and not 'sheek') and their full name. Government ministers of the ruling line are 'Your Excellency, Minister of …' and other ministers simply 'Your Excellency' followed by the full name. Lesser members of ruling families and those in religious authority are addressed as 'Sheikh' followed by their full name. In Saudi Arabia, the title has somewhat less significance and is also being used by powerful members of the business community. The conventions for addressing rulers and members of ruling families are complex, and you should always check locally before being introduced to any dignitaries.

Hands & Feet

You should accept refreshment whenever it's offered, but note that you should always use your right hand for drinking and eating, as the left hand is regarded as unclean (as it's used for 'toilet purposes'). Similarly, you should avoid showing the soles of your shoes or feet, which implies that you think the other person is 'dirt', which is obviously highly offensive. You should therefore keep your feet flat on the ground and not cross your legs.

Invitations

If you're invited to the home of an Arab, you should always accept that. You should generally take every opportunity to become acquainted with local people and avoid the natural tendency to stay within the social and physical confines of your foreign 'ghetto'. Your Arab host will be interested in you and your views. However, you should avoid politics and religion as subjects for discussion; your opinions might be regarded as ill-informed or even offensive, even if they seem acceptable to you from a western perspective.

When you enter the *majlis*, the reception room for visitors, you should always remove your footwear, unless the host indicates otherwise (you should therefore ensure that there are no holes in your socks!). At this point, women are usually asked to join the women. You will almost certainly be offered something to drink and perhaps eat; accept the offer. Arabs are almost always polite and expect the same from those they meet, and believe that sharing a meal with a person positively affects the relationship.

The standard greeting is *Ahlan wa sahlan*-which means welcome -and this will become familiar to all who visit Saudi Arabia. It's certainly worth learning enough Arabic to communicate the pleasantries, greetings and responses of the country you're living in. You will enjoy people's reaction and your hosts invariably offer encouragement to those who attempt to speak their language. It's important to note, however, that the Arabic language has a special significance, having been designed to carry the word of God, so it's important to use it respectfully.

You should also never call at an Arab's house without warning him that you're coming. If the women of the family are present, this won't be appreciated, particularly in Saudi Arabia. You should also avoid expressing admiration for any of your host's possessions, as tradition dictates that he must then offer it to you. Although this tradition isn't followed by everybody, it can nevertheless cause embarrassment. What's more, the correct response is for the recipient to give an even more valued gift in return, so think twice before admiring an Arab's Rolls Royce!

Other Dos and Don'ts

You should also heed the following warnings:

• Don't offer alcoholic drinks to an Arab, unless you're certain that he drinks alcohol. This can cause great offence.

• Don't walk on a prayer mat or in front of any person at prayer and try not to stare at people who are praying.

• Don't try to enter a mosque without first asking permission. It's unlikely that you will be allowed in.

• In Saudi Arabia, don't try to enter the Holy sites of the areas surrounding Mecca and Medina. The roads are well signposted to notify everybody of this restriction. If a non-Muslim is found within the prohibited areas, he's likely to be assaulted and will be afforded no protection against the assailants.

• Avoid blasphemy, particularly in the presence of Muslims.

• Avoid putting an Arab in a position where he might suffer a 'loss of face' in front of other Arabs. He will appreciate this, if he notices your action.

• Don't beckon to people with a finger, as this is considered particularly impolite. Arabs might use such a gesture to summon a dog.

• Avoid shouting and displays of aggression or drunkenness at all times, as such behavior is rarely tolerated.

• During Ramadan, don't eat, drink or smoke anywhere where you can be seen by Muslims during the hours of daylight and don't engage in any noisy behavior or embrace or kiss anyone in public.

Unit 4
Economic Crisis in Egypt

Warm-Up Questions

1. What are the most important resources of Egypt's economy?
2. What do you think about Morsi and Mbarak? Do you think they have contributed to Egypt's economy?
3. If you were the president of Egypt, what would you do to make its economy recover?

Text

Egypt, a transcontinental country spanning the northeast corner of Africa and southwest corner of Asia, has a very diversified economy that comprises the sectors such as tourism, agriculture, industry and services at almost equal production levels. But the revolution which took place between January and February in 2011 nearly pushed it into the abyss. And its economy goes from bad to worse.

Egypt's Economy Going to the Dogs[①]

Annoyed at being skinned in a Cairo bazaar, a medieval Arab traveler sniffed that rascally Egyptians behaved "as if there were no Day of Judgment." The IMF (International Monetary Fund), which has been trying to extend a generous package of aid to Egypt since revolution pitched the country into turmoil two years ago, may have similar concerns. Along with its politics, Egypt's economy has lurched ever closer to ruin, yet successive governments have blithely ignored the looming danger.

Thecurrent one, dominated by the Muslim Brotherhood, is no exception. Nine months into office, President Muhammad Morsi has yet to devise an economic plan plausible enough to convince the IMF, whose proffered $4.8 billion standby agreement and stamp of approval could unlock as much as $15 billion in multilateral aid, mostly on generous terms, and slash borrowing costs overall.

Earlier this month Mr. Morsi's government also rejected suggestions that Egypt could dip into its own deposits at the fund for emergency financing. Fearful of imposing austerity ahead of a general election due later this year, it has instead borrowed at steep rates from local banks, beseeched friendly governments (mostly in the Gulf) for cash and fuel, and busied itself trying to push through legislation to allow for issuing "Islamic" bonds.

This has not stemmed the slide. Egypt's official foreign reserves, around $36 billion before the revolution of January 2011, have tumbled to around $13 billion, barely enough to cover three months' imports. Yet in theory much of even that sum cannot be touched, since it consists of recent deposits in Egypt's central bank from such brotherly states as Qatar ($4 billion), Saudi Arabia and Turkey ($1 billion each). Rich Gulf monarchies now say they are not in the mood to stump up more, so Mr. Morsi's government has turned to Iraq and, reportedly, Libya, to fill the central bank's vaults. Even should they cough up, this would improve only the numbers, not the reality.

With the value of Egypt's currency eroding by 10% since December, the bank has imposed increasingly stringent exchange controls. These are

---

① http://www.economist.com/news/.

beginning to throttle trade and foreign investment. Some imported medicines, for example, have vanished from pharmacies, and brokers now warn foreign clients of trouble repatriating funds. In any case, little new money is coming in. Even as Brotherhood salesmen talk up investment, Egypt's authorities persist in sounding hostile to foreign capital. Serial court rulings have overturned privatization deals from more than a decade ago, and taxmen have taken to imposing large bills retroactively.

The falling currency has pushed up inflation from an annual rate of less than 5% in December to 8% in February. That is particularlygrim for Egypt's growing number of unemployed. One labor group reports at least 4,500 factory closures since the revolution, which explains a rise in the official jobless rate from 9% to 13%. But far higher unofficial estimates are given credibility by evidence of a surge in crime and the plethora of unlicensed street markets that now swamp Egyptian cities.

Thousands of workers in tourism, which in good times contributed 12% of Egypt's GDP, have also been left idle. Though the beach resorts that attract most visitors have kept going by slashing prices, older tourist draws such as the Pyramids, the Valley of the Kings and cruise-boats on the Nile are eerily empty.

The government's budget deficit, meanwhile, looks set to approach a sickly 12% of GDP by the end of the fiscal year in June, above its earlier target of 9.5%. A single bill of around $20 billion accounts for the bulk of that shortfall: subsidies. Afraid of igniting popular unrest, Egyptian governments have shied for more than a decade from tackling a system that provides ungrateful consumers with such items as bread at the equivalent of less than an American cent a loaf, petrol at less than 20 cents a liter (barely a tenth of its price at pumps in Europe) and cooking gas at 7% of its actual cost.

Diesel fuel alone makes up nearly half the subsidy bill. It powers not only the country's commercial transport fleet but also the irrigation pumps used by millions of poor farmers; without it Egypt's precious farmland would wither. Yet the government has had to import a growing proportion of Egypt's diesel at world prices, in part because the state oil monopoly has had to export more crude oil to pay off pressing debts. Moreover, growing shortages of diesel fuel, prompted by smuggling and hoarding as well as by the government's inability to import enough, have created mile-long queues, replete with fisticuffs and shootings. Black marketers now charge double the official price.

Use your loaf

Subsidized bread is still plentiful. That is a good thing, since Credit Suisse, a Swiss bank, reckons that the average family spends nearly half its income on food. With the proportion of Egyptians under the official poverty line having risen from 21% in 2009 to 25% last year, nutritionists note with alarm that Egyptians have grown dangerously reliant on bread to feed their children. The local wheat harvest accounts for barely half of consumption, which is why Egypt is the world's largest importer of wheat. Even as government stocks have fallen to an unusually low level, the state commodity-supply board has cut back on imports and issued what some experts say are unrealistically optimistic forecasts for Egypt's own spring crop. "We expect a squeeze by early summer," says a private trader.

To be fair to Mr. Morsi's government, it has not been entirely oblivious of the impending crunch. It has raised a few customs duties and minor taxes, and mooted plans to ration some subsidized goods, perhaps as soon as June. Where it has really fallen short, however, is in meeting the request, politely framed in a statement from the IMF after one delegation's visit to Cairo, for Mr. Morsi to build "broad support" for wider-reaching economic reform.

Not only has his government failed to propose acoherent plan for reform or to prepare the public for it, Mr. Morsi and the Brotherhood have tried to muscle aside critics, using much the same methods as did Hosni Mubarak, the dictator overthrown in 2011 after 30 years in power. But Egyptians are no longer so easily cowed, so the result has been political paralysis accompanied by rising violence. Mr. Morsi has shown growing frustration with the limits to his power, leading opponents to suspect he may try even harsher tactics to thwart them. Many Egyptians now fear that a judgment day is indeed nearing.

New Words

skin [skɪn] v. to take the skin off an animal, a fruit or a vegetable; cheat 剥皮；欺骗

medieval [ˌmedɪ'i:vəl] adj. 中世纪的（公元1000年到1450年）

rascally ['ræskəlɪ] adj. 无赖的；坏蛋的

extend [ɪk'stend] v. to make sth. longer or larger 使伸长；扩大；扩展

pitch [pɪtʃ] v. to throw sb./sth. with force 用力扔，投；抛

turmoil ['tə:mɔɪl] n. a state of great anxiety and confusion 动乱；骚动；混乱

lurch [lə:tʃ] v. 突然前倾（或向一侧倾斜）

loom [lu:m] v. to appear as a large shape that is not clear, especially in a frightening or threatening way 赫然耸现；（尤指）令人惊恐地隐现

current ['kʌrənt] adj. of the present time 当前的；现在的

devise [dɪ'vaɪz] v. to invent sth new or a new way of doing sth 发明；设计；想出

plausible ['plɔ:zəbl] adj. reasonable and likely to be true 有道理的；可信的

proffer ['prɔfə] v. offer or give 提供；供给

multilateral [mʌltɪ'læt(ə)r(ə)l] adj. in which three or more groups, nations, etc. 多边的；多国的

dip [dɪp] v. to go downwards or to a lower level （使）下降；下沉

deposit [dɪ'pɔzɪt] n. money 订金；订钱

austerity [ɔ'sterətɪ] n. 节衣缩食

beseech [bɪ'si:tʃ] v. ask for or request earnestly 恳求；请求

legislation [ledʒɪs'leɪʃən] n. law 法规；法律

stem [stem] v. to stop sth that is flowing from spreading or increasing 阻止；遏止

tumble ['tʌmbl] v. fall down as if collapsing 使跌倒；暴跌

erode [ɪ'rəud] v. gradually destroy or remove 逐渐毁坏；削弱；损害

stringent ['strɪndʒənt] v. severe or strictly controlled 严格的；迫切的

throttle ['θrɔtl] v. 掐死；勒死

pharmacy ['fɑ:məsɪ] n. a shop that sells medicines and drugs 药房；药店

repatriate [ri:'pætrɪeɪt] v. to send money or profits back to your own country 寄（钱）回国；将（利润）调回本国

Mysterious Arab Countries
神秘的阿拉伯

privatization [ˌpraɪvətaɪˈzeɪʃn] n. 私有化

retroactively [retrəuˈæktɪvlɪ] adv. 追溯地；逆动地

grim [grɪm] adj. unpleasant and depressing 令人不快的；令人沮丧的

closure [ˈkləuʒə] n. the situation when a factory, school, etc. shuts permanently （永久的）停业；关闭；倒闭

plethora [ˈpleθərə] n. an amount that is greater than is needed 过多；过剩

swamp [swɒmp] v. fill up with water; be hard to deal with 使淹没；使疲于应对

slash [slæʃ] v. to reduce sth by a large amount 大幅度削减；大大降低

eerily [ˈɪərɪlɪ] adv. strangely, mysteriously, frighteningly 怪异地；神秘地；恐怖地

fiscal [fɪskəl] adj. connected with government or public money, especially taxes 财政的；国库的

subsidy [ˈsʌbsədɪ] n. 津贴；补助

ignite [ɪgˈnaɪt] v. cause to start burning or arouse 点燃；激起

unrest [ʌnˈrest] n. 动荡；动乱；骚动

tackle [ˈtækl] v. to deal with a difficult problem or situation 应付；处理；解决（难题或局面）

equivalent [ɪˈkwɪvələnt] adj. equal in value, amount, meaning, importance, etc. （价值、数量、意义等）相等的；相同的

irrigation [ɪrɪˈgeɪʃn] n. 灌溉渠

wither [ˈwɪθə(r)] v. dry up, become weak and die 凋谢；衰弱；萎缩

proportion [prəˈpɔʃən] n. a part or share of a whole 部分；份额

smuggling [ˈsmʌglɪŋ] n. 走私（罪）

inability [ˌɪnəˈbɪlətɪ] n. the fact of not being able to do sth 无能；无力

queue [ˈkju:] n. 队；行列

fisticuff [ˈfɪstɪkʌf] n. a fight in which people hit each other with their fists 拳斗；互殴

nutritionist [nju:ˈtrɪʃənɪst] n. 营养学家

optimistic [ɔptɪˈmɪstɪk] adj. expecting good things to happen or sth to be successful 乐观的；抱乐观看法的

oblivious [əˈblɪvɪəs] adj. being unaware of 不知道的；不清楚的

crunch [ˈkrʌntʃ] n. an important and often unpleasant situation 紧要关头；困境

Unit 4 Economic Crisis in Egypt

duty [ˈdjuːtɪ] n. 税收
ration [ˈræʃn] v. restrict the consumption of a relatively scarce commodity 限量供应；配给供应
delegation [delɪˈgeɪʃən] n. 代表团
coherent [kəuˈhɪərənt] adj. logical and well organized 合乎逻辑的；有条理的
muscle [ˈmʌsl] v. make one's way by force 硬挤
critic [ˈkrɪtɪk] n. 批评家；评论家
overthrow [ˈəuvəθrəu] v. cause the downfall of rulers 推翻
paralysis [pəˈrælɪsɪs] n. 麻痹；瘫痪
opponent [əˈpəunənt] n. a person that you are playing against 对手；竞争者
harsh [haːʃ] adj. cruel, severe and unkind 残酷的；严厉的
tactic [ˈtæktɪk] n. a plan or measure for attaining a particular goal 策略；手段
thwart [θwɔːt] v. to prevent sb. from doing what they want to do 阻止

Phrases & Expressions

go from bad to worse	江河日下
dip into	动用
stump up	掏腰包；付清
cough up	掏出；勉强说出（某事）
talk up	热烈讨论
push up	推升
make up	组成；补足
provide with	提供；供应
pay off	付清；偿清
cut back on	削减
fall to	下降到

Proper Names

MohamedMorsi [ˈməuˈhæmed ˈmɔʃsɪ]　　穆罕默德·穆尔西
Credit Suisse [swis]　　瑞士信贷

Mysterious Arab Countries
神秘的阿拉伯

Qatar [ˈkʌtɑː(r)]   卡塔尔
Saudi Arabia   沙特阿拉伯
Turkey [ˈtəːkɪ]   土耳其
the Muslim Brotherhood   穆斯林兄弟会
IMF   国际货币基金组织
Hosni Mubarak [ˈhɔsnɪ ˈmubærək]   胡斯尼·穆巴拉克

Background Information

1. Day of Judgement

Day of the Last Judgment is when God will decree the fates of all men according to the good and evil of their earthly lives (New Testament) (末日)

2. The Muslim Brotherhood

The Muslim Brotherhood is also called the Society of the Muslim Brothers, which is the largest Islamic movements, and is the most influential political opposition organization in the Arab world. Founded in Egypt in 1928 as a religious, political and social movement by Hassan al-Banna, the Muslim Brotherhood had an estimated two million members by the end of World War II. The organization seeks to make Muslim countries become Islamic caliphates and to isolate women and non-Muslims from public life. The movement is also known for engaging in political violence. Muslim brotherhood members are suspected to have assassinated political opponents like Egyptian Prime Minister Mahmoud an-Nukrashi Pasha.

3. Hosni Mubarak

Muhammed Hosni Mubarak, the Former President of Egypt and the chairman of the National Democratic Party of Egypt. In October 1981, he was elected as the fourth president of Egypt, a series of whose reform has significantly improved the overall national strength in Egypt. And he resigned his position and turned over his power to the military on February 11, 2011. In the end he was sentenced to life imprisonment.

4. Mohamed Morsi

He was elected to be a councilor of the People's Assembly in 2000, and was appointed as a member of the Discipline Board of the Brotherhood. At the end of April 2011, he took the charge of organizing the Freedom and Justice Party and became its leader. And then in June 24, 2012, he was announced to have won the final election and became the first president after Mubarak's step-down. Then six days later, he officially swore in his president position in the Plenary Session of the Supreme Constitutional Court, starting his four-year presidential tenure.

Study & Practice

I. Read Aloud and Memorize

Read the following paragraph aloud until you have learned them by heart.

With the value of Egypt's currency eroding by 10% since December, the bank has imposed increasingly stringent exchange controls. These are beginning to throttle trade and foreign investment. Some imported medicines, for example, have vanished from pharmacies, and brokers now warn foreign clients of trouble repatriating funds. In any case, little new money is coming in. Even as Brotherhood salesmen talk up investment, Egypt's authorities persist in sounding hostile to foreign capital. Serial court rulings have overturned privatization deals from more than a decade ago, and taxmen have taken to imposing large bills retroactively.

II. Answer the Following Questions

1. Why does the medieval Arab traveler sniff like that?
2. What did the IMF do to help Egypt since the revolution?
3. Does Morsi's government mean anything to Egyptian economy?
4. Why did the Morsi's government borrow at steep rates from local banks instead?
5. Did the external loan from the local bank and friendly governments save Egyptian economy from sliding down?
6. Why has the bank imposed increasingly stringent exchange controls?
7. What did the Egyptian government do for fear of igniting popular unrest?
8. How much does the diesel fuel make up in the subsidy bill?
9. Why has the government had to import a growing proportion of Egypt's diesel?
10. Why is Egypt the world's largest importer of wheat?

III. Cloze

Complete the following paragraphs according to your own understanding, and change the forms where necessary.

Paragraph 1 [①]

It was hard enough before. The Middle East has strikingly few companies, which is _____ (1) one-third of the number per person in Eastern Europe. Everywhere the state dominates the economy. In Egypt the public sector _____ (2) for 40% of value-added outside agriculture — an unusually large share for a middle-income country. Such _____ (3) firms as do exist tend to be large and closely connected to the state. The average Middle Eastern company is ten years older than that in East Asia or Eastern Europe because new entrants are kept out by pervasive red tape. The

---

① http://www.kekenet.com/menu/201305/241074.shtml.

authors _____ (4) it costs roughly 20 times the average _____ (5) income to start a firm in Syria and Yemen (assuming anyone would want to), just over twice the average globally. In a few _____ (6) countries, like Tunisia, some notorious personifications of crony capitalism have fallen foul of political change but the practice has by no _____ (7) ended.

Paragraph 2[①]

On the Kuwaiti economic level also, a global news agency "Reuters" has _____ (1) last week, a report which stated that "Kuwait is a very rich country, but the economy is _____ (2) especially for catching up the Gulf countries which _____ (3) from high oil prices." The report noted that "no advancement in the country, except with a strong and solid private sector, as the country is now at a crossroads, either to take _____ (4) of its enormous potential, or remain underdeveloped on the economic and developmental levels, especially as the gap _____ (5) its wealth and level of the development is still _____ (6) The report described Kuwait that "it has cracked infrastructure and an unfavourable business environment, its dependence almost completely on oil, putting it at a very low level for a development side and dynamics of its economy, especially when compared it _____ (7) the rest of the Gulf countries, which working harder to develop its _____ (8) and diversifying its economies through the private sector investments." There is no _____ (9) that this painful situation which listed by the report are not new on Kuwaiti's regard. But it reflects a clear increasing in the power of criticism from the international bodies to Kuwait's economic management, which its performance significantly decreased than the level of events in the past years, leaving the Kuwaiti economy for more unjustified _____ (10) which leads to a very bad _____ (11) on the domestic economic situation.

IV. Spot Dictation

In this part, you will hear a passage three times. When the passage is read

---

① http: //www. businesstendersmag. com/economy/arabic-economy/.

Mysterious Arab Countries
神秘的阿拉伯

for the first time, you should listen carefully for its general idea. When the passage is read for the second time, you are required to fill in the blanks numbered from 1 to 10 with the exact words you have heard. Finally, when the passage is read for the third time, you should check what you have written.

Egypt is the biggest of the nations hit by recent _____ (1) in North Africa and the Middle East. One of the causes of this spreading wave of popular _____ (2) is a lack of economic progress.

Egypt is not a major oil _____ (3) and its economy is not big enough to affect world economic growth. But important _____ (4) cross Egypt. And Egypt controls the Suez Canal. About eight percent of world shipping passes through this link between Europe and Asia. That includes two million _____ (5) of oil each day, mainly to Europe. Many experts say they expect the _____ (6) to remain open. Still, _____ (7) about the Suez have pushed oil prices to their highest levels since two thousand and eight.

Fariborz Ghadar heads the Center for Global Business Studies at Penn State University. He says _____ (8) in Egypt remains high — up to forty percent in some areas. Yet Egypt is not alone. Foreign _____ (9) worry about _____ (10) mismanagement and security problems across North Africa and the Middle East.

Every year millions of young people enter the job market. Populations are young and fast growing. In Egypt, the economy grew about five percent last year — too little growth to create enough jobs.

V. Translation

Turn the following sentences into English, using as many words and phrases you have learned from the text as possible.

1. 我似乎无法使儿子明白，现在花在学习上的额外时间将来会有回报的。

2. 经济衰退时期，这家工厂解雇了许多工人。

3. 爸爸失业时，我们必须减少娱乐开销。

4. 该调查报告指出旅游业在不少阿拉伯国家的经济中占有重要地位，同时也很容易受环境变化的影响。

5. 没有经济管理体制的改革，我们的工业就会逐渐衰退。

6. 他们必须采取通货膨胀的方法来刺激国内经济。

7. 这次金融危机使亚洲国家的经济大伤元气。

8. 但我认为，如果双方就世界经济的形势，特别是亚洲经济的走向等问题交换意见，也完全在情理之中。

VI. Oral Practice

Find a partner or partners, and discuss with them about the following questions.

1. Do you know the building in the following picture? Please tell your partner (s) whatever you know about it.
2. Which Arab country are you familiar with? Can you share some information with your partner (s)?
3. There has been economic interaction between China and the Arab world since ancient times. Can you offer some facts about this?

Mysterious Arab Countries
神秘的阿拉伯

图片来源: https: //www. newshour. press/business/epc-giant-punj-lloyd-wins-rs-308-crore-infrastructure-project-in-dubai/.

VII. Language Enhancement

A Brief History of the Veil in Islam[①]

Scarves and veils of different colors and shapes were customary in countless cultures long before Islam came into being in the seventh century in the Arabian Peninsula (which includes present-day Saudi Arabia) . To this day, head coverings play a significant role in many religions, including Orthodox Judaism and Catholicism.

Since the seventh century, Islam has grown to be one of the world major religions. As it spread through the Middle East to Saharan and sub-Saharan Africa, to Central Asia, and to many different societies around the Arabian Sea, it incorporated some local veiling customs and influenced others. But it is only recently that some Islamic states, such as Iran, have begun to require all women to wear the veil (in Iran it is called the chador, which covers the entire body).

Critics of the Muslim veiling tradition argue that women do not wear the veil by choice, and they are often forced to cover their heads and bodies. In contrast, many daughters of Muslim immigrants in the West argue that the veil symbolizes devotion and piety (虔诚) and that veiling is their own choice. To them it is a question of religious identity and self-expression.

---

① http: //civicdilemmas. facinghistory. org/content/brief-history-veil-islam.

What are the origins of the obligation to wear the Islamic veil? Do all Muslim women wear the veil? Do they have to? Also, are all veils the same, or do they take different forms and shapes? And, finally, what objections does the veil raise in some countries in the West? Sociologist Caitlin Killian explains that, in the past as in the present, the tradition of veiling has been influenced by different religious interpretations as well as by politics.

Muslim religious writings are not entirely clear on the question of women veiling. Various statements in the *Qur'an* and the Hadith (穆罕默德言行录) (statements attributed to the prophet Muhammad) make reference to Muhammad's wives veiling, but it is debatable whether these statements apply only to the Prophet's wives or to all Muslim women.

While the need for women to be modest is mentioned, the area women must cover depends on the source and ranges from "the bosom" to the whole body except the face and hands. The veil is a vehicle for distinguishing between women and men and a means of controlling male sexual desire. Muslim men are also urged to be modest and to cover themselves between the waist and the knees··· [In some Islamic societies] an immodest woman brings dishonor not only on herself but also on her male family members. The veil itself, however, predated Islam and was practiced by women of several religions. It also was largely linked to class position: Wealthy women could afford to veil their bodies completely, whereas poor women who had to work [in the field] either modified their veils or did not wear them at all.

The numerous styles of Islamic dress throughout the world today reflect local traditions and different interpretations of Islamic requirements. Muslim women in France, therefore, exhibit a wide range of dress and head coverings. Many wear nothing that distinguishes them as Muslims. A number of immigrant women practice modesty, not by donning traditional dress, but rather by wearing long-sleeved shirts and skirts that reach the ankles. For those who do veil, some simply wear brightly colored scarves on their heads, sometimes even allowing hair to show; others pin unicolor (单色的) veils tightly around the face; and still others adopt long, flowing Islamic dress and occasionally cover the entire face except for the eyes. The girls at the center of the controversy usually wear Western clothing with a veil pinned around the face to cover their hair.

The struggle over Maghrebian women's dress began long before their immigration to France in the 1970s. French and British colonizers encouraged Muslim women to remove the veil and emulate European women. Consequently, in Algeria and other North African and Middle Eastern countries, the veil became a symbol of national identity and opposition to the West during independence and nationalist movements.

The hijab [喜佳伯（穆斯林妇女戴的面纱或头巾）] is one name for a variety of similar headscarves. It is the most popular veil worn in the West. These veils consist of one or two scarves that cover the head and neck. Outside the West, this traditional veil is worn by many Muslim women in the Arab world and beyond.

The niqab（尼卡伯）covers the entire body, head and face; however, an opening is left for the eyes. The two main styles of niqab are the half-niqab that consists of a headscarf and facial veil that leaves the eyes and part of the forehead visible and the full, or Gulf, niqab that leaves only a narrow slit for the eyes. Although these veils are popular across the Muslim world, they are most common in the Gulf States. The niqab is responsible for creating much debate within Europe. Some politicians have argued for its ban, while others feel that it interferes with communication or creates security concerns.

The chador（卡多尔）is a full-body-length shawl held closed at the neck by hand or pin. It covers the head and the body but leaves the face completely visible. Chadors are most often black and are most common in the Middle East, specifically in Iran.

The burqa（布尔卡）is a full-body veil. The wearer's entire face and body are covered, and one sees through a mesh screen over the eyes. It is most commonly worn in Afghanistan and Pakistan. Under the Taliban regime in Afghanistan（1996 - 2001）, its use was mandated by law.

Unit 5
Education in Egypt

Warm-Up Questions

1. What do you think of the English proverb "The education of a man never completes until he dies"?
2. Suppose you were the Minister of Education in Egypt, what suggestions would you offer?
3. How much do you know about the education in Egypt? Any similarities and differences in education system between Egypt and China?

Text

The importance of education has always been acknowledged in Egypt, which, as we know it today, has an excellent education system and the government has been particularly keen on developing the literacy levels in the country. The following is an introduction about its educational system.

Education in Egypt[1]

Egypt has the largest overall education system in the Middle East and North Africa and it has grown rapidly since the early 1990s. In recent years the Government of Egypt has accorded even greater priority in improving the education system.

According to the Human Development Index (HDI), Egypt is ranked 123 in the HDI and 7 in the lowest 10 HDI countries in the Middle East and Northern Africa, in 2009. With the help of the World Bank and othermultilateral organizations Egypt aims to increase access in early childhood to care and education and the inclusion of ICT at all levels of education, especially at the tertiary level. The government is responsible for offering free education at all levels. The current overall expenditure on education is about 12.6 percent as of 2007 Investment in education as a percentage of GDP rose to 4.8 in 2005 but then fell to 3.7 in 2007. The Ministry of education is also tackling with a number of issues: trying to move from a highly centralized system to offering more autonomy to individual institutions, thereby increasing accountability. The personnel management in the education also needs to be overhauled and teachers should be hired on merit with salaries attached to the performance.

Basic education

The basic education consists of pre-primary, primary and preparatory levels of education. In Egypt, the Ministry of Education coordinates the preschool education. In 1999 - 2000 the total enrollment rate of pre-primary students was 16 percent and that increased to 24 percent in 2009. Irrespective of private or state run, all preschool institutions come under Ministry of Education. It is the Ministry's duty to select and distribute textbooks. According to the Ministry's guidelines, the maximum size of a preschool should not exceed more than 45 students. Ministry of Education is also getting

---

[1] http://en.wikipedia.org/wiki/Education_in_Egypt.

support from the international agencies, such as the World Bank to enhance the early childhood education system by increasing access to schools, improving quality of education and building capacity of teachers. At the primary level students could attend private, religious or government schools. Currently, there are 7.8 percent of students enrolled at primary level in private schools as of 2007. The total enrollment of students at primary level is 105 percent in 2007. The examinations at grade 3 are on district level.

The second tier of basic compulsory education is the preparatory stage or lower secondary which is three years long. Completion of this tier grants students the Basic Education Completion Certificate. The importance of completion of this level of education is to safeguard students against illiteracy as early dropouts at this stage easily recede into illiteracy and eventually poverty.

Secondary education

Secondary education consists of three tracks: general, vocational/technical and the dual-system vocational education known as Mubarak-Kohl schools. The general secondary stage includes 3 years of education, whereas the secondary vocational track could be for 3 – 5 years, and 3 years for the dual system vocational education. To enter the secondary level, the students must pass a national exam which is given at end of the secondary stage. As of year 2004 the 77.3 percent of students completing preparatory stage are estimated to be enrolled in secondary education. At this level, students have formative and summative assessments during the first year and the average of the end of year national standardized exams for year two and three qualifies the students to take the Certificate of General Secondary Education, which is one of the requirements for admission into the universities. So far efforts are underway with the support of multilateral organizations to make the general and vocational secondary system less rigid and provide equal opportunities to students of various wealth quintiles in the two tracks to opt for higher education. This is also being implemented by the World Bank led secondary enhancement project in Egypt.

Technical and vocational secondary education

Technical education, which is provided in three-year and five-year programs, includes schools in three different fields: industrial, commercial and agricultural. The UN and other multilateral organizations are working towards improving the technical and vocational training system in Egypt. It is recommended to the Ministry of Education to introduce broad vocational skills in the curricula of general secondary schools. In this way students will be able to gain certification in practical skills needed in the job market. The Ministry of Education controls pre-tertiary, school-based programs that can start after grade 6 and that enroll the largest number of students in TVET (Technical And Vocational Education And Training) —over 2 million students. The Ministry of Higher Education controls the middle technical institutes. These draw their enrollments from MoE's (Ministry of Education) general secondary schools or technical schools and have much smaller enrollment numbers. Graduates of the MoE's vocational programs can enter vocational training centers.

Al-Azhar system

Another system that runs in parallel with the public educational system is known as the Al-Azhar system. It consists of six years of primary stage, a three-year preparatory stage and finally three years of secondary stage. The Ministry of education reduced the number of secondary school years from four to three years in 1998, so as toalign the Al Azhar system with the general secondary education system. In this system as well, there are separate schools for girls and boys. Al Azhar education system is supervised by the Supreme Council of the Al-Azhar Institution. The Azhar Institution itself is nominally independent from the Ministry of Education, but is ultimately under supervision by the Egyptian Prime Minister. Al Azhar schools are named "institutes" and include primary, preparatory, and secondary phases. All schools in all stages teach religious subjects and non-religious subjects, to a certain degree—not as intensively as the state schools. The bulk of the curriculum, however, consists of religious subjects. All the students are Muslims, and males and females are separated in the prep and secondary stages. Al-Azhar schools are all over the country, especially in rural areas. The graduates of Al-Azhar secondary schools are eligible to continue their studies at the Al-Azhar University. As of 2007 and 2008, there are 8272 Al-Azhar schools in Egypt. In the early 2000s, Al-Azhar schools accounted for less than 4% of the total enrollment. The graduates of this system are then automatically accepted into Al-Azhar University. In 2007, the Pre-University enrollment in Al-Azhar institutes is about 1, 906, 290 students.

Education and the community

There were a few attempts to make a positive impact and educational reform from the civil community in Egypt but those efforts remained very limited on their impact on the educational process. Education crisis in Egypt is very complicated, public education is not capable of providing quality education and is hardly providing any education with the shortage infacilities, lack of trained educators and inflation in classes. Private (including international) is still incapable of reform for the lack of interest, shortage in trained educators, defective curricula, commercialization of education and finally a customized accreditation system that involves the irrevocable licensure of international schools based on candidacy for accreditation while candidacy for accreditation is originally based on the initial efficiency of the school in providing the educational services including its status as a legal education provider that it doesn't get to get unless it's a candidate school, which is setting the cart before the horse.

No community efforts have been done toaddress the crisis of education in Egypt until 2008, when the International-Curricula Educators Association (ICEA) was established with modest financial resources but great expectations.

The Community addressed itself to contributing to solving the educational problems in Egypt including the shortage in research, statistics and entrepreneurship in the field of education

Mysterious Arab Countries
神秘的阿拉伯

New Words

accord [əˈkɔːd] v. allow to have 给予

priority [praɪˈɔrətɪ] n. status established in order of importance; preceding in time 优先；优先权

multilateral [ˈmʌltɪˌlætərəl] adj. having many parts or sides 多边的；多国的

tertiary [ˈtəːʃərɪ] n. from 63 million to 22 million years ago 第三纪；第三修道会会员；第三级教士

current [ˈkʌrənt] adj. occurring in or belonging to the present time 现在的；最近的

centralized [ˈsentrəlaɪzd] adj. drawn toward a center or brought under the control of a central authority 集中的；中央集权的

accountability [əˌkauntəˈbɪlɪtɪ] n. responsibility to someone or for some activity 负有责任；应做解释

overhaul [ˈəuvəhɔːl] v. make repairs, renovations, revisions or adjustments to 分解检查；追上并超过

coordinate [kəuˈɔːdɪnɪt] v. bring order and organization to 协调；调整；整合

distribute [dɪˈstrɪbjuːt] v. give out and make available 分配；散布

exceed [ɪkˈsiːd] v. go beyond 超过；胜过

agency [ˈeɪdʒənsɪ] n. an administrative unit of government 代理；中介

capacity [kəˈpæsɪtɪ] n. ability to perform or produce 能力；资格

tier [tɪə] n. a relative position or degree 等级；层；列

compulsory [kəmˈpʌlsərɪ] adj. required by rule 义务的；必修的

grant [grænt] v. let or allow to have 授予；承认；允许

certificate [səˈtɪfɪkeɪt] n. 证书；执照；文凭

illiteracy [ɪˈlɪtərəsɪ] n. ignorance resulting from not reading 文盲；无知

dropout [ˈdrɔpaut] n. someone who quits school before graduation 辍学学生

recede [rɪˈsiːd] v. pull back or move away or backward 后退；减弱

vocational [vəuˈkɪʃnl] adj. of or relating to an occupation especially providing or undergoing training in special skills 职业的；行业的

dual [ˈdjuːəl] adj. consisting of two parts 双重的；双倍的

estimate [ˈestɪmeɪt] v. judge to be probable 估计；判断

formative ['fɔːmətɪv] adj. forming or capable of forming or molding or fashioning 形成的；发展的

summative ['sʌmətɪv] adj. of or relating to a summation 总结的；总结性的

assessment [ə'sesmənt] n. the act of judging 评定；估价

quintile ['kwɪntail] n. 五分之一

enhancement [ɪn'haːnsmənt] n. improvement that makes something more agreeable 增加；放大

industrial [ɪn'dʌstrɪəl] adj. of or relating to or resulting from industry 工业的；产业的

curricula [kə'rɪkjulə] n. an integrated course of academic studies 课程

align [ə'laɪn] v. place in a line or arrange so as to be parallel or straight 使结盟；匹配

supervise ['sjuːpəvaɪz] v. watch and direct 监督；指导；管理

supreme [sjuː'priːm] adj. greatest in status or authority or power 最高的；至高的

nominally ['nɒmɪnəlɪ] adv. in name only 名义上地

eligible ['elɪdʒəbl] adj. qualified for or allowed or worthy of being chosen 合格的；符合条件的

automatically [ɔːtə'mætɪkəlɪ] adv. in the mechanical manner 自动地；机械地

facility [fə'sɪlətɪ] n. a building or place that provides a particular service or is used for a particular industry 设施；设备

inflation [ɪn'fleɪʃən] n. a general and progressive increase 膨胀

defective [dɪ'fektɪv] adj. having a defect or not working properly 有缺陷的；不完美的

commercialization [kə,məːʃəlaɪ'zeɪʃən] n. 商业化；商品化

accreditation [ə'kredɪ'teɪʃən] n. 鉴定合格；信任

irrevocable [ɪrɪ'vəukəbl] adj. incapable of being retracted or revoked 不可改变的；不能取消的；不能挽回的

address [ə'dres] v. be busy with or work on 从事；忙于

establish [ɪ'stæblɪʃ] v. bring about or set up or accept 制定；建立

entrepreneurship [,antrəprə'nəːʃɪp] n. 企业家精神

Phrases & Expressions

tackle with	处理；解决
rise to	上升到；升迁
get support from	从…得到支持
irrespective of	不论；不考虑
safeguard against	防范；预防
drop out	退出；退学
recede into	后退；衰退
opt for	选择；抉择
so as to	以便；为了
in parallel with	与…平行；与…同时
account for	（比例）占
contribute to	有助于；为…出力

Proper Names

Human Development Index	人类发展指数
Basic Education Completion Certificate	基础教育合格证书
Al-Azhar system	爱资哈尔体系
ICEA	国际课程教育工作者协会

Background Information

Human Development Index[①]

The Human Development Index (HDI) is a simple, approximate statistic devised by Mahbub ul Haq and Amartya Sen to introduce non-income factors and rival traditional economic indicators within a framework of international development. It is annually published by the United Nations Development

---

① http://en.wikipedia.org/wiki/Human_Development_Index.

Programme since 1990.

The first Human Development Report introduced a new way measuring development by combining indicators of life expectancy, educational attainment and income into a composite human development index, the HDI. The breakthrough for the HDI was the creation of a single statistic which was to serve as a frame of reference for both social and economic development. The HDI sets a minimum and a maximum for each dimension, called goalposts, and then shows where each country stands in relation to these goalposts, expressed as a value between 0 and 1.

The education component of the HDI is now measured by mean of years of schooling for adults aged 25 years and expected years of schooling for children of school entering age. Mean years of schooling is estimated based on educational attainment data from censuses and surveys available in the UNESCO Institute. Expected years of schooling estimates are based on enrolment by age at all levels of education and population of official school age for each level of education. Expected years of schooling is capped at 18 years. The indicators are normalized using a minimum value of zero and maximum values are set to the actual observed maximum value of mean years of schooling from the countries in the time series, 1980 − 2012, that is 13.3 years estimated for the United States in 2010. Expected years of schooling is maximized by its cap at 18 years. The education index is the geometric mean of two indices.

The life expectancy at birth component of the HDI is calculated using a minimum value of 20 years and maximum value of 83.57 years. This is the observed maximum value of the indicators from the countries in the time series, 1980 − 2012. Thus, the longevity component for a country where life expectancy birth is 55 years would be 0.551.

For thewealth component, the goalpost for minimum income is $100 (PPP) and the maximum is $87,478 (PPP), estimated for Qatar in 2012.

The decent standard of living component is measured by GNI per capita (PPP $) instead of GDP per capita (PPP $) The HDI uses the logarithm of income, to reflect the diminishing importance of income with increasing GNI. The scores for the three HDI dimension indices are then aggregated into a composite index using geometric mean. Refer to the Statistics for more details. The HDI facilitates instructive comparisons of the experiences within and between different countries.

Study & Practice

I. Read Aloud and Memorize

Read the following paragraph aloud until you have learned them by heart.

There were a few attempts to make a positive impact and educational reform from the civil community in Egypt but those efforts remained very limited on their impact on the educational process. Education crisis in Egypt is very complicated, public education is not capable of providing quality education and is hardly providing any education with the shortage in facilities, lack of trained educators and inflation in classes. Private (including International) is still incapable of reform for the lack of interest, shortage in trained educators, defective curricula, commercialization of education and finally a customized accreditation system that involves the irrevocable licensure of International schools based on candidacy for accreditation while candidacy for accreditation is originally based on the initial efficiency of the school in providing the educational services including its status as a legal education provider that it doesn't get to get unless it's a candidate school, which is setting the cart before the horse.

II. Answer the following questions

1. What are the Egypt's ambitions for education?
2. What are the shortcomings during the development of the education in Egypt?
3. Why is the second tier of basic compulsory educational the longest?
4. What's the present situation of the basic education in Egypt?
5. How many types does secondary education consist of in the passage? Please describe them.
6. What must students do to enter thesecondary schools and the universities? Why are far efforts underway with the support of

multilateral organizations?
7. What does "it" mean in the 6th paragraph? What does the control of the MoE cause?
8. Why is the bulk of the curriculum consisting of religious subjects?
9. Why is education crisis in Egypt very complicated?

III. Cloze

Complete the following paragraphs according to your own understanding, and change the forms where necessary.

Paragraph 1 [①]

Although significant progress has been made to _____ (1) human capital base through improved education system, still the _____ (2) of education experience is low and unequally distributed. Due to lack of good quality education at the basic and secondary levels, there has been a mushrooming market for _____ (3) tutoring. Now to take private tuition has become more of an _____ (4) than a remedial (补救的) activity. According to the Egypt Human Development Report, 58 percent of surveyed families stated that their children take private tutoring. The CAPMAS survey showed that households spend on average around 61 percent of total education expenditure on private tutoring _____ (5) per household expenditure of the richest quintile on private tutoring is more than seven times that of the poorest. Among the issues is the lack of sufficient education in public schools and the need for private tuition. As of 2005, 61%–70% of Egyptian students attend private tuition. Other _____ (6) issues include: theft of public educational funds and leakage of exams. Egypt also has a _____ (7) of skilled and semi-skilled workforce. But there has been an _____ (8) of low-skilled laborers. Even if there are any high-skilled workers available, their quality of training is quite poor. This is mostly a problem in small-medium companies and large public industries that work in "protected" domestic markets. The average gross production per worker is

---

① http: //en. wikipedia. org/wiki/Education_ in_ Egypt.

Mysterious Arab Countries
神秘的阿拉伯

lower than other North African countries: Morocco and Tunisia. Youth unemployment is also very high, _____ (9) due to lack of education system in providing _____ (10) training under TVET programs.

Paragraph 2①

Most importantly, Egyptian education _____ (1) a main challenge because of the quality of teachers that teach in public schools. An _____ (2) study conducted by Sarah Hartmann in 2008 concluded that most teachers in Egypt resort to teaching for _____ (3) of better options and because the nature of the job does not _____ (4) with their more important gender role as mothers. The low salaries offered by the public schooling system in Egypt _____ (5) low-skilled employees. A study _____ (6) in 1989 documenting the bureaucracy of the Egyptian Ministry of Education concluded that teachers' annual salary in Egypt is, on average, $360. A later study conducted in 2011 showed that teachers earn an average annual salary of $460 which is _____ (7) than half the country's average annual per-capita income. Following the low quality of teachers in Egypt, they lack basic psychological background that would allow them to deal _____ (8) students. Corporal punishment is a common practice in Egyptian schools even though it has not been deeply discussed in literature. A recent example was _____ (9) to media's attention in 2011 when a pre-K teacher was caught on video consistently beating his students harshly. The teacher was sent to court but the parents and students _____ (10) for questioning him expressing that this is what they believe to be the best way to deal with their youngsters.

IV. Spot Dictation

In this part, you will hear a passage three times. When the passage is read for the first time, you should listen carefully for its general idea. When the passage is read for the second time, you are required to fill in the blanks numbered from 1 to 10 with the exact words you have heard. Finally, when the

---

① http://en.wikipedia.org/wiki/Education_in_Egypt.

passage is read for the third time, you should check what you have written.

Ancient Egyptian Education[①]

In Ancient Egypt the child's _____ (1) was not as clearly separated from the adult's as it tends to be in modern Western society. As the years went by childish pastimes would give way to _____ (2) of grown-up behavior. Children would more and more _____ (3) be found lending a hand with the less onerous tasks and gradually _____ (4) practical skills and knowledge from their elders.

By precept and example, parents would _____ (5) into them various educational principles, moral attitudes and views of life. Thus from a tender age they would _____ (6) their basic education in the bosom of the family. For girls, this was usually all the schooling they would get, but for boys it would be _____ (7) by proper training in whatever line they chose, or was chosen for them. Education, of course, covers both the general _____ (8) of a child and its training for a particular vocation. The upbringing of boys was left largely in the hands of their fathers, that of girls was entrusted to their mothers. Parents _____ (9) their children with their ideas about the world, with their religious outlook, with their ethical principles, with correct behavior toward others and toward the super-natural beings in whom everyone believed. They taught them about _____ (10) rituals and so forth.

V. Translation

Turn the following sentences into English, using as many words and phrases you have learned from the text as possible.

1. 埃及也存在受过训练的劳动力匮乏的问题。

_____

_____

[①] http: //en. wikipedia. org/wiki/Education_ in_ Egypt.

2. 埃及政府有责任提供给各个教育阶段免费的教育，比如小学、初中、高中、大学。

3. 埃及有着全中东最庞大的教育机构，并且从1990年以来一直在不断扩大。

4. 技术教育项目提供三年和四年两种，而教育科目分为化学、工业、农业。

5. 不要觉得做这件事情很困难，只要你愿意，你可以利用一切可以利用的资源。

6. 埃及民间社团的几次教育改革尝试产生了一定的积极影响，但这些影响对于教育改革进程的作用仍然十分有限。

VI. Oral Practice

Find a partner or partners and discuss with them the Egypt education. The following questions may help you to start the discussion.

1. After reading the text, have you got a brief understanding of the education system of Egypt? What are they?
2. What difficulties is Egypt education facing now?
3. Do you want to get education in Egypt? Why or why not?

VII. Broaden Your Horizon

Education of Women in the Arab World[①]

The population of the Arab world today is around 150 million, inhabiting an area stretching from Mauritania on the Atlantic Ocean, to Iraq on the Arab Gulf. Education has been seen as the primary means by which the desired goals to develop can be accomplished. Without expanding and improving educational opportunities for both men and women, political, social and economic development, cannot be reached.

The education of women in particular is seen to be essential and necessary for the construction of the new society. Women comprise half of the total population, and their contribution to the nation building process is a must.

Modern education for women in the Arab world is of relatively recent origin. The first modern schools were opened in Egypt (1829), Lebanon (1835) and Iraq (1898). In other countries like Kuwait, Yemen and Saudi Arabia, modern education for women is a product of the 20th century. Progress in female education until recently was slow and extremely limited. Most of the Arab world was under colonial domination. In several places political independence was incomplete and foreign troops remained in the country until many years later. The colonial powers were not interested in expanding educational facilities or making them available to women and, as a result, the illiteracy rate among Arab women remained extremely high. For instance, the illiteracy rate was 96% in Tunisia in 1956 and over 90% in Algeria in 1962.

With political independence and emancipation (解放) from foreign domination, education received a big boost. Both the government and the public considered education as the most important means to develop the Arab world and to improve the conditions of the Arab people. There was a

---

① http://www.library.cornell.edu/colldev/mideast/awomeduc.htm.

substantial increase in the allocation of funds for education in nearly all Arab countries, ranging from twenty to thirty percent of the public budget. Most Arab governments have proclaimed the goal of universal literacy and many possess laws making education free at all levels, compulsory at the first level, and available to as many as possible at the second and third levels.

Governments of some oil producing countries allot stipends（津贴）both to students in school as well as to their parents, thus reducing any economic burden. The stipend serves as an added incentive to pursue an education.

I. Overall development

A quick glance at the overall development of female education in the Arab world reveals that education in all Arab countries expanded enormously on every level in a very short time. Enrollment jumped from approximately one million in 1950, to over eight million in 1975; in other words the rate of growth expanded over eight times.

The ratio of female enrollments to the total registration increased from 30 percent to 36 percent. While this represents a definite change for the better, it also suggests that opportunities for female education are still much more limited and restricted than male education. In other words, the status of women's education still has room for improvement.

The greatest expansion occurred at the first level where total enrollment rose from less than one million to over six million, but the subsequent rate of increase tends to be smaller than those at the second and third levels. This can be explained by two factors; first, the primary level has a larger base with which to start and thus the growth rate tends to be smaller despite the enormous numerical increases. Second, Arab governments paid more attention to the two upper levels. These had been neglected in the past and the resultant need for qualified manpower became acute as the individual countries began to implement development programs aiming at improving social and economic conditions.

The proportion of female enrollment to the total female population of the same age group improved at all levels. On the other hand, the figures also show that there are still large numbers of women who do not have access to schools and for whom universal education at the first level is still a dream. Effort, energy and money need to be invested in the field of education to make it fully accessible.

II. Development of female education in different Arab countries

Enrollment in the primary grades grew steadily in all Arab countries and in fact doubled in most of them. It tripled in some, as in the case of Oman, Qatar, United Arab Emirates, Djibouti and it quadrupled in places like Saudi Arabia, Libya, and South Yemen.

Enrollment differences between boys and girls greatly narrowed in 1975. Seven countries nearly achieved sex parity in enrollment; Bahrain, Jordan Kuwait, Libya, Lebanon, Qatar and the United Arab Emirates. All of these countries are small in area, with the exception of Libya. Libya, Qatar, and the United Arab Emirates achieved near sex parity only recently. Kuwait, Libya, Qatar and the United Arab Emirates, oil producing countries with a very high per capita income exceeding $10, 000 in 1978, are better able to allocate substantial amounts of money for expanding educational facilities.

Second level—Secondary

Secondary school enrollment experienced a remarkable expansion over the last two decades. Enrollments tripled in Iraq, quadrupled in some, and in states like Qatar grew eight times. Three countries, Bahrain, Jordan, Qatar, and United Arab Emirates, experienced the highest growth in female enrollment and toward achieving sex parity. Despite the numerical improvements, the majority of Arab countries still exhibit a high degree of disparity in educational opportunities for male and female on the secondary level. The difference can be explained partly by the outdated but dying tradition which tends to discourage women from going to school, and partly to the lack of educational facilities and teachers.

Third level—College

In 1960, several Arab countries like Kuwait, Qatar, Yemen and United Arab Emirates had no college education. Today practically all Arab states, with the exception of Oman and Djibouti, have developed their own college system.

The disparity between male and female enrollment is highest in North Yemen. Female enrollment was only 10% in 1975, followed by Somalia, where enrollment was 11% the same year. In Bahrain, Kuwait, and Qatar, a curious phenomenon appears; female enrollment exceeded male enrollment (53% in Bahrain, 57% in Qatar, and 56% in Kuwait). There seem to be two reasons for these unusual statistics. First, male students are urged to study abroad while girls are discouraged by tradition or marriage. Accordingly, scholarships or grants to study abroad are rarely granted to women. Nevertheless, these figures signify that Arab women are eager to learn and to obtain the qualifications necessary to enter the labor force in their own societies.

Female enrollments at the third level are represented in all fields with the heaviest concentration in the liberal arts, humanities, social sciences and law. For example, in many Arab countries the ratio of women studying in these areas is over 50%. This to some extent is due to the fact that it is easier and cheaper to expand liberal arts facilities than to augment technical field facilities, and partly to the prevailing attitudes and traditions that the liberal arts are more suitable for women. Recently, enrollment in the liberal arts started to decline in some countries such as Algeria and Syria. The change came partially in response to concentrated efforts to expand the technical facilities and to encourage women to enroll in them. More importantly, employment opportunities are far better in technical and related fields and financially more rewarding. A third reason is that prospective employers often pay salaries in advance to students as an incentive to complete their training in technical fields.

The fields of medicine, dentistry, pharmacy, and nursing have attracted a large number of Arab women. They constitute a considerable percentage of the enrollment in Egypt, Algeria, Kuwait, Lebanon, Iraq, Syria, and Tunisia. Medicine is a prestigious and lucrative profession, and is considered a very acceptable and fitting occupation for women, as most Arab women prefer to be treated by women doctors particularly in gynecology and obstetrics.

Evaluation

Current statistics underscore the significant improvement and the remarkable expansion of educational opportunities at all levels for Arab women in the last two decades. A new born girl in the Arab world today has much better chance than her mother to attend school and finish college. Arab governments are committed and determined to augment educational opportunities and to make them accessible to all eligible women. It is firmly believed that without emancipating women from the bondage of illiteracy no real political, social or economic development can take place. Several studies in the Arab world show that the education of women is the most powerful weapon for improving their status as well as the most potent force of social change, and will touch every aspect of their life from the family to economics. For example, it was discovered that women's education is the best weapon against the population explosion.

Investigations in Egypt, Tunisia, Morocco, and Jordan have shown that illiterate mothers tend to have a larger number of children than educated mothers. Furthermore, these analyses revealed that education in effect delays and postpones marriage by at least two years. It was also shown that the educational attainment of the women determines the attitudes of others toward women and their role in their society. Men whose mothers had no formal education are inclined to oppose the notion of granting women equal political rights and equal employment opportunities. Quite the opposite is true of men whose mothers attended a university. Furthermore, women's participation in public life is proportionately related to the degree of education.

Educational opportunities increase for women in the Arab world, so do their chances for integration in the labor force and moving up the employment ladder.

Mysterious Arab Countries
神秘的阿拉伯

Unit 6
Travel in Dubai

Warm-Up Questions

1. Which country do you want to travel most? Please list your reasons.
2. Do you know anything about Dubai? What comes to you instantly at the thought of Dubai?
3. Do you have the intention of visiting Dubai someday?

Text

As one of the most famous tourist attractions in the Middle East and the Persian Gulf region, Dubai has shining attraction herself all along. Being one of the few cities in the world that has undergone such a rapid transformation — from a humble beginning as a pearl-diving centre — to one of the fastest growing cities on earth, Dubai has recently attracted world attention through many innovative large construction projects. Dubai has emerged as a cosmopolitan metropolis that has grown steadily to become a tourism and trade hub, which has become symbolic for its skyscrapers and high-rise buildings.

Unit 6 Travel in Dubai

Dubai: Ostentatious and Beckoning[1]

I expected the infinite blue sky. I expected the intense, unrelenting heat. I even anticipated that the city sprawl would stop abruptly to make way for rolling, barren dunes. What I didn't expect from Dubai, however, was the luxury, the slick modernity. I certainly did not expect the gleaming metropolis that has sprung up in the desert in the 34 years since seven small kingdoms joined to form the United Arab Emirates.

If there is one word to describe Dubai, it's "ostentatious". So many of the attractions here appear to have been created simply as a means of saying to the rest of the world: "Look how much money we've got".

Take, for example, The Palm. An immense man-made island — in the shape of a palm tree — off the coast of the fashionable Jumeirah beach district, it comprises the homes of multi-millionaires, as well as luxury apartments, shopping malls and the world's biggest hotels. The Palm 2 is already under construction. Further along is the just-begun The World, 300 individual islands which, when viewed from the air, look like a world map. If I had the bank balance, I could assuage my homesickness by snapping up "South Australia" and building my own modest seven-bedroom palace right where my native Adelaide should be. Dubai is already home to the world's only seven-star hotel, Burj Al-Arab, which has an underwater restaurant that guests are taken to via submarine. The city will soon also house an entirely underwater hotel.

Other plans afoot in Dubai are Dubailand, a Disneyworld-style theme park which, with its 45 separate "worlds", will be bigger than Dubai itself. The world's biggest shopping mall is also under construction, so is the world's tallest building, and everyone is very excited about the soon-to-be-built world's biggest indoor ski slope. Notice a pattern emerging?

But Dubai's feverish cash-splashing is not megalomania; rather, it is part of a very shrewd plan for sustainability hatched by its ruler, Sheik Mohammed, and his family.

Unlike its closest neighbor and the UAE's capital, Abu Dhabi, Dubai has

---

[1] http://www.holidaycityflash.com/traveladvise/dubai_future.htm.

very limited oil reserves. It has cleverly secured its future by positioning itself as a business and finance hub and, more recently, a tourist idyll. It's a city with a lot to offer but, above all else, Dubai deserves credit for its unabashed ambition.

At this very moment, there are 2800 building projects underway in the city. Just 20 per cent of Dubai's population are Emirati — the rest are expatriates keeping the well-oiled wheels of commerce turning — and, of these, a hefty proportion are construction workers who toil in shifts day and night to transform the city from building site to world-beater.

Even the harsh desert interior — for centuries home only to the nomadic Bedouin tribes — is considered ripe for money-spinning development. Forty-five minutes from Dubai is the sumptuous Al Mahaj desert resort, where rooms are in fact stand-alone luxury huts, each with its own infinity pool.

Here, guests rise at dawn — the only time when being outside is bearable — for activities including camel trekking, falconry and archery. During the daylight hours, when desert temperatures top 50 degrees centigrade, there's nothing to do but indulge in all manner of delicious treatments in the day spa.

At night, when the temperature drops to a positively chilly 30 degrees, there are dune dinners and more camel treks to be enjoyed. Or, if that all seems a little too active, Al Mahaj boasts a deck with sweeping desert views where it's easy to while away an entire evening watching the oryx, gazelles and lizards who call the 2000 km sq conservation site home.

Dubai is a destination which aims to cater for everyone, so it is, of course, possible to have an authentic desert experience without the Al Mahaj price tag. Tour company Arabian Adventures, a subsidiary of the Emirates airline group, offers a dune safari dinner which is not to be missed. Diners travel in a convoy of 4WD jeeps in amongst the rolling dunes which look, ironically, like rippling water. Some rather hairy dune driving leads to a desert camp, where guests sit on intricately detailed carpets and cushions and eat traditional food from low tables. Belly dancers provide the entertainment and there are camel rides and a henna tattooist to complete the experience.

If all the opulence gets too much, head across Dubai Creek — the modestly named waterway is actually about as wide as the Thames! — to the old town, where haggling over prices at the gold and spice souks (markets) is the order of the day. The Kurama district is also a must-shop for fashion-and budget-conscious ladies.

The Dubai in the glossy tourist brochures is a relatively new invention but a city has existed here for hundreds of years, while the Bedouin and other desert people have lived in the region for millennia. A fantastic exploration of Middle Eastern history and culture, as well as the birth of Dubai as we know it, can be found in the innovative Dubai Museum.

I almost felt like I'd visited Dubai too soon. It's already an exciting destination and a city of fascinating contrasts — old versus new, ambition versus careful planning, progress versus history. But there's a pervading sense that in 5 or 10 years, when cranes no longer dominate the skyline and it's possible to see and touch all these fledgling developments, Dubai will be truly breathtaking.

New Words

infinite ['ɪnfɪnət] adj. having no limits or boundaries in time or space or extent or magnitude 无限的；无穷的

intense [ɪn'tens] adj. in an extreme degree 强烈的；紧张的；非常的

unrelenting [ˌʌnrɪ'lentɪŋ] adj. not to be placated or appeased or moved by entreaty 无情的；不屈不挠的

anticipate [æn'tɪsɪpeɪt] v. regard something as probable or likely 预期；期望；盼望

sprawl [sprɔːl] n. a continuous network of urban communities 蔓延；伸开手足躺；无计划地扩展

abruptly [ə'brʌptlɪ] adv. quickly and without warning 突然地；唐突地

barren ['bærən] adj. providing no shelter or sustenance, completely lacking 贫瘠的；无益的；空洞的

luxury ['lʌkʃərɪ] n. something that is an indulgence rather than a necessity 奢侈；奢华；奢侈品

slick [slɪk] adj. having a smooth, gleaming surface 光滑的；华而不实的

metropolis [mɪ'trɔplɪs] n. 大都市；首府

Mysterious Arab Countries
神秘的阿拉伯

ostentatious [ɔsten'teɪʃəs] adj. intended to attract notice and impress other 招摇的；夸耀的；惹人注目的
immense [ɪ'mens] adj. unusually great in size or amount or degree 巨大的；广大的；无边无际的
palm [pɔ:m] n. 棕榈树
multi-millionaire ['mʌlti mɪljə'neə] n. 千万富翁
individual [ɪndɪ'vɪdjuəl] adj. separate and distinct from others of the same kind 个人的；个别的；独特的
assuage [ə'sweɪdʒ] v. provide physical relief, as from pain 缓解；减轻
homesickness ['həumsɪknɪs] n. a longing to return home 乡愁
snap ['snæp] v. to grasp hastily or eagerly 抓
guest [gest] n. a visitor to whom hospitality is extended 客人；来宾
submarine ['sʌbməri:n] n. 潜水艇
separate ['sepəreɪt] adj. independent; not united or joint 单独的；分开的
emerge [ɪ'mə:dʒ] v. to come into view 新兴；出现
feverish ['fi:vərɪʃ] adj. marked by intense agitation or emotion 极度兴奋的
megalomania [megələu'meɪnɪə] n. 狂妄自大
shrewd [ʃru:d] adj. able to understand and judge a situation quickly and to use this understanding to their own advantage 精明的；机灵的
sustainability [sə'steɪnəbɪləti] n. the property of being sustainable 持久性；持续
hatch [hætʃ] v. devise or invent 策划
idyll ['aɪdɪl] n. 田园生活
unabashed [ʌnə'bæʃt] adj. not embarrassed 不害羞的；不畏惧的
expatriate [eks'pætrɪeɪt] n. someone who is living in a country that is not their own 侨居者；移居国外者
commerce ['kɔmə:s] n. the activities and procedures involved in buying and selling things 商业；贸易
hefty ['heftɪ] adj. of considerable weight and size 重的；肌肉发达的；强有力地
toil [tɔɪl] v. work hard 辛苦工作；费力地做
harsh [ha:ʃ] adj. unpleasantly stern 严厉的；粗糙的
interior [ɪn'tɪərɪə] n. the region that is inside of something 内部；本质
nomadic [nəu'mædɪk] adj. tending to travel 游牧的；流浪的；游动的

sumptuous ['sʌmptjuəs] adj. rich and superior in quality 华丽的；奢侈的
infinity [ɪn'fɪnətɪ] n. time without end 无穷；无限大；无限距
trek [trek] v. make a long and difficult journey 艰苦跋涉
temperature ['tempərɪtʃə] n. the somatic sensation of cold or heat 温度
centigrade ['sentɪgreɪd] n. a temperature scale on 摄氏温度
indulge [ɪn'dʌldʒ] v. give free rein to 满足；沉迷于…
positively ['pɔzətɪvlɪ] adv. extremely 肯定地；明确地；断然地
chilly ['tʃɪlɪ] adj. uncomfortably cool 寒冷的；怕冷的
oryx ['ɔrɪks] n. 大羚羊
gazelle [gə'zel] n. 瞪羚
destination [destɪ'neɪʃən] n. the place designated as the end 目的地；终点
subsidiary [səb'sɪdɪərɪ] n. furnishing added support 子公司；辅助者
safari [sə'fɑːrɪ] n. an overland journey by hunters (especially in Africa) 旅行队
ironically [aɪ'rɔnɪklɪ] adv. contrary to plan or expectation 讽刺地；说反话地
rippling ['rɪplɪŋ] adj. having a small wave on the surface of a liquid 使起涟漪；呈波状起伏
henna ['henə] n. a reddish brown dye used especially on hair 指甲花；红褐色
tattooist [tə'tuːɪst] n. 有纹身的人
opulence ['ɔpjuləns] n. wealth as evidenced by sumptuous living 富裕；丰富
haggle ['hægl] v. argue about the price 讨价还价；争论（价格）
brochure ['brəuʃə] n. a small book usually having a paper cover 印刷资料（或广告）手册、小册子
millennia [mɪ'lenɪə] n. 千年期
innovative ['ɪnəvətɪv] adj. ahead of the times 革新的；创新的
versus ['vəːsəs] prep. in the teeth of 与…相对；对抗
pervading [pə:'veɪdɪŋ] adj. spreading through 普遍的
crane [kreɪn] n. 起重机
skyline ['skaɪlaɪn] n. the outline of objects seen against the sky 地平线；空中轮廓线
fledgling ['fledʒlɪŋ] adj. young and inexperienced 初出茅庐的；无经验的

Mysterious Arab Countries
神秘的阿拉伯

Phrases & Expressions

make way for	让路
spring up	如雨后春笋般涌现
snap up	抢购；抢先弄到手
appear to	出现；似乎
as a means of	作为一种手段
the rest of	其余的；剩下的
take…for example	以…为例
in the shape of	…的形状
as well as	以及
throw down	丢下
look like	像
above all	首先
in fact	事实上；其实
aim to	旨在；目的是
as we know	就我们所知
no longer	不再

Proper Names

Dubai [ˈdjuːbaɪ]	迪拜
United Arab Emirates [ˈemɪreɪts]	阿拉伯联合酋长国
Jumeirah beach [ˈjuːmɪrə ˈbiːtʃ]	朱美拉海滩
Adelaide [ˈædəleɪd]	阿德莱德（南澳大利亚州首府）
Abu Dhabi [ˌaːbuːˈdaːbiː]	阿布扎比（阿拉伯联合酋长国之一）
Sheik Mohammed [ˈʃeɪk muˈhæməd]	谢赫·穆罕默德
Dubai Creek [ˈdjuːbaɪ ˈkriːk]	迪拜湾

Unit 6　Travel in Dubai

Background Information

1. The United Arab Emirates（阿拉伯联合酋长国）

　　The United Arab Emirates, sometimes simply called the Emirates or the UAE, is an Arab country located in the southeast end of the Arabian Peninsula on the Persian Gulf, bordering Oman（阿曼）to the east and Saudi Arabia to the south, as well as sharing sea borders with Qatar（卡塔尔）and Iran. The UAE is a federation of seven emirates（equivalent to principalities）. Each emirate is governed by a hereditary emir who jointly form the Federal Supreme Council which is the highest legislative and executive body in the country. One of the emirs is selected as the President of the United Arab Emirates. The constituent emirates are Abu Dhabi（阿布扎比）, Ajman（阿治曼）, Dubai（迪拜）, Fujairah（富查伊拉）, Ras al-Khaimah（哈伊马角）, Sharjah（沙迦）, and Umm al-Quwain（乌姆盖万）. The capital is Abu Dhabi, which is one of the two centers of commercial and cultural activities, together with Dubai. Islam is the official religion of the UAE, and Arabic is the official language. UAE is a hot desert climate with little rainfall. Oil and gas resources are very rich.

2. The Palm Islands

　　Palm Islands（棕榈岛）are artificial islands which called the eighth wonder of the world, "the astonishing imagination of ancient hanging gardens of Babylon（巴比伦）and ancient Arab rich combination of luxury and style". Palm Islands by reclaimed completed plans to build more than 12,000 private homes and more than 10,000 apartments, also includes more than 100 more luxury hotels, as well as ports, water theme parks, restaurants, shopping centers and places of diving facilities.

3. Abu Dhabi

　　Abu Dhabi（阿布扎比）is the capital of the United Arab Emirates

Emirate of Abu Dhabi（阿拉伯联合酋长国阿布扎比酋长国）, is also the capital of the United Arab Emirates. The western coast of Abu Dhabi is in the United Arab Emirates, a t-shaped island in the Persian Gulf. While Abu Dhabi is mostly desert, the city of Abu Dhabi is a green paradise because of deep, wide streets, beautiful park full of trees in the distance, and vision.

4. The Bedouin（贝都因人）

The Bedouin are a part of a predominantly desert-dwelling Arabian ethnic group traditionally divided into tribes, or clans. Later with the development of pastoral industry they gradually spread to West Asia, North Africa in many countries, most of them being Muslims desert nomads. Bedouins living in the desert, wasteland and hills and agricultural area edge on camels for a living. Many has given up the nomadic Bedouin tribes（贝都因部落）and lived in urban areas and lived a semi-nomadic（半游牧）life.

Study & Practice

I. Read Aloud and Memorize

But Dubai's feverish cash-splashing is not megalomania; rather, it is part of a very shrewd plan for sustainability hatched by its ruler, Sheik Mohammed, and his family.

Unlike its closest neighbor and the UAE's capital, Abu Dhabi, Dubai has very limited oil reserves. It has cleverly secured its future by positioning itself as a business and finance hub and, more recently, a tourist idyll. It's a city with a lot to offer but, above all else, Dubai deserves credit for its unabashed ambition.

Unit 6 Travel in Dubai

II. Answer the Following Questions

1. Which word did the author use to describe Dubai?
2. Is the real life in Dubai the same as what the author expected? Why?
3. What's the function of the example — an immense man-made island?
4. Why did the author say: "If I had the bank balance, I could assuage my homesickness by snapping up South Australia, and building my own modest seven-bedroom palace right where my native Adelaide should be."
5. How can you know the luxury of Dubai through this passage?
6. Is Dubai feverish cash-splashing megalomania? Why?
7. Dubai has very limited oil reserves, how can it secure its future?
8. Why do the people do nothing during the daylight times in Al Mahaj desert resort, yet active at night?
9. What's the author's conclusion at the end of the article?
10. After reading the passage, what do you think of Dubai?

III. Cloze

Complete the following paragraphs according to your own understanding, and change the forms where necessary.

Paragraph 1 [①]

Truth is, there's no such thing as a seven-star establishment. You can't officially go _____ (1) than five. The Burj Al Arab's seven-star rating may be an urban myth that got out of hand, but _____ (2) dominates the Dubai skyline and tourists' imagination quite like it. It's the world's tallest hotel and _____ (3) its least subtle — gold-leaf is applied as liberally as undercoat, there's a _____ (4) of white Rolls Royce on the forecourt and dancing fountains in the foyer, and fireworks launch from the bridge to

---

① http://content.time.com/time/travel/cityguide/article/0, 31489, 1849667 _ 1849594 _ 1849205, 00. html.

Mysterious Arab Countries
神秘的阿拉伯

announce the _____ (5) of VVIPs (very important doesn't cut it here) — but nobody ever came to Dubai in _____ (6) of understatement. The only way to get inside without paying for a room is to _____ (7) a table at one of the hotel's costly eateries. Al Muntaha is on the top floor but its bafflingly bright interior prevents you from seeing the views outside; Al Mahara is an expensive fish restaurant with an aquarium _____ (8) than most people's apartments; and Sahn Eddar serves afternoon tea. Best of the lot is the beach-based Majlis Al Bahar. From here you can admire the Burj's impressive exterior (the hotel's beauty is on the outside) _____ (9) instructing the maître (管家) that you'll be taking your nightcap in the top-floor cocktail bar, _____ (10) you can gaze at the city's garishness.

Paragraph 2[①]

The _____ (1) audacious of all of Dubai's megaprojects is the collection of reclaimed islands just offshore. First came the palm-tree shaped Palm Jumeirah, _____ (2) the city bills as the eighth wonder of the world. And there are two more islands, Jebel Ali and Deira, in _____ (3) stages of development. In an outlandish stroke, Jebel Ali will feature a breakwater that spells out a line of poetry by Dubai's ruler Sheikh Mohammed bin Rashid Al Maktoum ("It takes a man of vision to write on water"). Last, but certainly not the _____ (4) is the world, an archipelago of islands _____ (5) forms a world map in miniature; the islands are for sale, so if you can _____ (6) it, you can buy a "country" for yourself. _____ (7) you're one of the few who bought property early, you'll have to wait for hotels to open in 2009 to set foot on the reclaimed land. In the _____ (8) your best views are by boat. A _____ (9) of companies can get you out into the Gulf: Try Dusail, Bristol Marine or Art Marine, all of which offer stately yachts, motor boats and speed boats. It's not often that you can claim to have sailed around the _____ (10) world in an afternoon.

---

① http: //content. time. com/time/travel/cityguide/article/0, 31489, 1849667 _ 1849594 _ 1849205, 00. html.

IV. Spot Dictation

In this part, you will hear a passage three times. When the passage is read for the first time, you should listen carefully for its general idea. When the passage is read for the second time, you are required to fill in the blanks numbered from 1 to 10 with the exact words you have heard. Finally, when the passage is read for the third time, you should check what you have written.

The Traditional Dubai[①]

While vast swaths of the city have been demolished in the relentless _____ (1) toward the future, one neighborhood harks back to the quiet fishing village once was. The Bastakia Quarter, _____ (2) squeezes itself between the Dubai Creek and the buzzing Bur Dubai district, is a mini maze of wind-towered buildings, a clutch of which have been _____ (3) into art galleries and cafés. Start your tour at XVA Gallery, which _____ (4) in contemporary art from across the Gulf region. Continue your appreciation of Middle Eastern art at the Majlis Gallery before lunching on _____ (5) salads and a refreshing mint-and-lime juice in the neighboring Basta Art Cafe's sun-dappled courtyard.

Once _____ (6) weave through the textile souk — where you'll find magnificent bolts of fabric, _____ (7) with less inspiring tat — and on to the Creek where you can either join the commuters for a ride across the water or hire your own boat for a _____ (8) tour of the waterway. Back in port, head to the small but interesting Dubai Museum to see how oil and _____ (9) mixed to make this modern oasis. If you get hungry again, check out Bastakiah Nights, an atmospheric Lebanese restaurant with a great _____ (10) area.

[①] http: //content. time. com/time/travel/cityguide/article/0, 31489, 1849667 _ 1849594 _ 1849212, 00. html.

V. Translation

Turn the following sentences into English, using as many words and phrases you have learned from the text as possible.

1. 他浑身疲倦。

2. 许多巨大的高层建筑在这座城市拔地而起。

3. 从理论上来说直线可以无限地延伸。

4. 品德之美应列于其他美之上。

5. 只有摔倒过，才能学着如何站起来。

6. 暴风雨来临前，乌云笼罩着整座城市。

7. 在战争期间，政府禁止任何人与敌国通商。

8. 市政工人和志愿者在紧张地忙碌着，将积雪从房顶上除去。

VI. Oral Practice

Find a partner or partners and discuss with them thefollowing questions

and share your opinions with your classmates.
1. Do you know more about Dubai after studying the text? Share with your partners.
2. What do you think the differences between traditional and modern Dubai are?
3. As we all know, modern Dubai is famous for luxury. What contributes to Dubai's rapid economy development in your idea?

VII. Broaden Your Horizon

Dubai: More than Buildings[①]

The city of Dubai really knows how to create its headlines. This little fishing-village-that-could has built an entire tourist industry out of piquing people's curiosity. Its unstoppable, finely tuned PR machine has managed to overcome every downside to make the city a must-see location. Dubai has its virtues, so if you find yourself with 24 hours in the city, you'll have no shortage of things to do in addition to visiting famous architectures.

1. Cheap and Chic Eats

This is a city with the super rich and the super poor. You are unlikely to see a place where the division between the "have nots" and the "have yachts" is so apparent. The local-born Emiratis (阿联酋国民), who make up about 12% of the population, are typically extremely wealthy, but the town was built on the backs of a huge working-class population predominantly from the Indian subcontinent and from less prosperous areas of the Gulf. Sitting between the two groups is a burgeoning band of expats, mostly from the West, who are profiting to varying degrees from the city's modern day Gold Rush.

The best way to experience these distinct social strata (阶层) is through your stomach. At the top end is five-star cuisine of the highest order. British

---

① http: //content. time. com/time/travel/cityguide/article/.

chefs Gary Rhodes and Gordon Ramsay have culinary outposts in the Grosvenor House Hotel and the Hilton Dubai Creek, respectively, both offering Michelin star-courting cuisine. They are joined at the top of the tree by the excellent Chinese restaurant Noble House in the Raffles Hotel. In any one of these gilt-edged places you'll sample sensational fare in a high-end setting surrounded by Emiratis and those who have benefited most from Dubai's economic boom, all paying about AED 500 ($140) per person for the privilege.

On the other end of the social spectrum lies Al Dhiyafah Road, Dubai's cheap-eats street. Here restaurants catering to the city's less affluent residents spill out onto the sidewalk so you can people-watch while feasting on food from Lebanon, Iran and the Indian subcontinent. On the northern end of the street lies Sidra, with zesty salads and a gut-busting mixed grill that gives you a taste of the Levant.

2. Shopping Malls

The thing about shopping in Dubai is that the actual shopping is average, but the experience is intriguing. If you've shopped in New York or Paris, Dubai's malls will be a disappointment. Most of the shops are familiar and no cheaper (though you may find the odd bargain on electronics) than in other places in the world. But store trawling is only the tip of the Dubai shopping experience. Malls in this city are realizations of unrestrained fantasy, offering surreal attractions to lure you (and your credit card) in.

The Souk Madinat inside the Madinat Jumeirah Hotel, for example, boasts its own waterway to transfer people from its shops, bars and restaurants to the neighboring clutch of hotels. The gargantuan Mall of the Emirates has an indoor ski slope with real snow, should you fancy a quick slalom between shopping and hitting the beach. The recently opened Khan Murjan souk claims to be an example of "Islamic authenticity, unparalleled in the region"; it connects the Wafi Mall, home of Chanel, Marks & Spencer and Montblanc, with the brand new Raffles Hotel. All may be surpassed by the Mall of Arabia, open in 2008, as the largest mall in the world covering 10 million square feet with a real-life Jurassic Park, in which the beasts will be mechanical.

3. The Gold Souk

Dubai is known for really cheap gold — but you'll have to haggle for it. Whether or not you're ready to buy, a stroll through the dazzling Gold Souk is a must. The stores also offer platinum, diamonds and occasionally silver, and the government keeps tight control over the quality of all the merchandise, so rest assured that your purchases will be genuine. If something in the window catches your fancy, be sure to barter — persistent protest capped with a walk-away will get merchants to drop their asking price by as much as half.

Less atmospheric, but even cheaper, is the Gold & Diamond Park, where you can find unique designs or get jewelers to recreate pieces for you at a fraction of the cost of the original.

4. Champagne Brunch

This is a Muslim state, but alcohol flows liberally. By law, it can be served only within the confines of a hotel, but with an estimated 450 hotels in the emirate, some with up to 26 bars, restaurants and clubs, you won't be left thirsty.

If your stay in Dubai takes in a Friday (the first day of the Arabic weekend) then you can experience first-hand the city's strange relationship with the bottle. While it is the holiest day of the week for Muslims, many of the city's restaurants throw their doors open for "champagne brunch." This brunch is not the sedate culinary experience it is elsewhere; in Dubai, it is an exercise in excess, with free-flowing booze and heaping buffets that would have even the most indulgent glutton begging for mercy.

If you're just in the mood for an evening tipple, the places to head are the open-air 360 Degrees, an out-to-sea rooftop bar within spitting distance of the famed Burj Al Arab.

Mysterious Arab Countries
神秘的阿拉伯

5. The Beach

You'll definitely want to see the shore while you're in town. The posher (豪华的) beach hotels have partitioned off the majority of the sand, so if you're not staying on the Jumeirah beach strip, your best bet is Al Mamzar, a public beach near the neighboring emirate of Sharjah. The clogged artery of a road that connects the cities means it's frustratingly inaccessible during the work week. Other good alternatives are Jumeirah Beach Park with its small coffee shop and AED 5 ($1.30) entrance fee, or the free stretch of sand running the length of Umm Suqeim, known as Kite Beach due to its popularity with the city's kite-surfers. If you insist on a more luxurious beach experience, then a few hotels will allow you to sit on their sand for a fee: Try Le Meridien Mina Seyahi (AED 250, or $70).

6. The Desert

A visit to the desert isn't as peaceful as you'd think. The easiest way to get at the dunes outside the city is on a four-wheel-drive safari. The tours are incredibly popular, but your enjoyment will depend on your tolerance for being thrown around the sand in a Jeep, touristy BBQs in the desert replete with a belly dancer and henna painting services and lots of other tourists. If you can handle all the three, then a number of expeditions are awaiting. The same outfit also has hot-air balloon flights over the sand at sunrise—a statelier desert experience. If you just want to see some sand without vertigo or nausea, then head out to the Bab Al Shams Resort hotel. Here you can sit on the rooftop and enjoy a cocktail as the sun dips below the dunes.

7. Golf

Golf is an obsession in Dubai. If you want to rub elbows with celebrities on the green, try the courses designed by Colin Montgomerie and Ernie Els. Better yet, head to the city's most famous course, the Emirates Golf Club, which hosts the annual Dubai Desert Classic (total prize money is a cool

$2.5 million). It's a stunning course, whose 18th hole has one of the finest approaches in the world. Almost as impressive is the Dubai Creek Golf and Yacht Club, which boasts a challenging par-72 course along with a fun "pitch and putt" (an amateur sport very similar to golf) course, plus an impressive clubhouse whose architecture echoes that of the Sydney Opera House. Tee times go quickly, so you'd be wise to book in advance, especially if you want to be among the first to take a swing at Tiger's tees: the first holes designed by Woods—the Tiger Woods Dubai, a private golf community and resort.

Mysterious Arab Countries
神秘的阿拉伯

Unit 7
Belly Dance

Warm-Up Questions

1. Do you know any kind of Arabic dance?
2. What do you know about belly dance? Have you ever tried it?
3. Do you agree with the opinion that belly dance is performed mainly for the purpose of entertaining men?

Text

Arabic dance is generally equivalent to belly dance due to the latter's worldwide popularity. However, actually there are many other dance forms in the Arab world. But belly dance's popularity is most widely acknowledged throughout the world.

Belly Dance[1]

The Arab world is home to numerous dance traditions. There are many styles of traditional Arabic dance[2]. Stretching across North Africa and the Middle East, the Arabic world is a large and diverse region. As with the varieties in cuisine, dress, dialect and landscape present all across the Arab world, the dance traditions are rich and varied as well.

Most of the dancing that goes on in the Arab world happens at weddings and other celebrations. Certain dance styles, such as the hagalla step from Western Egypt and Eastern Libya, are specific wedding dances; though many dance forms are danced at celebrations. Even small parties and social gatherings in the Arab world will be accompanied by music and dance. Professional dancers are often present at Arabic weddings as part of the celebration, though guests participate in celebratory dances as well.

Arabic dance choreography varies much from country to country. You can even find distinctive regional dance styles within the same country. Many of the traditional dance forms in the Arab world focus on movements of the hips, shoulders, arms and feet. Many forms involve using props or an artistic manipulation of the costume.

Though most traditional Arabic dances are primarily social dance forms, some dancers perform these styles in formaltheatrical venues as part of cultural preservation and education. Many of the Arab countries have national dance troupes that tour internationally to perform and share their cultural traditions. Arab communities in the United States, Europe and Australia also form local troupes dedicated to preserving and accurately representing Arabic dance traditions.

Men are as involved with dance in the Arabic world as women. In addition to taking part in social dance traditions, several men are famous worldwide in

---

[1] http: //www. bellydance. org/articles/what _ is _ bellydance. html & http: //www. esto. es/bellydance/english/history. htm.

[2] All the content about traditional Arabic dances are cited from the website: http: //www. ehow. com/about_ 6720485 _ traditional-arabic-dance. html.

the fields of choreography, teaching and the performance of Arabic traditional dances.

The term "Arabic dance" is often associated with the style of belly dance. Though this is an inaccurate label, belly dance's popularity is most widely acknowledged.

Belly dance has been around for ages and is thought to be a women's dance. Many experts say belly dancing is the oldest form of dance, having roots in all ancient cultures from the orient to India to the mid-East. It is at least 6,000 years old dating back to Mesopotamia time. Probably the greatest misconception about belly dancing is that it is intended to entertain men. Throughout history, this ritualized expression has usually been performed for other women, it is thought to be originated from fertility dances, and men were not allowed. Groups of women would perform belly dance in parties preparing a young woman for marriage or during birth to aid the mother in the childbirth process, and women would dance for goddess celebrations or special occasions. In most cases, the presence of men is not permitted.

Belly dancing is natural to a woman's bone and muscle structure with movements emanating from the torso rather than in the legs and feet. The dance often focuses upon isolating different parts of the body, moving them independently in sensuous patterns, weaving together the entire feminine form. Belly dancing is generally performed barefoot, thought by many to emphasize the intimate physical connection between the dancer, her expression, and Mother Earth.

Belly dancing costumes are often colorful, flowing garments, accented with flowing scarves and veils. Finger cymbals (made of brass and known as zills) are common, dating back to 200 B.C. as well as exotic jewelry, including intricate belts made of coins that, in earlier days, comprised the family's wealth so that it might be portable in the event the woman needed to move quickly or flee. Other interesting accessories used during the dance are swords, snakes, large vessels, and even huge candelabras, complete with flaming candles.

The exact origin of this dance form is actively debated among dance enthusiasts, especially given the limited academic research on the topic. Much of the research in this area has been done by dancers attempting to understand their dance's origins. However, the often overlooked fact that most dancing in the Middle East occurs in the social context rather than the more visible and glamorous context of the professional nightclub dancers, has led to an overall misunderstanding of the dance's true nature and has given rise to many conflicting theories about its origins. Because this dance is a fusion of many dance styles, it undoubtedly has many different origins — many of them in ethnic folk dances.

Many dancers subscribe to one or another of a number of theories regarding the origins of the dance form. The most well-known theory is that it descended from a religious dance temple priestesses once practiced. This idea is usually the one referred to in mainstream articles on the topic, and has enjoyed a large amount of publicity. Another theory is referring to its part of traditional birthing practices, which covers a sub-set of dance movements in modern Raqs Sharqi. Strongly publicized by the research of the dancer/layperson anthropologist Morocco (also known as Carolina Varga Dinicu), it involves the rework of movements traditionally utilized to demonstrate or ease childbirth. Although lacking an "origin point", this theory does have the advantage of numerous oral historical references, and is backed by a commentary in the work *The Dancer of Shamahka*. Besides, two points suggest Roma dance as its origin. The Roma, and other related groups, are seen as either having brought the form over as they traveled, or picked it up along the way and spread it around. Thanks to the conflation of Roma forms of dance into the Raqs Sharqi sphere in the West, these theories enjoy a vogue in the West that is not necessarily reflected in their origin countries — although some of that may be due to strongly-held prejudices against the Roma. Whatever the origin point, belly dance has a long history in the Middle East.

Egyptian belly dance is one of the most elegant dance styles of belly dance. It is a slow and sensual style with a lot of isolations, shimmies and layering. The central home of belly dance today is in Egypt, more specifically, Cairo. It is there that Egyptian Cabaret had originated in. Cairo is like Hollywood. It is filled with Egyptian dancers, shops, musicians and anything remotely related to Oriental dance (another name for belly dance). Cairo is home to the most famous belly dancers in the entire world. It is also a very good place to tour during the belly dance season. There are shops at every corner, and costume designers are famous for their designs.

Egyptian style is an all body dance experience. When you dance Egyptian everything from your toes to the top of your head should be dancing. This means that you must actually feel the music, and you must dance with it. Egyptian dance is graceful, exciting and energized all at the same time. In Egypt the dancers don't do veil work, but in America an Egyptian dancer performing in a restaurant may throw around the veil a bit before going into her routine. Veil work is normally minimal and will last between 1 and 2 minutes at most.

Practice layering shimmies, belly rolls, undulations, chest thrust and circles. Mix these with snake arms, shoulder rolls and shimmies. Know how to transition into different moves. Practice really does make perfection! Limit your spins and kicks when dancing Egyptian. It's okay to do a few, but if you get excessive with it then you are more than likely going to look like a Turkish dancer.

In Palestine, this social dance is called Raks Baladi, and is performed by people of all ages and both sexes during festive occasions such as weddings and other social gatherings for fun and celebration. It is the theatricalized version, performed by male and female professional dancers and called Raks Sharki in Arabic that is most popular in America today.

In its native lands boys and girls learn the dance from an early age. As with all social dances, it is learned informally through observation andimitation of their elders during family and community celebrations, as well as during informal gatherings with friends. Today, Middle Eastern dance classes are offered throughout the world, and skilled dancers are able to share their knowledge of the dance during studio classes and workshops.

In America, belly dancing enjoyed its first significant renown when the famous dancer Little Egypt performed at the Chicago World's Fair in 1893. Americans found themselves fascinated by the exotic body rhythms and music, eventually including them in many silent films made just a few years later. Costumes and dancing styles were given a distinctive Hollywood flare and, in turn influenced dancers in the Middle East, thus evolving the art form to a new level. For example, belly dance with flowing veils wasn't documented before the 1900s but is now quite popular throughout the world.

Unit 7 Belly Dance

Since the turn of the century, belly dancing has grown enormously in popularity across the U. S. and worldwide. Belly dance festivals, workshops, andseminars take place constantly, attracting large audiences of interested, involved men and women. Many dancers now study the art form intensively, traveling to the mid-East and elsewhere to experience it where it originated in.

New Words

equivalent [ɪ'kwɪvələnt] adj. equal in amount or value 相等的；同意义的
numerous ['nju:mərəs] adj. amounting to a large indefinite number 许多的；很多的
stretch [stretʃ] v. extend to a greater or the full length 伸展；张开
present ['prezənt] adj. being or existing in a specified place 出席的；在场的
participate [pɑ:'tɪsɪpeɪt] v. be involved in; share in something 参与；分享
choreography [kɔrɪ'ɔgrəfɪ] n. 舞蹈艺术
distinctive [dɪ'stɪŋktɪv] adj. of a feature that helps to distinguish a person or thing 有特色的；与众不同的
props [prɔps] n. 小道具
manipulation [mənɪpju'leɪʃn] n. the action of touching with the hands or by the use of mechanical means 操作；处理
costume ['kɔstju:m] n. the attire worn in a play or at a fancy dress ball 服装；装束
theatrical [θɪ'ætrɪkl] adj. 1. of or relating to the theater 戏剧性的
venue ['venju:] n. the scene of any event or action 地点
preservation [prezə'veʃn] n. the activity of protecting something from loss or danger 保存；保留
troupe [tru:p] n. 剧团
represent [reprɪ'zent] v. express indirectly by an image, form, or model; be a symbol 代表；表现
orient ['ɔ:rɪənt] n. 东方；东方国家
entertain [entə'teɪn] v. amuse, interest or give sb. pleasure 招待；娱乐
ritualized ['rɪtjuəlaɪzd] adj. making or evolving into a ritual rather than natural 仪式化的

Mysterious Arab Countries
神秘的阿拉伯

fertility [fə'tɪlɪtɪ] n. the state of being fertile; capable of producing offspring 丰饶；多产

presence ['prezəns] n. the state of being present; current existence 出席；存在

emanate ['eməneɪt] v. give out (breath or an odor) 发散；发出

torso ['tɔ:səu] n. 躯干

isolate ['aɪsəleɪt] v. place or set apart; set apart from others 孤立；隔离

sensuous ['sensjuəs] adj. giving pleasure to the mind or body through the senses 感觉上的；给人快感的

feminine ['femɪnɪn] adj. being related to or are considered typical of women 女性的；阴柔的

intimate ['ɪntɪmət] adj. having or fostering a warm or friendly and close relationship 亲密的

accent ['æksənt] v. to stress, single out as important 强调；重读

cymbal ['sɪmbəl] n. (乐器) 铙钹

exotic [ɪg'zɔtɪk] adj. being or from or characteristic of another place or part of the world 外国的；有异国情调的

intricate ['ɪntrɪkət] adj. having many complexly arranged elements 复杂的；错综的

accessory [ək'sesərɪ] n. clothing that is worn or carried, but not part of your main clothing 配件

candelabra [kændə'lɑbrə] n. 枝状大烛台

enthusiast [ɪn'θju:zɪæst] n. a person having a strong liking for something 狂热者

given ['gɪvən] prep. 考虑到

overlook [əuvə'luk] v. fail to notice 忽略

glamorous ['glæmərəs] adj. having an air of allure, romance and excitement 迷人的；有魅力的

fusion ['fju:ʒən] n. an occurrence that involves the production of a union 融合

subscribe [səb'skraɪb] v. adopt as a belief 赞成；签署

descend [dɪ'send] v. move downward and lower, but not necessarily all the way; come from 下降；遗传

anthropologist [ænθrə'pɔlədʒɪst] n. 人类学家

historical [hɪ'stɔrɪkl] adj. of or relating to the study of history 历史的；基

Unit 7 Belly Dance

于史实的
commentary ['kɔmentərɪ] n. 评论；说明
conflation [kən'fleɪʃn] n. 合并
vogue [vəug] n. fashion 时尚；流行
prejudice ['predʒudɪs] n. a partiality that prevents objective consideration of an issue or situation 偏见；歧视
shimmy ['ʃɪmɪ] n. lively dancing with much shaking of the shoulders and hips 摇动
cabaret ['kæbəreɪ] n. 卡巴莱歌舞表演
undulation [ˌʌndju'leɪʃn] n. a gentle rising and falling in the manner of waves 波动；起伏
excessively [ek'sesɪvlɪ] adv. to an excessive degree 过分地；极度
imitation [ˌɪmɪ'teɪʃn] n. copying someone else's actions 模仿
fascinate ['fæsɪneɪt] v. cause to be interested or curious 使着迷
seminar ['semɪnɑː] n. 进修班；研讨会
intensively [ɪn'tensɪvlɪ] adv. in an intensive manner 强烈地；集中地

Phrases & Expressions

dedicate to doing sth.	把（时间、精力等）用于
be involved with	涉及；与…有关联
intend to	打算做；想要
in most cases	大部分情况下
complete with	包括；连同
give rise to	使发生；引起

Proper Names

hagalla ['hægəlɑ]	肚皮舞的一种舞步
Tito Seif of Egypt ['tiːtəu 'siːf]	提托·赛义夫（肚皮舞大师）
Raqs Sharqi ['ræks 'ʃɑːkɪ]	肚皮舞
Morocco (Carolina Varga Dinicu) [mə'rɔkə]	卡罗莱纳·瓦尔加·旦尼库（肚皮舞大师）

Mysterious Arab Countries
神秘的阿拉伯

Background Information

1. Hagalla[①]

The "Hagalla" is a woman's folk dance step that originated in western Egypt/eastern Libya. Women (usually one girl, 'el hagalla') did this one step, resembling something like a three-quarter shimmy or a meringue (梅伦格舞,海地和多米尼加的一种交际舞) step, while men clapped accompaniment. However, because watching an entire song done with one step would not be interesting to an audience, additional movements, including dancing by the men, were added.

The traditional costume for the dance would be a simple long dress with long sleeves, with a heavy unadorned scarf wrapped around the hips. For performances, the dress may be shorter (calf or knee length), the sleeves may be shorter, and the hip scarf looks like more of a ruffled apron and may be fringed.

There are a couple of stories about this dance found on the web. One from Egypt cites it as a pre-wedding dance, where a woman (not the bride) dances this step for whichever of the groups of men clap the loudest. Another from Libya has it as a coming-of-age for the dancing girl, and she dances for whichever of the clapping men she pleases. The men chant about how lovely she is as she grows into a mature woman who will marry and have children.

2. Tito Seif

Tito Seif is an internationally acclaimed instructor and one of the world's premier belly dance artists. He's an amazing Egyptian dancer, teacher, choreographer, who is regularly featured as a special guest dancer on numerous international TV stations and networks. Born in 1971, Tito began to belly dance at the age of 14. Within a very short period of time he became one of the biggest names in the business. A prominent, technically

---

① http://voices.yahoo.com/an-introduction-three-middle-eastern-dances-the-3077709.html? cat =2.

proficient, innovative and mesmerizing belly dancer, he is recognized as a leader in the belly dance world. Tito's talents as an entertainer and a gifted prolific instructor are sought after all over the world. In 2004 Tito started teaching and performing outside Egypt (Germany, Australia, Sweden, Canada, Japan, Russia and recently the USA). Many belly dancers worldwide have raved about his workshops; he has a proven track record of imparting his clever techniques to dancers worldwide.

3. Morocco (Carolina Varga Dinicu)

Carolina Varga Dinicu was born in Romania while her parents were trying to help relatives escape from the Nazis. It was five years before the family could return to New York. She was a teenager before she discovered that her family were Rom. She studied flamenco and became a "belly dancer" by accident in 1960.

Named "Morocco" from her first gig, her curiosity took her to watch Moroccan dance first in New York and later "other there". Today she is a widely respected researcher as well as dancer and teacher.

4. Little Egypt

Little Egypt was the stage name for three popular belly dancers. They had so many imitators, and the name became synonymous with belly dancers generally. The three famous belly dancers are Farida Mazar Spyropoulos, Ashea Wabe, and Fatima Djemille.

Study & Practice

I. Read Aloud and Memorize

Read the following paragraph aloud until you have learned them by heart.

Mysterious Arab Countries

神秘的阿拉伯

> Belly dancing is natural to a woman's bone and muscle structure with movements emanating from the torso rather than in the legs and feet. The dance often focuses upon isolating different parts of the body, moving them independently in sensuous patterns, weaving together the entire feminine form. Belly dancing is generally performed barefoot, thought by many to emphasize the intimate physical connection between the dancer, her expression, and Mother Earth.

II. Answer the Following Questions

1. Under what circumstances are Arabic dances usually performed?
2. What is the choreography of Arabic dance?
3. Is Arabic dance equivalent to belly dance?
4. According to some experts, what is the root of belly dance?
5. What is the greatest misconception about belly dance?
6. Is there a widely accepted origin of belly dance?
7. What are the characteristics of Egyptian belly dance?
8. When you are practicing Egyptian belly dance, what should you focus on?
9. What will make a dancer look like a Turkish dancer?
10. When and how did belly dance begin to get popular in America?

III. Cloze

Complete the followingpassages according to your own understanding, and change the forms where necessary.

Passage 1①

Raqs sharqi is performed both by women and men, usually solo, to _____ (1) spectators in public or private settings. _____ (2) its alias, "belly dance", Raqs Sharqi dancing involves movements from the entire

---

① http://www.experiencefestival.com/a/Belly_dance/id/1930065.

body. It is fundamentally an improvisational dance with its _____ (3) dance movement vocabulary, fluidly integrating into the rhythm of the music.

In Raqs sharqi, the dancer internalizes and expresses the emotions evoked by the music. _____ (4), the music is integral to the vocabulary of the dance movements. The most revered of dancers are those _____ (5) can best project their emotions through the dance, even if their movement vocabulary is very simple. The dancer _____ (6) to the audience visually the _____ (7) and sounds of the music.

Many see it as a woman's dance, celebrating sensuality and power of _____ (8) a woman. Sohair Zaki, Fifi Abdou, Lucy, Dina, who are all popular dancers in Egypt, are above the age of 40. Many feel that you have _____ (9) life experiences to use as a catalyst for _____ (10) until you reach "a certain age".

Paragraph 2[①]
Health and Belly Dancing

The _____ (1) of belly dance are both mental and physical. Dancing is a good cardio-vascular _____ (2), helps increase flexibility and focuses _____ (3) the torso or "core muscles". It is _____ (4) for all ages and body types and can be as physical as the participant chooses to make _____ (5) Individuals would be wise to _____ (6) a doctor before starting belly dance, just as with starting any new exercise routine. It is also advised that one talk with the instructor to see _____ (7) level his or her classes are _____ (8) Mental health benefits, for many belly dancers, include an improved sense of wellbeing, elevated body image and self-esteem _____ (9) a generally positive outlook that _____ (10) regular, enjoyable exercise.

IV. Spot Dictation

In this part, you will hear a passage three times. When the passage is read for the first time, you should listen carefully for its general idea. When the

---

① http://www.experiencefestival.com/a/Belly_dance/id/1930065.

Mysterious Arab Countries
神秘的阿拉伯

passage is read for the second time, you are required to fill in the blanks numbered from 1 to 10 with the exact words you have heard. Finally, when the passage is read for the third time, you should check what you have written.

Belly Dance[①]

During the course of history many of the dances we _____ (1) with belly dance today were _____ (2) as separate dances; men for men, women for women. There are few _____ (3) of co-ed dances. For many years this made it so that a "good" woman would not be seen dancing by any but her husband, her close family or the women she was with at a get-together. This _____ (4) to separate the musicians so that only female musicians could _____ (5) for female dancers. This custom continues in much of the Middle East, _____ (6) on which country you are in. In some areas the _____ (7) dancer will go to a woman _____ (8) with the musicians, get the women up and dancing then go to the men's _____ (9) of the house and perform for the male guests at a _____ (10).

V. Translation

Turn the following sentences into English, using as many words and phrases you have learned from the text as possible.

1. 尽管天气闷热,他还是穿了一套深色的衣服,并配上了一件背心。

_____

_____

2. 他打算参加游行,但后来临阵退缩了。

_____

_____

3. 我不想让我的儿子与坏人混在一起。

_____

_____

---

① Ditto.

Unit 7 Belly Dance

4. 他始终觉得医学是他能够为之献身的最重要的事业。

5. 这个提议可能产生一个有意义的探索领域。

6. 这些观点来源于那些非常著名的人类学家的思想。

7. 这部小说的情节错综复杂，引人入胜。

8. 冒失和自大在不久的将来会等同于挫折和失败。

VI. Oral Practice:

Find a partner or partners, and discuss with them about the following questions.

1. Keeping fit and loosing weight are increasingly popular nowadays, what do you usually do to work out?
2. Do you think it is weird for men to practice belly dance?
3. Along with regular exercises, what other things should we do to keep fit?

VII. Broaden Your Horizon

10 Things You Should Not Miss While Travelling to the Arab World[①]

In one of my inquisitive thoughts of what symbolises the Arab World and

---

① http://www.crescentrating.com/explore-the-world/muslim-heritage/.

sets it apart from the rest of the world, I put up on a Social Media site the question: "What is the first thing that comes to your mind when you say "The Arab World". After a lot of discussions and comments, I have decided to compile the 10 things that symbolises the Arab world and that you should not miss while travelling there.

1. Keffiyeh / Shemagh Scarfs (阿拉伯头巾)

This scarf is a cotton square cloth with checked woven patterns. It is worn around the head to protect oneself from the heat, dust and sand of the Arabian desserts. It is been used for centuries in Arabia, Iraq & Jordan. The patterned scarf available in all colours has evolved as a symbol of fashion across the world. The best thing I love about this scarf is— it is worn by peasants and princes alike— a universal brotherhood symbol. So the next time you wrap the scarf around yourself as a fashion statement, You should know that you are flaunting one of the symbols of all things Arab.

2. Sahan Food

Having food in a Sahan (a big plate) where people sit together and have food from the same plate is one of the etiquettes that set Muslims apart. When you order food in the Arab countries for example Mandi, they serve you in a Sahan where you have to sit in 2, 3 or 4 to finish it. So before you think of ordering individual portions in some small food outlets, go to the real traditional restaurants and have food served in the traditional Sahan way.

3. Attars (精油)

There's no doubt the first thing that comes into mind when you say the Arab world are its alcohol-free concentrated perfume. It is the small, delicately designed attar bottles with concentrated essential oils inside that takes the Attar to another class. It is also always the first thing that comes to mind when you think of souvenirs to buy home for friends and family.

4. Kebabs(烤肉串)

Kebabs have become a world phenomenon from America to Russia. This word means meat grilled in bite size pieces. Its history can be traced back to the 7th century. Every country you visit in the Arab world hasits own version of Kebab. (Gives us more excuses to taste all the varieties available!) The thing in common however is the meat marinated till tender with spices and herbs and heated in skewers over a flame be it charcoal, gas, wood etc.

5. Surma /Kohl(眼影)

If there is one thing that sets the Arabs apart, it is their huge black eyes. So Surma or Kohl which is made of powdered antimony and other ingredients have been used since time immemorial. The application of Kohl/ Surma to eyes has been around since 300BC in Egypt. It is believed to strengthen the eyes and protect the eyes against ailments. It also beautifies the eye. So stock up on some Kohl/ Surma and bring some back home for your friends and family.

6. Hummus(鹰嘴豆泥)

Hummus is also a famous dish known worldwide. Its origin can be traced back to the 13th century and believed to have originated in Egypt. However it is served in almost all Arab countries and has become a dip served in all homes. It is a dip made from grinding chickpeas, olive, lemon and tahini(芝麻酱).

7. Al-Qahwa / The Arabian Coffee

Coffee is a world phenomenon but if you go to the Arab world and ask for the normal espresso, or instant coffee-You are missing out on the real treat. Al-Qahwa is a unique blend of coffee beans roasted and blended with cardamom, saffron, cinnamon and some other spices in various proportions for different blends. It is generally served in small cups with no handles called Fenjan.

8. Dates（枣子）

Dates are the fruit which grows mostly in the Middle Eastern countries and is a symbolic fruit. The dates which are high in energy were sometimes the only form of sustenance for ancient travellers because it doesn't spoil easily. When you are in the Arab world try out the raw dates which are in yellow and red colour for an ultimate treat.

9. Arabian Carpets & Rugs（地毯）

The Arabian carpets and rugs wovenin the traditional Arabian pattern and design using traditional technique is something you need to buy to bring back home. Known for its patterns and designs, it clearly sets the place apart. Recently a carpet dating back to 7th century has been excavated from Ma'rib （马里卜省）, Yemen.

10. Hijab & Turbans（面纱、头巾）

In any corner of any city in any street in the Arab world there will always be a shop greeting you with Hijab and Turbans. One thing that sets the Arab world apart from the rest is you will always find shops selling these things almost everywhere. From traditional turban cloth to ready-mades for men and colourful stoles, scarves and shawls for women. With a million varieties to choose from, you indeed have to get some for sure!

Unit 8
Arabia Music

Warm-Up Questions

1. Do you know anything about the Arabic music? Say a few words about it.
2. Which musician do you admire most? Why?
3. In your opinion, what's the difference between Arabic music and Chinese music? Give your opinion.

Text

Broadly speaking, Arabic music can be divided into two styles, which can be clearly differentiated from one another: popular music, and so-called classical music. The following article serves as a simple introduction to the basics of Arabic music.

Mysterious Arab Countries
神秘的阿拉伯

Arabic Music and Its Development[1]

In the ninth century Arabic music was already highly developed. At that time the Arabs already had anextensive musical repertoire. In Arabic music the scale, like that in the West, consists of tones and semitones, but can also move in quartertones. Whereas in European music the smallest interval is the semitone, it is therefore possible in Arabic music to make far smaller tonal steps.

Two of the most important things all Arabic music has in common are a delight in improvisation, and thepredominance of melodic forms. A melody is usually sung by a solo voice, which may also be accompanied by a choir. Polyphony, such as we are accustomed to in Western orchestral music, does not exist in classical Arabic music. The basis of Arabic music is the maqam or mode. The term maqam originally means "pedestal", "step", or simply "location". It was also used to designate a gathering in which poems were recited; later, a musical gathering was also called a maqam. In classical Arabic music theory, the maqam indicates the pitch of an Arabic scale, comparable with the ancient ecclesiastical modes, or the two modes of flat and sharp in European music, although the individual shifts in tone can, as mentioned above, be smaller than a semitone. Arabic music, however, has more than ten different modes. Furthermore, as a complete piece of music, what differentiates the maqam entirely from its European counterparts is that the musician has complete freedom with regard to the rhythm and the potential for introducing variations. This is hardly possible in European music. Here a particular rhythm is prescribed, the melody for which can be modified freely.

Many musicians and music theorists of the Arab world ascribe specific states of feeling to particular maqam. Thus, for example, mourning is often expressed by the maqamat "hijaz" and "saba". The mesmerizing beauty of the beloved and all her charms are usually dwelt on in the maqam "bayati".

Arabic music does not measure itself in terms of technical perfection, but by the degree of intensity and emotion in the tone, feeling, or namentation,

---

[1] http://www.goethe.de/ges/phi/prj/ffs/the/a96/en8626486.htm.

performance and singing. The Western musician repeatedly practices a piece as it is written in the sheet music until he is able to play and interpret it perfectly. The classical Arabic musician, on the other hand, is only able to access the music through its "soul" if he touches this "soul", he surmounts all other difficulties. He improvises, not sticking to the basic form of the piece of music but varying it according to the time of day or the occasion-for the same piece can sound quite different played at midday or at night, as it is being performed in a completely different atmosphere.

This has far-reaching consequences. Classical European music was written down in notes, which to this day is not the case for classical Arabic music, as the same maqam is always improvised and performed in a different way.

One of the most important classical music forms in the east of the Arab world is the waslat. It consists of a series of compositions and improvised instrumental and vocal pieces, which are all played in one and the same maqam series. The waslat always begins with an instrumental piece, which may be a sama or a bashraf. Both forms are played by the entire orchestra and are similar in form, but differ in rhythm. They could, however, be compared with the overture in a European suite. Between the individual songs of the waslat, taqsim are played: these are solo pieces for one instrument only, which enable individual soloists to demonstrate the range of their improvisational skill.

In northern African countries another form of classical music hasestablished itself: the nouba. This is a specific, large-scale musical form of Arabic-Andalusian music. In the cities of the Maghreb countries Morocco, Tunisia, Algeria and Libya, the nouba has retained its characteristic form to this day. The nouba is an important large-scale musical form comparable with the European suite. It usually consists of five parts, called mizan, which are each characterized by a particular fundamental rhythmic pattern. The nouba consists of different musical themes, which are not woven together as is often the case in European music; however, stylistically and melodically, as in the European suite, they create a whole.

The key starting point for Arabic music is song. In Arabic musical tradition there is hardly any music without song. Music and poetry are so closely woven together that to this day it is difficult to discover the names of

Mysterious Arab Countries
神秘的阿拉伯

the composers of classical Arabic music. We often only know the names of the singers and poets. If purely instrumental pieces are played at all, it is usually as an introduction to a song. Polyphonic elements, like those typical in European music, have therefore scarcely been able to establish themselves.

In the Arab world the musical experience a singer, with her ensemble, conveys to her audience is referred to as tarab. It is a mood created by the song and the music, which culminates in a feeling of happiness bordering on intoxication. The tarab can transport the entire audience; sometimes people weep or groan in pain when the singer sings of her lost love. Other listeners jump up and loudly cheer on the performers. The degree of intensity of the tarab depends primarily on the voice and manner of performance of the singer. According to temperament, mood, and occasion, the singer not only allows herself the freedom of creative artistic interpretation but does in fact improvise.

A singer's career is usually characterized by a thorough training in Koran recitation according to the traditional rules of song. There are hardly any singers who have subsequently become famous who have not undergone the hard schooling of Koran recitation; for the musically modulated performance of the suras is part of the cultural heritage of classical Arabic music. Just as many European singers who want to specialize in baroque music make a thorough study of Renaissance and baroque choral music, many Arab classical music singers choose the route of Koran recitation. This is why until the 1950s almost all well-known singers and musicians bore the title "Sheikh".

The traditional orchestra for classical music, called al tacht, consists of three main instruments: the oud, the qanoun and the nay, to which was later added the Arab violin, the kamanija. The oud, the Arab short-necked lute, provides both the rhythm and the melody in Arabic music. It has been celebrated by many Arab poets, and is the foundation of Arabic music theory.

New Words

extensive [ɪkˈstensɪv] adj. large in spatial extent or range or scope or quantity 广泛的；大量的；广阔的

repertoire [ˈrepətwaː] n. the entire range of skills or aptitudes or devices

Unit 8 Arabia Music

used in a particular field or occupation 全部节目
semitone ['semɪtɔn] n. 半音程；半级音
interval ['ɪntəvəl] n. a definite length of time marked off by two instants 间隔；间距；幕间休息
tonal ['təunəl] adj. employing variations in pitch to distinguish meanings of otherwise similar words 音调的
predominance [prɪ'dɔmɪnəns] n. the quality of being more noticeable than anything else 优势；主导地位
melodic [mə'lɔdɪk] adj. containing or characterized by pleasing melody 有旋律的；音调优美的
accompany [ə'kʌmpənɪ] v. be associated with 陪伴；陪同（be accompanied by）vi. 伴奏；伴唱
choir ['kwaɪə] n. a chorus that sings as part of a religious ceremony 唱诗班；合唱队
polyphony [pə'lɪfənɪ] n. music arranged in parts for several voices or instruments 复调；复调音乐；多音
orchestral [ɔ:'kestrəl] adj. relating to or composed for an orchestra 管弦乐的；管弦乐队的
designate ['dezɪgneɪt] v. assign a name or title to 指定；指派；标出；把…定名为
pitch [pɪtʃ] n. the property of sound that varies with variation in the frequency of vibration 音高
ecclesiastical [ɪˌkli:zɪ'æstɪkl] adj. of or associated with a church (esp. a Christian Church) 教会的；神职的；基督教的
counterpart ['kauntəpa:t] n. a person or thing having the same function or characteristics as another 副本；配对物；相对物
variation [ˌeərɪ'eɪʃn] n. an instance of change; the rate or magnitude of change 变化；（生物）变异；变种
prescribe [prɪ'skraɪb] v. issue commands or orders for 指定；规定 vi. 建立规定；开处方
modify ['mɔdɪfaɪ] v. cause to change, make different 修改；修饰；更改
ascribe [ə'skraɪb] v. attribute or credit to 归因于；归咎于
mourn ['mɔ:n] vi. feel sadness 哀痛；服丧
mourning: n. state of sorrow over the death or departure of a loved one 悲痛；

Mysterious Arab Countries
神秘的阿拉伯

哀悼

mesmerize ['mezməraɪz] (mesmerize) v. attract strongly, as if with a magnet 使…入迷；使…目瞪口呆

intensity [ɪn'tensətɪ] n. the property of being intense 强度；强烈

ornamentation [ˌɔːnmen'teɪʃn] n. something used to beautify; the act of adding extraneous decorations to something 装饰物

surmount [sə'maunt] v. get on top of; deal with successfully 克服；越过；战胜

overture ['əuvetʃue(r)] n. orchestral music played at the beginning of an opera 前奏曲；序幕

suite [swiːt] n. a musical composition of several movements only loosely connected 组曲；套件

retain [re'teɪn] v. keep or remember 保持；记住

stylistically [staɪ'lɪstɪklɪ] adv. in a rhetorically stylistic manner 在文体上

ensemble [aːn'zaːmbl] n. a group of musicians playing or singing together 全体；总效果；合奏组

culminate ['kʌlmɪneɪt] v. end, especially to reach a final or the highest point 到绝顶；达到顶点；使结束

intoxication [ɪnˌtɔksɪ'keɪʃn] n. a quality of something that makes you feel very excited 陶醉

groan [grəun] n. an utterance expressing pain or disapproval 呻吟；叹息

temperament ['tempərəmənt] n. excessive emotionalism and excitability especially when displayed openly 性情；性格

subsequently ['sʌbsɪkwəntlɪ] adv. happening at a time subsequent to a reference time 随后；其后；后来

modulate ['mɔdjuleɪt] v. fix or adjust the time, amount, degree, or rate of 调节；（信号）调制；调整

suras ['suərə] n. one of the sections (or chapters) in the Koran 节；章

bear [beə] (bore, borne/born) v. have or put up with 忍受；具有；支撑

Phrases & Expressions

in common   共同的；共有的
be accustomed to   习惯于

with regard to	关于；就；说起
dwell on/upon	老是想着；详述
in terms of	就…而言；根据
stick to	坚持
be characterized by	…的特点在于；…的特点是
differ in	不同在；在…方面存在不同
be part of	成为…的一部分
be comparable with	可比较的，比得上的；可同…比较

Proper Names

quartertone ['kwɔ:tətəun]	四分音
maqam ['meɪkəm]	木卡姆（阿拉伯音乐的组曲或调式、乐音）
Andalusian [ˌændə'lu:zjən]	安达卢西亚人；安达卢西亚语
Algeria [æl'dʒɪərɪe]	阿尔及利亚（北非国家）
Tunisia [tju:'nɪzɪə]	突尼斯（非洲国家）
Morocco [mə'rɔkəu]	摩洛哥（非洲国家）
Maghreb ['meɪgrəb]	马格利布（北非的一地区）
Libya ['lɪbɪə]	利比亚（埃及以西的北非地方古名）
Koran [kɔ'ra:n]	《古兰经》（伊斯兰教）
Baroque [bə'rɔk]	巴洛克风格；巴洛克艺术

Background Information

Qur'an (Koran)

The Qur'an (literally meaning "the recitation") is the central religious text of Islam, which Muslims believe to be a revelation from God (Allah). It is widely regarded as the finest piece of literature in the Arabic language. Muslims consider the Qur'an to be the only book that has been protected by God from distortion or corruption.

Mysterious Arab Countries
神秘的阿拉伯

Muslims believe that the Qur'an was verbally revealed from God to Muhammad through the angel Gabriel, gradually over a period of approximately 23 years, beginning on 22 December 609 CE, when Muhammad was 40, and concluding in 632 CE, the year of his death. Shortly after Muhammad's death, the Qur'an was collected by his companions using written Qur'anic materials and everything that had been memorized of the Quran.

Muslims regard the Qur'an as the most important miracle of Muhammad, the proof of his prophethood and the culmination of a series of divine messages that started with the messages revealed to Adam and ended with Muhammad. The Qur'an assumes familiarity with major narratives recounted in the Jewish and Christian scriptures. It summarizes some, dwells at length on others and, in some cases, presents alternative accounts and interpretations of events. The Qur'an describes itself as a book of guidance. It sometimes offers detailed accounts of specific historical events, and it often emphasizes the moral significance of an event over its narrative sequence. The Qur'an is used along with the hadith to interpret sharia law. During prayers, the Qur'an is recited only in Arabic.

Study & Practice

I. Read Aloud and Memorize

Read the following paragraph aloud until you have learned them by heart.

One of the most important classical music forms in the east of the Arab world is the *waslat*. It consists of a series of compositions and improvised instrumental and vocal pieces, which are all played in one and the same *maqam* series. The waslat always begins with an instrumental piece, which may be a *sama'i* or a *bashraf*. Both forms are played by the entire *orchestra* and are similar in form, but differ in rhythm. They could, however, be compared with the overture in a European suite. Between the individual songs of the *waslat*, *taqsim* are played: these are solo pieces for one instrument only, which enable *individual* soloists to demonstrate the range of their improvisational skill.

II. Answer the Following Questions

1. When did the Arabic music highly develop?
2. What is the basis of Arabic music?
3. What is the Arabic music measured by?
4. What are the most important classical music forms in the east of the Arab world?
5. What is the key starting point for Arabic music?
6. How to characterize a singer's career?
7. What is the smallest interval in the European music?
8. Why were many musicians trained by means of Koran recitation?
9. What are the main instruments in the traditional orchestra for classical music?
10. What are the Arabic music notices?

III. Cloze

Complete the following paragraphs according to your own understanding, and change the forms where necessary.

Paragraph 1 [①]

Another popular form of *West meets East*, Arabic jazz is also _____ (1) with many songs using jazz instruments. Early jazz influences _____ (2) with the use of the saxophone by _____ (3) like Samir Suroor, in the "oriental" style. The use of the saxophone in that manner can be found in Abdel Halim Hafez's songs, as well as Kadim Al Sahir and Rida Al Abdallah today. The first mainstream jazz _____ (4) were incorporated _____ (5) Arabic music by the Rahbani brothers. Fairuz's later work was almost exclusively _____ (6) up of jazz songs, composed by her son Ziad Rahbani. Ziad Rahbani also _____ (7) today's oriental jazz movement, to _____ (8) singers including Rima

---

① http://en.wikipia.org/wiki/Arabic_music.

Khcheich, Salma El Mosfi, _____ (9) (on occasion) Latifa adhere. We can also find a lot of jazz music in Mohamed Mounir's songs starting _____ (10) his first album which was in 1977.

Paragraph 2

Rock music is popular all _____ (1) the world, the Arab world being no _____ (2) There have been many Arab rock bands _____ (3) the years that fused rock, metal and alternative rock sounds with traditional Arab _____ (4) Arabic Rock has been gaining a lot of _____ (5) lately in the Middle East with _____ (6) like JadaL and Akher Zapheer of Jordan, Mashrou' Leila and Meen of Lebanon, Massar Egbari, Sahara, Wyvern and Cartoon Killerz of Egypt, Khalas and Chaos (band) of Palestine and Acrassicauda of Iraq. The band Hoba Hoba Spirit from Morocco is also _____ (7) popularity, _____ (8) in the Maghrebi region. Rachid Taha, _____ (9) Algerian musician, plays a _____ (10) of rock and roll.

IV. Spot Dictation

In this part, you will hear a passage three times. When the passage is read for the first time, you should listen carefully for its general idea. When the passage is read for the second time, you are required to fill in the blanks numbered from 1 to 10 with the exact words you have heard. Finally, when the passage is read for the third time, you should check what you have written.

Arabic music is also known as Arab music which includes several styles and genres of music that _____ (1) from pop music to classical (Arabic) and also from secular to sacred music. Though Arab music will be very independent and also _____ (2) they have a very good _____ (3) with other music genres and styles.

Arabic music has _____ (4) through the ages and several people are now _____ (5) in this genre of Arabic music. It has been around for several years now but the main tweak in the sounds of Arabic music came when Ahmad Baba Rachid _____ (6) traditional music with pop sounds to create a new type of sound. Male singers of the Arabic music genre are called as cheb or cheba for _____ (7) singers. There are several different styles of Rai Arabic music styles present and singers _____ (8) in them to ensure popularity. There is no doubt about the fact that Arabic music surely sounds a far lot different than any form of Western music. A _____ (9) clear drum beat is heard most of the times in the sound without any particular musical or vocal _____ (10) Descriptions about Arabic music often are attached with a lot of technicalities.

V. Translation

Turn the following sentences into English, using as many words and phrases you have learned from the text as possible.

1. 毫无疑问，这将是很困难的，特别是对那些习惯于只想要正确答案的学生。

2. 众所周知，阿拉伯音乐是一个进化的艺术形式，或许和希腊文明开始得一样早。

3. 他的脑子里现在只记住了她所讲的那几句热烈的爱情诉说。

4. 在中东，人们认为马尔瓦是最有名的具有阿拉伯风格的流行音乐艺术家，甜美的声音是其最大的特点。（Marwa）

5. 每个周末我们在家举办的聚会都充满阿拉伯的传统食品、音乐，以及大多用阿拉伯语进行的高谈阔论。

Mysterious Arab Countries
神秘的阿拉伯

6. 他对她的态度虽然是认真的、批判的，但并不是明智的。
_____
_____

7. 鸟类的歌唱和人类的语言之间很可能有我们意想不到的共同之处。
_____
_____

8. 那些孩子成绩方面的差异不能完全从社会背景来解释。
_____
_____

9. 欧文·柏林的音乐作品难以同贝多芬的相比。（Irving Berlin）
_____
_____

10. 如果我们每天背一点章节，到我们高中毕业的时候就可以记住整本经典著作，这是一项多么特殊的荣誉。
_____
_____

VI. Oral Practice

Find a partner or partners and discuss with them about the following questions.

1. What's your hobby? Are you good at playing a kind of musical instrument in your spare time?
2. Can you sing Arabic songs? Show it to your classmates and talk about your understanding of the Arab music with your classmates.
3. Talk about the impact of foreign music on Arabic music.

VII. Language Enhancement

The Arabian Nights is a work that has enthralled readers for centuries. The origins of *The Arabian Nights* are obscure. About a thousand years ago a vast number of stories in Arabic form various countries began to be brought together; only much later was the collection called *The Arabian Nights* or *The Thousand and One Nights*. All the stories are told by Shahrazad

Unit 8　Arabia Music

(Scheherazade), who entertains her husband, King Shahryar, whose custom was to execute his wives after a single night. Shahrazad begins a story each night but withholds the ending until the following night, thus postponing her execution. The following is one of the stories.

The Little Hunchback[①]
Part I

In the kingdom of Kashgar, which is, as everybody knows, situated on the frontiers of Great Tartary, there lived long ago a tailor and his wife who loved each other very much. One day, when the tailor was hard at work, a little hunchback came and sat at the entrance of the shop, and began to sing and play his tambourine. The tailor was amused with the antics of the fellow, and thought he would take him home to divert his wife. The hunchback having agreed to his proposal, the tailor closed his shop and they set off together.

When they reached the house they found the table ready laid for supper, and in a very few minutes all three were sitting before a beautiful fish which the tailor's wife had cooked with her own hands. But unluckily, the hunchback happened to swallow a large bone, and, in spite of all the tailor and his wife could do to help him, died of suffocation in an instant. Besides being very sorry for the poor man, the tailor and his wife were very much frightened on their own account, for if the police came to hear of it the worthy couple ran the risk of being thrown into prison for willful murder. In order to prevent this dreadful calamity they both set about inventing some plan which would throw suspicion on someone else, and at last they made up their minds that they could do no better than select a Jewish doctor who lived close by as the author of the crime. So the tailor picked up the hunchback by his head while his wife took his feet and carried him to the doctor's house. Then they knocked at the door, which opened straight on to a steep staircase. A servant soon appeared, feeling her way down the dark staircase and inquired what they wanted.

"Tell your master," said the tailor, "that we have brought a very sick man for him to cure; and," he added, holding out some money, "give him this in

---

① http://ishare.iask.sina.com.cn/download/explain.php? fileid = 11723728. (Its Chinese version can be checked out in Appendix II.)

advance, so that he may not feel he is wasting his time." The servant remounted the stairs to give the message to the doctor, and the moment she was out of sight the tailor and his wife carried the body swiftly after her, propped it up at the top of the staircase, and ran home as fast as their legs could carry them.

Now the doctor was so delighted at the news of a patient (for he was young, and had not many of them), that he was transported with joy. "Get a light," he called to the servant, "and follow me as fast as you can!" and rushing out of his room he ran towards the staircase. There he nearly fell over the body of the hunchback, and without knowing what it was gave it such a kick that it rolled right to the bottom, and very nearly dragged the doctor after it. "A light! A light!" he cried again, and when it was brought and he saw what he had done he was almost beside himself with terror.

"Holy Moses!" he exclaimed, "why did I not wait for the light? I have killed the sick man whom they brought me; and if the sacred Ass of Esdras does not come to my aid I am lost! It will not be long before I am led to jail as a murderer."

Agitated though he was, and with reason, the doctor did not forget to shut the house door, lest some passers-by might chance to see what had happened. He then took up the corpse and carried it into his wife's room, nearly driving her crazy with fright.

"It is all over with us!" she wailed, "if we cannot find some means of getting the body out of the house. Once let the sun rise and we can hide it no longer! How were you driven to commit such a terrible crime?"

"Never mind that," returned the doctor, "the thing is to find a way out of it."

For a long while the doctor and his wife continued to turn over in their minds a way of escape, but could not find any that seemed good enough. At last the doctor gave it up altogether and resigned himself to bear the penalty of his misfortune. But his wife, who had twice his brains, suddenly exclaimed, "I have thought of something! Let us carry the body on the roof of the house and lower it down the chimney of our neighbor the Mussulman." Now this Mussulman was employed by the Sultan, and furnished his table with oil and butter. Part of his house was occupied by a great storeroom, where rats and mice held high revel.

The doctor jumped at his wife's plan, and they took up the hunchback, and passing cords under his armpits they let him down into the purveyor's bedroom so gently that he really seemed to be leaning against the wall. When they felt he was touching the ground they drew up the cords and left him.

Scarcely had they got back to their own house when the purveyor entered his room. He had spent the evening at a wedding feast, and had a lantern in his hand. In the dim light it cast he was astonished to see a man standing in his chimney, but being naturally courageous he seized a stick and made straight for the supposed thief. "Ah!" he cried, "so it is you, and not the rats and mice, who steal my butter. I'll take care that you don't want to come back!"

So saying he struck him several hard blows. The corpse fell on the floor, but the man only redoubled his blows, till at length it occurred to him it was odd that the thief should lie so still and make no resistance. Then, finding he was quite dead, a cold fear took possession of him.

"Wretch that I am," said he, "I have murdered a man. Ah, my revenge has gone too far. Without the help of Allah I am undone! Cursed be the goods which have led me to my ruin." And already he felt the rope round his neck.

But when he had got over the first shock he began to think of some way out of the difficulty, and seizing the hunchback in his arms he carried him out into the street, and leaning him against the wall of a shop he stole back to his own house, without once looking behind him.

A few minutes before the sun rose, a rich Christian merchant, who supplied the palace with all sorts of necessaries, left his house, after a night of feasting, to go to the bath. Though he was very drunk, he was yet sober enough to know that the dawn was at hand, and that all good Mussulmen would shortly be going to prayer. So he hastened his steps lest he should meet some one on his way to the mosque, who, seeing his condition would send him to prison as a drunkard. In his haste he jostled against the hunchback, who fell heavily upon him, and the merchant, thinking he was being attacked by a thief, knocked him down with one blow of his fist. He then called loudly for help, beating the fallen man all the while.

Mysterious Arab Countries
神秘的阿拉伯

hunchback n. 驼背
swallow v. 咽下
on one's own account 为自身利益
prop up 支撑；支持
purveyor n. 承办商；伙食承办商
sober v. 使酒醒；使清醒

tambourine n. 狭长形鼓
suffocation n. 窒息；闷死
calamity n. 灾难
agitate v. 使…激动
at length 最终
jostle v. 推挤；撞

Unit 9
Egyptian Clothing

Warm-Up Questions

1. Do you know any kinds of clothes the Egyptian wears, and where do you get the message?
2. In Arab countries, are all of the people dressed in the same style? Why or why not?
3. Are there any big changes in the clothes in Egypt from ancient to now? What kind of clothes do you like best?

Text

Arab countries have a long history, splendid culture and traditions, along with social progress, scientific and technological development, and the exchange of cultural penetration of the East and the West, people who follow traditional practices evolve a lot during the process, so does their clothing in terms of the color and flavor.

Garments[①]

Clothing materials

The Egyptian climate with its hot summers and mild winters favored light clothing made from plant fibers, predominantly linen and in Roman times occasionally cotton, an import from India. Wool was used to a lesser extent, and seldom by Egyptians proper.

Small amounts of silk were traded to the eastern Mediterranean possibly as early as the second half of the second millennium and traces of silk have been found in Egyptian tombs.

Animals' skins, above all leopard skins, were sometimes worn by priests and by pharaohs in their role as first servants of the god. Such outfits were found in Tutankhamen's tomb and were depicted quite frequently on the walls of tombs. At times kings and queens wore decorative ceremonial clothing adorned with feathers.

Production

The most important textile was linen. It was produced from flax, the quality ranging from the finest woven linen, the byssus for royalty, to the coarse cloth peasants wore. The first stages of the linen production were performed by men: They reaped the plants and by beating and combing the plants they extracted fibers from them, which could be spun into thread. When the cloth was still woven on horizontal looms, which were often just pegs rammed into the ground and where the weavers had to crouch on the floor, it was generally women who performed the task. During the New Kingdom vertical looms were invented. These new loom were physically more demanding and were generally operated by men.

As the sewing of clothes was very labor intensive and the art of tailoring to fit in its infancy — the tightly fitting dresses which the incredibly shapely

---

① www. reshafim. org. il/ad/egypt/timelines/topics/clothing. htm.

women displayed — many garments consisted simply of a pieces of cloth draped around the body and held together by a belt. But the cloth was often hemmed to prevent fraying, with either simple, or rolled and whipped hems. At times garments had parts, which had to be stitched on such as sleeves or shoulder straps. The seams used were generally simple or lap-over, though run-and-fell and overcast seams were also known. The number of different stitch types was also limited: running stitch, overcast stitch, and twisted chain stitch.

The tools used such as knives and needles changed over the centuries. Blades were made from stone during the Neolithic, then from copper, from bronze during the Middle Kingdom and finally from iron, though flint knives, which had sharper edges than iron ones, continued to be used to an ever decreasing extent until Roman times. Needles were fashioned from wood, bone and metal. The Egyptians succeeded in making eyes in millimeter thick copper needles. Scissors came into general use late in Egypt's history though the principle was known since the second millennium BC.

Articles of dress

Tutankhamen's tomb yielded many pieces of clothing: tunics, shirts, kilts, aprons and sashes, socks, head-dresses, caps, scarves, gauntlets and gloves, some of them with fine linen linings, others with separate index and middle fingers and a hole for the thumb. Underwear in the form of a triangular loincloth was also found.

If royals had a garment for every body part and for any occasion — even though statues and relieves often show them wearing only the so-called kilt, and a crown — most of their subjects had to make do with much less. Clothes were expensive and in the hot Egyptian climate people often wore as little as possible. If we are to believe the depictions, at parties servants and slave girls wore little more than skimpy panties and jewellery, though one may assume that the reason for this undress was not a lack of funds. Working women mostly dressed in a short kind of kalasiris. Men doing physical labor wore a loin cloth, wide galabiyeh-like robes or, if they were working in the water, nothing at all. Children usually ran around nude during the summer months, and wore wraps and cloaks in winter when temperatures might fall below 10 ℃.

The gods had to be dressed as well. This was the duty of a small number of priests allowed to enter the holiest of holies, where the god's statue was. Nesuhor, commander of the fortress at Elephantine under Apries, took care that the temple of Khnum had all the servants necessary to serve the needs of the god:

I appointed weavers, maid-servants and launderers for the august wardrobe of the great god and his divine ennead.

Fashion

The clothes were generally made of linen and kept simple: a short loincloth resembling a kilt for men, a dress with straps for women. These basic garments with minor variations accounting for fashion, social status and wealth did not change fundamentally throughout Egypt's history. Very little sewing was done. The cloth was wrapped round the body and held in place by a belt. Its color was generally whitish, in contrast to the colorful clothes foreigners wore in Egyptian depictions, although dyed cloth was not unknown.

Everyday clothing was mostly undecorated, though pleating was known since the Old Kingdom, when some dresses of upper class Egyptians were pleated horizontally. In the New Kingdom the pleats were oftenvertical, but pleating could be quite intricate. A Middle Kingdom piece of clothing displays three different types of pleating: one part is pleated with pleats a few centimeters apart, another with very narrow pleats and a third part is chevron-patterned, with horizontal and vertical pleats crossing each other. How the pleating was done is not known, but it is generally supposed to have been very labor intensive.

The length of the kilts varied, being short during the Old Kingdom and reaching the calf in the Middle Kingdom, when it was oftensupplemented with a sleeveless shirt or a long robe. The robes worn by both sexes in Egypt were called kalasiris by Herodotus. Material and cut varied over the centuries, though the cloth of choice was always linen.

The kalasiris women wore might cover one or both shoulders or be worn with shoulder straps. While the top could reach anywhere from below the breast up to the neck, the bottom hem generally touched the calves or even the ankles. Some had short sleeves, others were sleeveless. The fit might be very tight or quite loose. They were often worn with a belt which held together the folds of cloth.

They were sewn from a rectangular piece of cloth twice the desired garment length. An opening for the head was cut at the centre of the cloth, which was then folded in half. The lower parts of the sides were stitched together leaving openings for the arms.

Women's dresses were at times ornamented with beads. They covered the breasts most of the time, though there were periods when fashion left them bare.

Circular capes date back as far as the Old Kingdom. They were generally made of linen and had an opening for the head cut at the centre. They were often dyed, painted or otherwise decorated and covered little more than the shoulders. Shawls were sometimes worn during the New Kingdom.

The ancient Egyptians knew how to use starch. They used it to stick sheets of papyrus together. According to Pliny they made starch by mixing some of the finest wheaten flour with boiling water. They also soaked linen bandages in starch which became hard and stiff when dried. It would be tempting to assume that they achieved the pleats in their clothes by using starch, but there is no evidence for that.

Headdresses

If depictions are anything to go by, then ordinary Egyptians did not wear any headdress as a rule, similar to African peoples further south. The better-off put on wigs — perhaps just on special occasions. These grew to a remarkable size during the New Kingdom.

The pharaohs are always represented wearing crowns, but whether this is a pictorial convention or whether they did so in every day life can not be decided.

New Words

favored ['feɪvəd] adj. preferred above all others and treated with partiality 受

Mysterious Arab Countries
神秘的阿拉伯

到优待的；得到宠爱的；有天赋的

predominantly [prɪˈdɒmɪnəntlɪ] adv. much greater in number or influence 主要地；显著地

linen [ˈlɪnɪn] n. a fabric woven with fibers from the flax plan 亚麻布；亚麻线；亚麻制品

Trad [træd] n. traditional jazz as revived in the 1950s 传统主义

Mediterranean [ˌmedɪtəˈreɪnɪən] n. the largest inland sea; between Europe and Africa and Asian. 地中海

millennium [mɪˈlenɪəm] n. a span of 1000 years 千禧年；一千年；千年纪念

trace [treɪs] n. a just detectable amount 痕迹；踪迹；微量

tomb [tu:m] n. a place for the burial of a corpse (especially beneath the ground and marked by a tombstone) 坟墓；死亡

leopard [ˈlepəd] n. the pelt of a leopard 豹；美洲豹

pharaoh [ˈfeərəu] n. the title of the ancient Egyptian kings 法老；暴君

decorative [ˈdekərətɪv] adj. serving an esthetic rather than a useful purpose 装饰性的；装潢用的

ceremonial [ˌserɪˈməunɪəl] n. a formal event performed on the special occasion 仪式；礼节

adorned [əˈdɔ:nd] adj. provided with something intended to increase its beauty or distinction 被修饰的

reap [ri:p] v. gather, as of natural products 收获；获得；收割

fiber [ˈfaɪbə] n. a slender and greatly elongated solid substance 纤维；光纤

labor [ˈleɪbə] n. a social class comprising those who do manual labor or work for wages 劳动力；人工

belt [belt] n. a band to tie or buckle around the body (usually at the waist) 腰带

hem [hem] v. fold over and sew together to provide with a hem 缝边；包围；约束 n. 褶边

blade [bleɪd] n. especially a leaf of grass or the broad portion of a leaf as distinct from the petiole 叶片；刀片，刀锋；剑

Neolithic [ˌni:əuˈlɪθɪk] adj. of or relating to the most recent period of the Stone Age (following the Mesolithic) [古] 新石器时代的；早先的

millimeter [ˈmɪlɪˌmi:tə] n. a metric unit of length equal to one thousandth of

Unit 9 Egyptian Clothing

a meter 毫米；公厘

yield [ji:ld] vi. be the cause or source of 屈服，投降；给出，产出

scarf [ska:f] n. a garment worn around the head or neck or shoulders for warmth or decoration 围巾；嵌接；头巾领巾

index ['ɪndeks] n. a numerical scale used to compare variables with one another or with some reference number 指标；指数；索引

triangular [traɪ'æɡjulə] adj. having three angles; forming or shaped like a triangle 三角的；[数]三角形的

loincloth ['lɔɪnklɔθ] n. a garment that provides covering for the loins 缠腰带；腰布

resemble [rɪ'zembl] v. appear like; be similar or bear a likeness to 类似；像

fundamentally [ˌfʌndə'mentəlɪ] adv. at bottom or by one's (or its) very nature 根本地；从根本上；基础地

whitish ['waɪtɪʃ] adj. resembling milk in color or cloudiness; not clear 带白色的；发白的

vertical ['və:tɪkəl] n. something that is oriented vertically 垂直线；垂直面 adj. right angles to the plane of the horizon or a base line 垂直的；直立的

intricate ['ɪntrɪkət] adj. having many complexly arranged elements; elaborate 复杂的；难懂的

ornament ['ɔ:nəmənt] n. make more attractive by adding ornament, color, 装饰；装饰物；教堂用品

circular ['sə:kjulə] n. an advertisement (usually printed on a page or in a leaflet) intended for wide distribution 通知；传单；adj. 循环的；圆形的；间接的

starch [sta:tʃ] n. an advertisement (usually printed on a page or in a leaflet) intended for wide distribution 淀粉；刻板；生硬

headdresses ['heddres] n. 头巾；头饰

Phrases & Expressions

spun into	纺成
horizontal looms	横织机
vertical looms	垂直织机

Mysterious Arab Countries
神秘的阿拉伯

drape around	将松松地披在…上；周围悬挂
make do	将就着使用；凑合着用
be stitched on	被缝上
nothing at all	一无所有；什么都不是
supplement with	用…增补
maid-servants	女仆
go by	判断

Proper Names

the Middle Kingdom	集古村（古埃及中王国时期，公元前 2040 -前 1640 年）
Tutankhamen [ˌtu:tənˈka:men]	图坦卡蒙（公元前 1361—前 1352 年在位，古埃及第十八王朝法老，其陵墓于 1922 年被完整发现）
Herodotus [heˈrɔdətəs]	希罗多德（希腊历史学家）
Egyptian [ɪˈdʒɪpʃən]	埃及人

Background Information

1. Tutankhamen

His name is also spelled as Tutankhamun, an Egyptian pharaoh of the 18th dynasty (ruled 1333 BC – 1323 BC in the conventional chronology), during the period of Egyptian history known as the New Kingdom. His original name, Tutankhaten, means "Living Image of Aton（埃及太阳神阿托恩）", while Tutankhamun means "Living Image of Amun（埃及生命和繁殖之神亚蒙神）".

He was known chiefly for his intact tomb, discovered in the Valley of the Kings in 1922 by Howard Carter and George Herbert. The 5th Earl of Carnarvon of Tutankhamun's nearly intact tomb received worldwide press coverage. It sparked a renewed public interest in ancient Egypt, for which Tutankhamun's burial mask remains the popular symbol. Exhibits of artifacts from his tomb have toured the world.

2. 2nd Millennium BC

The 2nd millennium BC marks the transition from the Middle to the Late Bronze Age. Its first half is dominated by the Middle Kingdom of Egypt and Babylonia. The alphabet develops. Indo-Iranian migration onto the Iranian plateau and onto the Indian subcontinent propagates the use of the chariot. Chariot warfare and population movements lead to violent changes at the center of the millennium, and a new order emerges with Greek dominance of the Aegean and the rise of the Hittite Empire. The end of the millennium sees the transition to the Iron Age. World population begins to rise steadily, reaching some 50 million towards 1000 BC.

3. Horizontal Loom

European tapestry may be woven on either a vertical loom (high-warp, or haute-lisse in French) or a horizontal loom (low-warp, or basse-lisse). In early high-warp looms the warps were attached to a beam at the top, and groups of warp threads were weighted at the bottom. The weft was beaten up (i. e., pushed) toward the top as the weaving progressed.

4. Kalasiri (Clothing)

This is a long, one-piece form-fitting dress. Usually either high-necked, or asymmetrically (不对称地) - cut, one-sleeved, ankle length garment, which is typically worn by Allanak nobility or upper class.

Study & Practice

I. Read Aloud and Memorize

Read the following paragraph aloud until you have learned them by heart.

Mysterious Arab Countries
神秘的阿拉伯

Everyday clothing was mostly undecorated, though pleating was known since the Old Kingdom, when some dresses of upper class Egyptians were pleated horizontally. In the New Kingdom the pleats were often vertical, but pleating could be quite intricate. A Middle Kingdom piece of clothing displays three different types of pleating: one part is pleated with pleats a few centimeters apart, another with very narrow pleats and a third part is chevron-patterned, with horizontal and vertical pleats crossing each other. How the pleating was done is not known, but it is generally supposed to have been very labor intensive.

II. Answer the Following Questions

1. What was the dominant material of Egyptian clothing?
2. In Egypt, how was the first stage of garment production performed?
3. What were the garments like?
4. What were found in Tutankhamun's tomb?
5. What did the man doing physical strength wear?
6. Were the clothes in ancient Egypt colorful?
7. What is the meaning of "Herodotus" in the text?
8. How were the kalasiris women wore usually made?
9. What is the usage of "starch"?
10. According to the text, did the depictions clearly show whether Egyptians wear headdress?

III. Cloze

Complete the following passages according to your own understanding, and change the forms where necessary.

Passage 1[①]

Bridal hijab of Arabic brides is usually _____ (1) with beautiful

---

[①] http: //www. latestasianfashions. com/arabic-bridal-dresses-2013/.

Unit 9 Egyptian Clothing

jewels and gems in which usually diamonds and real gem stones are used. As far as wedding dress of Arabic _____ (2) or Muslim women are concerned their dresses are usually very modest. Arabic Bridal _____ (3) of Muslim girls are designed in such a way that they cover the whole body of brides. For these _____ (4) long wedding gowns are made on which embroidery, bead work etc. has been done. Nowadays Arabic bridal dresses have _____ (5) of western or European wedding gown but they are modified in such a way that they _____ (6) full covering to the body. Today we have also selected Arabic _____ (7) dresses 2013. Our Arabic bridal collection is best for all modest Islamic or Muslim brides. Our collection have Arabic bridal dresses of _____ (8) Asian countries, like Malaysian bridal dresses, Omani bridal dresses, Indonesian bridal dresses and bridal dresses from many other Arab _____ (9) hope you will like our bridal collection of Arabian _____ (10) .

Passage 2[①]

The majority of Arab women dress conservatively. In the Arabic countries you will find a _____ (1) of traditions. Many women dress in clothes that do not cover their _____ (2) or _____ (3), while others cover them and it all depends on the country they reside, their personal choice, or social level.

A very _____ (4) woman might wear a long black garment called "Abayah" that covers the body from the _____ (5) down to feet. Under this cover she could be wearing a traditional Arabian dress, "thawb", or she could be wearing the latest style designer clothes. In addition to the Abayah, a very conservative woman would wear a face and head cover. Some women would wear the Abayah _____ (6) the head and face cover, while others might wear a scarf-like cover called "Hejab" to cover the hair only and not the face.

_____ (7), many women wear the latest style clothes without an Abayah or Hejab depending on the country they reside in. In some countries, like Saudi Arabia, you _____ (8) find women in the streets without the

---

① http://www.canadianarabcommunity.com/traditionalclothing.php.

Mysterious Arab Countries
神秘的阿拉伯

Abayah whereas in other countries such as Jordan, Iraq, Syria, Lebanon and Egypt you find a _____ (9) of women either wearing the Hejab, Abayah, or casual jeans, shirts, long and short _____ (10).

IV. Spot Dictation

In this part, you will hear a passage three times. When the passage is read for the first time, you should listen carefully for its general idea. When the passage is read for the second time, you are required to fill in the blanks numbered from 1 to 10 with the exact words you have heard. Finally, when the passage is read for the third time, you should check what you have written.

Ancient Egyptian Clothing[①]

Ancient Egyptian _____ (1) is quite different from the ancient Mediterranean type. The Egyptians usually worn _____ (2) that were sewn to fit them. These were like a long T-shirt that reached the _____ (3) in case of men or up to the ankles in case of women. The material was generally linen and has white color. The heads were left bare. The feet were also bare and _____ (4) leather sandals were worn. Those men who worked outside _____ (5) short skirts rather than tunics. A piece of cloth was covered around the _____ (6) and legs. Men and women wore blue and green _____ (7) and black kohl eyeliner when it was aimed to dress up fancy. Men kept their hair short and did not prefer _____ (8) beards and _____ (9) Women grew their hair so that they reached the shoulders. As for their affordability, _____ (10) of either sexes used gold jewelry.

V. Translation

Turn the following sentences into English, using as many words and phrases you have learned from the text as possible.

[①] http://www.buzzle.com/articles/ancient-egyptian-clothing.html.

Unit 9　Egyptian Clothing

1. 在社会生活中，男女分工往往不同。

2. 我们当代所研究的古埃及人服饰的资料大多来自于考古及图书文献。

3. 现有的设备还能应付两三年。

4. 图坦卡蒙的陵墓里各式各样的服饰体现了古埃及人无与伦比的智慧。

5. 如何使在线学习与传统教育的优势进行互补是我们面临的巨大挑战。（Supplement with）

6. 服装设计是一个有趣而又漫长的过程。一方面，它在培养你不断钻研探索的精神；另一方面，又在考验你的毅力。

7. 其实，在不同的场合人们的着装有着很大的区别。

8. 假如自信是成功的前提，那么不懈努力就是成功唯一的途径。

VI. Oral Practice

Find a partner or partners and discuss with them the traditional Egypt clothing. The following questions may help you to start the discussion.

1. What's your favorite way of dressing?
2. "What you wear changes the way you think." is a typical idea in

Enclothed Cognition. What's your opinion on it?

3. What is "Dress Code"? Explain your understanding with the help of the picture.

图片来源：https://www.google.com/search?q=dress+code&rlz=1C1EJFC_zh-CNIE808IE808&source=lnms&tbm=isch&sa=X&ved=0ahUKEwi7vo_nhePhAhXsY98KHTvqBqgQ_AUIDygC&biw=1024&bih=488#imgrc=99wsZYkTgyXQjM.

VII. Language Enhancement

The Arabian Nights is a work that has enthralled readers for centuries. The following is one of the stories for reading and thinking.

The Little Hunchback[1]
Part II

The chief policeman of the quarter came running up, and found a Christian ill-treating a Mussulman. "What are you doing?" he asked indignantly.

"He tried to rob me," replied the merchant, "and very nearly choked me."

"Well, you have had your revenge," said the man, catching hold of his arm. "Come, be off with you!"

As he spoke he held out his hand to the hunchback to help him up, but the hunchback never moved. "Oho!" he went on, looking closer, "so this is the way a Christian has the impudence to treat a Mussulman!" and seizing the

---

[1] http://ishare.iask.sina.com.cn/download/explain.php?fileid=11723728.

merchant in a firm grasp he took him to the inspector of police, who threw him into prison till the judge should be out of bed and ready to attend to his case. All this brought the merchant to his senses, but the more he thought of it the less he could understand how the hunchback could have died merely from the blows he had received.

The merchant was still pondering on this subject when he was summoned before the chief of police and questioned about his crime, which he could not deny. As the hunchback was one of the Sultan's private jesters, the chief of police resolved to defer sentence of death until he had consulted his master. He went to the palace to demand an audience, and told his story to the Sultan, who only answered, "There is no pardon for a Christian who kills a Mussulman. Do your duty." So the chief of police ordered a gallows to be erected, and sent criers to proclaim in every street in the city that a Christian was to be hanged that day for having killed a Mussulman. When all was ready the merchant was brought from prison and led to the foot of the gallows. The executioner knotted the cord firmly round the unfortunate man's neck and was just about to swing him into the air, when the Sultan's purveyor dashed through the crowd, and cried, panting, to the hangman,

"Stop, stop, don't be in such a hurry. It was not he who did the murder, it was I."

The chief of police, who was present to see that everything was in order, put several questions to the purveyor, who told him the whole story of the death of the hunchback, and how he had carried the body to the place where it had been found by the Christian merchant.

"You are going," he said to the chief of police, "to kill an innocent man, for it is impossible that he should have murdered a creature who was dead already. It is bad enough for me to have slain a Mussulman without having it on my conscience that a Christian who is guiltless should suffer through my fault."

Now the purveyor's speech had been made in a loud voice, and was heard by all the crowd, and even if he had wished it, the chief of police could not have escaped setting the merchant free.

"Loose the cords from the Christian's neck," he commanded, turning to the executioner, "and hang this man in his place, seeing that by his own confession he is the murderer."

The hangman did as he was bid, and was tying the cord firmly, when he was stopped by the voice of the Jewish doctor beseeching him to pause, for he had something very important to say. When he had fought his way through the crowd and reached the chief of police,

"Worshipful sir," he began, "this Mussulman whom you desire to hang is unworthy of death; I alone am guilty. Last night a man and a woman who were strangers to me knocked at my door, bringing with them a patient for me to cure. The servant opened it, but having no light was hardly able to make out their faces, though she readily agreed to wake me and to hand me the fee for my services. While she was telling me her story they seem to have carried the sick man to the top of the staircase and then left him there. I jumped up in a hurry without waiting for a lantern, and in the darkness I fell against something, which tumbled head-long down the stairs and never stopped till it reached the bottom. When I examined the body I found it was quite dead, and the corpse was that of a hunchback Mussulman. Terrified at what we had done, my wife and I took the body on the roof and let it down the chimney of our neighbor the purveyor, whom you were just about to hang. The purveyor, finding him in his room, naturally thought he was a thief, and struck him such a blow that the man fell down and lay motionless on the floor. Stooping to examine him, and finding him stone dead, the purveyor supposed that the man had died from the blow he had received; but of course this was a mistake, as you will see from my account, and I only am the murderer; and although I am innocent of any wish to commit a crime, I must suffer for it all the same, or else have the blood of two Mussulmans on my conscience. Therefore send away this man, I pray you, and let me take his place, as it is I who am guilty."

On hearing the declaration of the Jewish doctor, the chief of police commanded that he should be led to the gallows, and the Sultan's purveyor go free. The cord was placed round the Jew's neck, and his feet had already ceased to touch the ground when the voice of the tailor was heard beseeching the executioner to pause one moment and to listen to what he had to say.

indignantly adv. 愤怒地
ponder v. 仔细考虑
defer v. 推迟
slain v. 杀死（slay 的过去分词）
beseech v. 哀求
stoop v. 屈服

impudence n. 厚颜无耻
summon v. 召集
gallows n. 绞刑架
conscience n. 良心
tumble v. 摔倒

Mysterious Arab Countries
神秘的阿拉伯

Unit 10
Cuisine in Arabia

Warm-Up Questions

1. How many kinds of Arab diet do you know? Can you talk about it?
2. Do you know the differences between Arab diet and Chinese diet?
3. If you are going to travel to Arab countries, what would you like to eat or drink?

Text

As we know, Arab countries are mysterious, so is the cooking. Essential to any cooking in the Arabian Peninsula is the concept of hospitality and generosity. Meals are generally large family affairs, with much sharing and a great deal of warmth over the dinner table. Now, let's know them through their diets.

Middle Eastern Cuisine[①]

Elements

  Cereals constitute the basis of the Middle Eastern diet, both historically and today. Wheat and rice are the major and preferred sources of staple foods. Barley is also common in the region and maize has become common in some areas as well. Bread is a universal staple in the region, eaten, in one form or another, by all classes and groups, practically at every meal.

  Aside from bread, wheat is also used in the forms of burghul and couscous. Burghul is cracked wheat, made by partially cooking the wheat grains in water, drying it in an oven or in the sun, then breaking it into pieces, in different grades of size. Typically, it is cooked in water, with flavorings, much like rice. Burghul is also used in making meat pies and as an ingredient in salads, notably in tabbouleh, with chopped parsley, tomato, lemon, and oil. Freekeh is another common grain, made from immature green wheat.

  There are many types of rice produced and consumed in the region. Plain rice is served undergrilled meats or with meat/vegetable stews. In more complex rice dishes, there are layers of meat, vegetables, sauces, nuts, or dried fruits.

  Butter and clarified butter (also known as ghee) are, traditionally, the preferred medium of cooking. Olive oil is prevalent in the Mediterranean coastal areas. Christians use it during lent, when meat and dairy products are excluded, and Jews use it in place of animal fats such as butter to avoid mixing meat and dairy products.

  Most regions in the Middle East use spices. Typically, a stew will include a small amount of cinnamon, cloves, cumin, and coriander. Black pepper is common, and chili peppers are used occasionally, especially as a separate sauce or as a pickle. Parsley and mint are commonly used in cooking and in salads. Varieties of thyme are common in Syria, Lebanon, and Palestine, and a mixture of dried thyme and sumac (crushed sour berries) is a common

---

① http: //en. wikipedia. org/wiki/Middle_ Eastern_ cuisine.

breakfast item with oil and bread. Sumac is also sprinkled over grilled meat. Garlic is common to many dishes and salads. Lamb and mutton have always been the favored meats of the region. Pork is prohibited in Islam and Judaism and is rarely eaten in the region. Prominent among the meat preparations were the grilled meats, or kebabs. There are a wide variety of these grills, with many regional specialties and styles. The most common are the cubed cuts on skewers, known as shish kebab in most places. Chicken may also be grilled in the same fashion. Another common variety is kofta and kebab, made from ground meat, sometimes with onions and spices, shaped around the skewer like a long sausage and grilled. Kebabs are typically a street or restaurant food, served with bread, salad, and pickles. It is not usually prepared in domestic kitchens.

Meat and vegetable stews, served with rice, bulgur, or bread, are another form of meat preparation in the region. Kibbeh is a pie or dumpling made with meat and cereal. The most common are made with ground meat (typically lamb) and burghul, worked together like a dough, then stuffed with minced meat that has been fried with onion, aromatics, and, sometimes, pine nuts or almonds and raisins. This can either be in the form of individual small dumplings (usually shaped like a torpedo), or in slices like a cake, baked on an oven tray with the stuffing placed between two layers of the dough. One variation is kibbeh, which is made by pounding raw meat and burghul together with seasoning and served with dips of lemon juice and chili sauce.

Vegetables and pulses are the predominant everyday food of the great majority of the people of the Middle East. They are boiled, stewed, grilled, stuffed, and cooked with meat and with rice. Among the green leaf vegetables, many varieties of cabbage, spinach, and chard are widely used. Root and bulb vegetables, such as onions and garlic, as well as carrots, turnips, and beets are equally common. Squash, tomato, eggplants, and okra are distinctive elements in the cookery of the region. Eggplant is often fried in slices and dressed in yogurt and garlic, or roasted over an open fire, then pulped and dressed with sesame paste, lemon juice, garlic, and cumin, a dish known as baba ghannoush. Tomato is the most ubiquitous ingredient in Middle Eastern cookery. It is used fresh in a variety of salads, cooked in almost every stew and broth, and grilled with kebab.

Beans and pulses are crucial to the diet of the region, second only to cereals. The fava beans are eaten green and dried. Dried, they are boiled in one of the most popular Egyptian foods of ful medames, a domestic and street food, eaten for breakfast or any other meal, mashed and dressed in oil, lemon, and chili. Similar dishes are found in all other parts of the region. The famous Falafel, now popular in Europe and America, was originally made from dried fava bean, crushed and formed into a rissole with herbs and spices, then fried. It is also made from chickpeas or a mixture of the two. Green fava beans are cooked like other green beans, boiled and dressed in oil, or stewed with meat. The haricot beans and black-eyed beans are also common. Lentils, split peas, and chickpeas are widely used in soups, with rice, in salads, or with meat. Hummus, made from chickpeas and sesame paste, originated in Syria/Lebanon.

Stuffed vegetables are a dish most associated with the Middle East in the popular mind. They are commonly called dolma, the Turkish word meaning "stuffed", but also the Arabic mahshi. Grape leaves, chard, and cabbage are stuffed with rice, ground meat, pine nuts, and spices, and then stewed in oil and tomato. Many vegetables are similarly stuffed and stewed or baked, such as squash, onion, tomato, eggplant, peppers, and even carrots.

Arabs commonly consume milk, fresh or soured. Yogurt, a Turkish contribution, is commonly consumed plain, used in cooking, used in salad dressing, or diluted as a drink. White cheese, like the Greek feta, is the most common in the region.

Meze is common throughout the Middle East. It consists of a number of small dishes that are picked at leisure: cheese, melon, nuts, various salads and dips, such as tabbouleh, hummus and pickles, and also more substantial items, such as grilled meat, kibbeh, and sausage.

Beverages

Turkish coffee is the most well known beverage of the region. It is thicker than regular coffee and is made by boiling finely ground coffee in water and then letting the grounds settle. In the 1980s, instant coffee also became popular. Aside from Middle Eastern coffee, there is also an alcoholic drink called arak. It is most famous for its potency and milky-white color when water is added, producing the drink nicknamed "the milk of lions". Water and ice are almost always added because of alcohol content between 30% and 60%. Arak is colorless in its pure form and is aniseed-flavored. In the Middle East, arak is served in social settings and with meze. A common drink served during Ramadan is Qamar El Deen, a thick and sweet apricot drink. The apricots are boiled with sugar and water until they are thick and placed on wooden planks left in the sun until dry. Fruit leather is left, which is then melted with water and sugar and drunk. Another popular drink is Jallab. It is made by diluting a mixture grape molasses, dates, and rose water and served with crushed ice. Some also serve it with raisins or pine nuts. Ayran is a beverage made from yogurt.

Etiquette

In some areas in the Middle East, especially in the Persian Gulf countries, it is common for people to take their food from a common plate in the center of the table. Rather than employing forks or spoons, people traditional dine without utensils; they scoop up food with their thumb and two fingers or pita bread. In and around the Arab world, the left hand is considered unclean. Even if you are left handed, eat only with your right hand. Follow your host's lead for the exceptions; the most common is to use your left hand to drink from a glass when eating greasy food with your right. It is proper etiquette to compliment the host on the food and his hospitality. Similarly, it is important to try every plate on the table. If a guest does not leave food on his plate, the host generally fills it immediately. The Middle East places emphasis on enjoying meals with family and friends. Ramadan is the month during which food consumption increases dramatically throughout Muslim communities. Breaking the fast becomes a banquet, with exchanges of invitation between kin and friends, and public banquets held by charities and associations. The cafes and pastry shops are open at night, and a carnival atmosphere prevails in the streets. Many Muslims, following the reported example of the Prophet, break their fast with a date, followed by a variety of dishes. Sweet pastries and puddings are always present on Ramadan nights everywhere. The end of Ramadan is marked by a festival, Id 'al-Fitr, a feast that breaks the fast, during which a great quantity and variety of sweets and pastries are consumed. The other major Muslim feast is that of 'Id al-Adha, feast of the sacrifice, which occurs during the pilgrimage month, and at which an animal, usually a sheep or a goat, is slaughtered in every household that can afford it, and great banquets are prepared, with an obligation to give food to the poor.

New Words

cereal ['sɪərɪəl] n. 谷物；谷类植物
constitute ['kɔnstɪtjuːt] v. form, compose or set up 构成；组成；制定
historically [hɪ'stɔrɪklɪ] adv. throughout history 历史上地；从历史观点上说
wheat [wiːt] n. annual or biennial grass having erect flower spikes and light brown grains 小麦；小麦色
staple [steɪpl] n. (food or activity) basic and important in people's everyday lives 主要的（食物，活动）
barley ['baːlɪ] n. 大麦
region ['riːdʒ(ə)n] n. the extended spatial location of something 地区；区域
maize [meɪz] adj. a strong yellow color 玉米色的 n. 玉米；玉米色
universal [juːnɪ'vəːsl] adj. of worldwide scope or applicability 普遍的；全世界的
practically ['præktɪk(ə)l] adv. almost; nearly 实际地；几乎；事实上
couscous [kuskus] n. 粟（俗称小米、谷子）
crack [kræk] v. break on the surface only; make a sharp sound 破裂；发沙哑声
ingredient [ɪn'griːdɪənt] n. a component of a mixture or compound 原料；组成部分 adj. 构成组成部分
tabbouleh [tə'buːl] n. 塔博勒色拉（一种黎巴嫩生菜）
grain [greɪn] n. 粮食；谷物
immature [ɪmə'tjuə(r)] adj. characteristic of a lack of maturity 不成熟的；未成熟的
grill [grɪl] v. cook over a grill 烧；烤
stew [stjuː] v. be in a huff, be silent or sullen 炖；炖汤；焖

Mysterious Arab Countries
神秘的阿拉伯

clarify ['klærɪfaɪ] v. make clear and (more) comprehensible 澄清；阐明
prevalent ['prev(ə)l(ə)nt] adj. encountered generally especially at the present time 流行的；普遍的；广传的
coastal ['kəustl] adj. of or relating to a coast 沿海的；海岸的
occasionally [ə'keɪʒnəlɪ] adv. now and then or here and there 偶尔；间或
thyme [taɪm] n. （用以调味的）百里香（草）
prominent ['prɔmɪnənt] adj. having a quality that thrusts itself into attention 突出的；显著的；杰出的
specialty [speʃətɪ] n. an asset of special worth or utility 专长；特性
kofta ['kɔftə] n. 肉丸
kebab [kɪ'bæb] n. 烤肉串
domestic [də'mestɪk] adj. of concern to or concerning the internal affairs of a nation 国内的；家庭的；驯养的
individual [ɪndɪ'vɪdju(ə)l] adj. being or characteristic of a single thing or person 个人的；个别的
n. a human being 个人
kibbeh [kɪb] n. 碎羊肉面饼
predominant [prɪ'dɔmɪnənt] adj. most frequent or common 主要的；卓越的
majority [mə'dʒɔrɪtɪ] n. the property resulting from being greater in number or the main part 多数
distinctive [dɪ'stɪŋtɪv] adj. of a feature that helps to distinguish a person or thing 有特色的；与众不同的
ubiquitous [juː'bɪkwɪtəs] adj. being present everywhere at once 普遍存在的；无所不在的
crucial ['kruːʃ(ə)l] adj. of extreme importance; vital 重要的；决定性的；决断的
herb [həːb] n. aromatic potherb used in cookery for its savory qualities 药草
fava ['faːvə] n. (fava bean) 蚕豆
dilute [daɪ'luːt] v. lessen the strength or flavor of a solution or mixture 稀释
cheese [tʃiːz] n. a solid food prepared from the pressed curd of milk 奶酪；干酪
meze [mez] n. 开胃菜；前菜
throughout [θruː'aut] adv. from first to last 自始至终；到处；全部
prep. 贯穿；遍及

Unit 10 Cuisine in Arabia

substantial [sʌb'stæʃl] adj. fairly large or essential 大量的；重大的
potency ['pəutnsɪ] n. capacity to produce strong physiological or chemical effects 效能；力量；潜力
arak [ə'ra:k] n. 亚力酒；麦芽糖化槽酒（等于arrack）
utensil [ju:'tensl] n. an implement for practical use（especially in a household）器具；器皿；用具
compliment ['kɔmplɪm(ə)nt] n. a remark（or act）expressing praise and admiration or praise v. 恭维；称赞；问候；道贺
hospitality [ˌhɔspɪ'tælətɪ] n. kindness in welcoming guests or strangers 热情；好客；款待
dramatically [drə'mætɪkəlɪ] adv. in a very impressive manner 戏剧地；引人注目地
banquet ['bæŋkwɪt] n. a ceremonial dinner party for many people 宴会；盛宴
carnival ['ka:nɪv(ə)l] n. a festival marked by merrymaking and processions 狂欢节；嘉年华会
atmosphere ['ætməsfɪə] n. a particular environment or surrounding influence 气氛；大气
feast [fi:st] v. 享受；款待；宴请 n. a ceremonial dinner party for many people 筵席；宴会
sacrifice ['sækrɪfaɪs] v. endure the loss of 牺牲；献祭 n. a loss entailed by giving up 牺牲；祭品；供奉
obligation [ˌɔblɪ'geɪʃ(ə)n] n. the social force that binds you to the courses of action demanded by that force 义务；职责

Phrases & Expressions

aside from	除…以外
be used in	适用于；被用于
be in place of	代替
varieties of	各种各样的
be prohibited	被禁止的
in the form of	以…形式
as well as	也；和…一样；不但…而且

at leisure　　　　　　　　　　空闲地；悠闲地

Proper Names

Mediterranean [ˌmedɪtəˈreɪnɪən]	地中海；地中海的
Jew [dʒu:]	犹太人；犹太教
Judaism [ˈdʒu:deɪɪzəm]	犹太教；（总称）犹太人；犹太主义
Egyptian [ɪˈdʒɪpʃən]	埃及的；埃及人的；埃及人
Arab [ˈærəb]	阿拉伯人
baba ghannoush	茄泥（阿拉伯菜中的酱料式的冷盘）
Falafel	沙拉三明治
dolma/mahshi	大米羊肉菜叶包
Qamar El Deen	杏子酒
Jallab	糖浆；果汁

Background Information

History and Influences

　　Originally the region of the fertile Crescent, the Middle East was where wheat was first cultivated, followed by barley, pistachios, figs, pomegranates, dates and other regional staples. Fermentation was also discovered here to leaven bread and make beer. As a crossroads between Europe, Asia and Africa, this area has long been a hub of food and recipe exchange. During the Persian Empire (ca. 550BC – 330 BC) the foundation was laid for Middle-Eastern food when rice, poultry and fruits were incorporated into their diets. Figs, dates and nuts were brought by Arabian warriors to conquered lands, and spices were brought back from the Orient.

　　Study & Practice The area was also influenced by dumplings from Mongol invaders; turmeric, cumin, garlic and other spices from India; cloves, peppercorns and allspice from the Spice Islands; okra from Africa; and tomatoes from the New World, via the Moors of Spain. Religion has also changed the cuisine as neither Jews nor Muslims eat pork, making lamb the primary meat. Since the Qur'an forbids alcohol consumption, the region isn't noted much for its wine—except in religiously mixed Lebanon, where vineyards like Chateau Ksara, Chateau Kefraya and Chateau Masaya have gained international fame for their wines. Chateau Ksara is also very popular for its arak, the Lebanese version of raki and ouzo. Al-Maza is also Lebanon's primary brewery, which was at one time, the Middle East's only beer-producing factory. Lebanon has always been well known in the region for its wines and arak, making it an exception when it comes to lack of alcohol in the region.

Study & Practice

I. Read Aloud and Memorize

Read the following poem aloud until you have learned them by heart.

My Heart Was Sad Seven Times
Kahlil Gibran, 1883—1931

The first time when I saw her being meek that she might attain height.

The second time when I saw her limping before the crippled.

The third time when she was given to choose between the hard and the easy, and she chose the easy.

The fourth time when she committed a wrong, and comforted herself that others also commit wrong.

The fifth time when she forbore for weakness, and attributed her patience to strength.

The sixth time when she despised the ugliness of a face, and knew not that it was one of her own masks.

And the seventh time when she sang a song of praise, and deemed it a virtue.

Mysterious Arab Countries
神秘的阿拉伯

II. Answer the Following Questions

1. Which are the major and preferred sources of staple foods?
2. What is a universal staple in the region?
3. Which kind of spices is common in Syria, Lebanon, and Palestine?
4. There are a wide variety of grills, what is the most common way?
5. What is the predominant everyday food of the great majority of the people in the Middle East?
6. What is the most ubiquitous ingredient in Middle Eastern cookery? Why?
7. What are the stuffed vegetables commonly called in the popular mind?
8. When did theinstant coffee become popular?
9. Why is the alcoholic drink "arak" nicknamed "the milk of lions"?
10. What else do you know about Middle Eastern cuisine?

III. Cloze

Complete the following paragraphs according to your own understanding, and change the forms where necessary.

Paragraph 1 [①]

Egyptian cuisine is a very rich cuisine _____ (1) has many unique customs. These customs may also vary within Egypt itself, _____ (2) in the coastal areas, _____ (3) the coast of the Mediterranean Sea and Canal, the diet of the people _____ (4) heavily on fish. In the more agriculture areas, the reliance on farm products is much _____ (5) Duck, geese, chicken, and river fish are the main animal protein sources. _____ (6) the surrounding Arab cuisines, _____ (7) place heavy _____ (8) on meat, Egyptian cuisine is rich in vegetarian dishes; both of the national dishes of Egypt; Ful medames, ta'amia (also known in other countries as *falafel*), and kushari, are generally vegetarian. Fruits are also greatly _____ (9) in Egypt: mango, grapes, bananas, apples, sycamore,

---

① http://en.wikipedia.org/wiki/Arab_ cuisinene.

Unit 10 Cuisine in Arabia

guava, and peach are very popular, especially because they are all domestically produced therefore are _____ (10) in relatively low prices.

Paragraph 2①

Islamic dietary laws _____ (1) the eating of pork and the drinking of _____ (2) beverage. This law is enforced throughout Saudi Arabia. According to Islamic law, animals must be _____ (3) in a halal way and blessed before they can be eaten. In 2008, Saudi Arabia was the world's fifth largest _____ (4) of both lamb and _____ (5).

According to the Saudi Arabian cultural mission, "guests are _____ (6) hot coffee and dates as a symbol of generosity and _____ (7) The same practice is carried out in the month of Ramadan. Muslims in Saudi Arabia break their _____ (8) with dates, water and Arabian coffee. The caffeine in the coffee and the protein and iron in dates _____ (9) the fasting person with a lot of energy. This helps them _____ (10) the Tarawhih (extended prayers) held in the evenings during Ramadan."

IV. Spot Dictation

In this part, you will hear a passage three times. When the passage is read for the first time, you should listen carefully for its general idea. When the passage is read for the second time, you are required to fill in the blanks numbered from 1 to 10 with the exact words you have heard. Finally, when the passage is read for the third time, you should check what you have written.

Middle Eastern Food②

Middle Eastern food first came became popular in the 1990s and the _____ (1) Mediterranean Diet. According to the Mayo Clinic, the _____ (2) included a reduced risk of heart disease, a reduced risk of Alzheimer's disease, and a reduced risk of cancer. _____ (3) with the rising _____ (4) rates, restaurants have become increasingly health

---

① http://en.wikipedia.org/wiki/Saudi_Arabian_cuisine.
② http://www.ecocn.org/thread-64297-1-1.html.

Mysterious Arab Countries
神秘的阿拉伯

_____ (5) and Middle Eastern food is exactly what so many are trying to _____ (6) into their menus. For example, Freekeh is a whole grain that has four times the fiber of brown rice, which helps keep blood sugar low. It also has more powerful vision _____ (7) than other grains and helps increase healthy _____ (8) in the digestive tract. Healthfulness and _____ (9) are central to the Middle Eastern diet, and these _____ (10) are becoming part of a change going on in the American diet as well.

V. Translation

Turn the following sentences into English, using as many words and phrases you have learned from the text as possible.

1. 这些不同的作物已从该地区各处收集起来。

2. 不合理饮食和过度吸烟会严重损害身体健康。

3. 这个村子有自己传统的服饰、烹调、民俗和手工艺。

4. 除了两三个窗户里有灯光偶尔闪烁一下，街上一片漆黑。

5. 当地人的善良、可爱和热情好客深深打动了来到佐治亚州的每位游客。

6. 置身其中，我们可以轻松地边漫步边了解这个国家丰富的艺术遗产。

7. 经济体系的第一要素是用来生产商品的自然资源。

Unit 10 Cuisine in Arabia

8. 职业安全训练项目应特别注重人与技术的互动。

_____

_____

VI. Oral Practice

Find a partner or partners and discuss with themabout the following questions.

1. Do you know anything about Vegetarian diet? Try to explain to your partner (s).
2. As the saying goes, "Food is the first necessity". Food security is related to people's health and safety of life and even economic development and social harmony. Please share with your partner (s) your ideas and advices about food security?
3. Describe the following picture first, show your opinion, and then give your suggestion.

图片来源：https: //www. banbaowang. com/shouchaobaochatu/list_ 31_ 18. html.

VII. Language Enhancement

The Arabian Nights is a work that has enthralled readers for centuries. The following is one of the stories for reading and thinking.

The Little Hunchback[①]
Part Ⅲ

"Oh, my lord," he cried, turning to the chief of police, "how nearly have you caused the death of three innocent people! But if you will only have the patience to listen to my tale, you shall know who the real culprit is. If someone has to suffer, it must be me! Yesterday, at dusk, I was working in my shop with a light heart when the little hunchback, who was more than half drunk, came and sat in the doorway. He sang me several songs, and then I invited him to finish the evening at my house. He accepted my invitation, and we went away together. At supper I helped him to a slice of fish, but in eating it a bone stuck in his throat, and in spite of all we could do he died in a few minutes. We felt deeply sorry for his death, but fearing lest we should be held responsible, we carried the corpse to the house of the Jewish doctor. I knocked, and desired the servant to beg her master to come down as fast as possible and see a sick man whom we had brought for him to cure; and in order to hasten his movements I placed a piece of money in her hand as the doctor's fee. Directly she had disappeared I dragged the body to the top of the stairs, and then hurried away with my wife back to our house. In descending the stairs the doctor accidentally knocked over the corpse, and finding him dead believed that he himself was the murderer. But now you know the truth, please set him free, and let me die in his stead."

The chief of police and the crowd of spectators were lost in astonishment at the strange events to which the death of the hunchback had given rise.

"Loosen the Jewish doctor," said he to the hangman, "and string up the tailor instead, since he has made confession of his crime. Really, one can not deny that this is a very singular story, and it deserves to be written in letters of gold."

The executioner speedily untied the knots which confined the doctor, and was passing the cord round the neck of the tailor, when the Sultan of Kashgar, who had missed his jester, happened to make inquiry of his officers as to what had become of him.

---

① http://ishare.iask.sina.com.cn/download/explain.php?fileid=11723728.

"Sire," replied they, "the hunchback having drunk more than was good for him, escaped from the palace and was seen wandering about the town, where this morning he was found dead. A man was arrested for having caused his death, and held in custody till a gallows was erected. At the moment that he was about to suffer punishment, first one man arrived, and then another, each accusing themselves of the murder, and this went on for a long time, and at the present instant the chief of police is engaged in questioning a man who declares that he himse of is the true assassin."

The Sultan of Kashgar no sooner heard these words than he ordered an usher to go to the chief of police and to bring all the persons concerned in the hunchback's death, together with the corpse, that he wished to see once again. The usher hastened on his errand, but was only just in time, for the tailor was positively swinging in the air, when his voice fell upon the silence of the crowd, commanding the hangman to cut down the body. The hangman, recognizing the usher as one of the king's servants, cut down the tailor, and the usher, seeing the man was safe, sought the chief of police and gave him the Sultan's message. Accordingly, the chief of police at once set out for the palace, taking with him the tailor, the doctor, the purveyor, and the merchant, who bore the dead hunchback on their shoulders.

When the procession reached the palace the chief of police prostrated himself at the feet of the Sultan, and related all that he knew of the matter. The Sultan was so much struck by the circumstances that he ordered his private historian to write down an exact account of what had passed, so that in the years to come the miraculous escape of the four men who had thought themselves murderers might never be forgotten.

Then came an old man, a barber who must have been at least ninety years of age. He said to the Sultan "Will your Highness graciously let me examine the body." He then knelt down, and took the head on his knees, looking at it attentively. Suddenly he burst into such loud laughter that he fell right backwards, and when he had recovered himself enough to speak, he turned to the Sultan. "The man is no more dead than I am," he said, "watch me." As he spoke he drew a small case of medicines from his pocket and rubbed the neck of the hunchback with some ointment made of balsam. Next he opened the dead man's mouth, and by the help of a pair of pincers drew the bone from his throat. At this the hunchback sneezed, stretched himself and opened his eyes.

The Sultan and all those who saw this operation did not know which to admire most, the constitution of the hunchback who had apparently been dead for a whole night and most of one day, or the skill of the barber, whom everyone now began to look upon as a great man. His Highness desired that the history of the hunchback should be written down, and placed in the archives beside that of the barber, so that they might be associated in people's minds to the end of time. And he did not stop there; for in order to wipe out the memory of what they had undergone, he commanded that the tailor, the doctor, the purveyor and the merchant, should each be clothed in his presence with a robe from his own wardrobe before they returned home. As for the barber, he bestowed on him a large pension, and kept him near his own person.

culprit n. 罪犯
custody n. 拘留
assassin n. 暗杀者
prostrate v. 拜倒
balsam n. 凤仙花
in one's stead 代替某人
accuse of 指控
errand n. 差事
ointment n. 油膏
bestow v. 授予

Unit 11
Arabia Marriage

Warm-Up Questions

1. What's your opinion on thepolygamy（多偶制）in the Arab regions?
2. Which one do you prefer, the free love marriage or blind date? Give you reasons.
3. Have you ever imagined your own wedding scene? What is your ideal style?

Text

Wedding customs vary from countries, Egypt has its own characteristics with respect to marriage, let's learn it.

Marriage in Ancient Egypt[①]

You may ask why I am writing an article about Egyptian weddings. You may think that an Egyptian wedding is like any other wedding, but I can assure you that an Egyptian wedding is a very special historical ceremony. It is the most important ceremony for Egyptian females. I am sure that there are certain rituals for marriage in many parts of the world but the Egyptian wedding ceremony has been carried on from generation to generation since the times of the Pharaohs. While there are many western aspects, the enthusiasm and grand festive atmosphere of an Egyptian wedding are simply amazing.

The ancient Egyptians were the first civilization to regard marriage as a legal relationship. Marriage in ancient Egypt was a religious imposition. The ancient Egyptian laws organized the marriage relationship and indicated all rights and duties for the couples. Many of the old marriage contracts have been found, and they were registered and signed by three officers. The ancient Egyptian laws gave the right of divorce to women as well as men, and the wife had great respect and a high degree of prestige.

Before marriage in ancient Egypt, there were many chances for men and women to meet in places such as the temples or at the common feasts. There was a custom in the Egyptian family which allowed the adult daughter to welcome guests who came to visit her parents. Even today there remains in some parts of rural Egypt a custom that the eldest daughter is to marry before the youngest. The ancient Egyptians had an engagement period in order for the couple to become familiar with each other. The groom-to-be and his parents would go to the bride's house and meet the head of the family. They would negotiate an agreement where the groom would pay a dowry and buy the bride a gift of precious stones or gold. On the day of the wedding there would be a great banquet where all the guests would eat, sing and dance. Then the bride and groom would be led to their home and on the way, green wheat would be tossed in the air as a symbol of fertility.

While time has altered modern Egyptian weddings, many of the traditions

---

① www. en. irisegypt. com.

remain. Christian and Islamic custom now dictates that the official wedding must take place in a church or mosque. However, the reception after the official wedding remains much the same as in ancient Egypt. Reception parties differ from place to place in Egypt but they all hold common features including singing, dancing, a banquet and a lot of guests. Most often the wealth of the family of the bride and groom dictates the number of guests invited to the reception.

Certain aspects of Egyptian weddings in urban cities are not unlike weddings anywhere in the world. The bride wears an ordinary bridal dress and the groom wears a black suit or a tuxedo. The ceremony starts with a car parade. The wedding car (as prestigious as possible) will be decorated with flowers and ribbons. Cars of both families move together in a noisy parade of continuous sounding of car horns to a wedding hall most often in a hotel. The honking is to announce that there is a wedding taking place. When the bride and groom reach the hotel they are received by a Zaffa. The Zaffa is another human parade of belly dancers and drummers surrounding the bride and groom, singing happy songs. The bride and groom will occasionally join in the dancing but the main aim is to walk as slowly as possible to the wedding hall. Some Zaffas will last an hour!

When the bride and groom finally reach their destination in the hall they sit in the Kosha. The Kosha usually consists of two comfortable seats in front of the guests where the bride and groom reign as though king and queen. As soon as the bride and groom are seated in the Kosha a rose sherbet drink is passed to the guests and all drink to their health. Then the bride and groom will switch rings from right index fingers to left index finger.

This is probably an old Christian tradition but it is done whether the couple is Moslem or Christian. With this ritual, the festivities begin. The bride and groom have the first dance after which the other wedding guests join in. Usually a belly dancer or a singer entertains the guests, but in more luxurious weddings there is more than one entertainer. Guests will dance and sing with the newly wed couple, and the groom will occasionally be tossed in the air by friends. The more the tossing of the groom the more popular he is! After the formal entertainment, a disc jockey is used to extend the festivities.

Then comes the cutting of the cake, as elsewhere in the world, the bride and groom cut the cake, which is several layers high. The bride then tosses her flower bouquet behind her back to other hopeful females. Whoever catches the bouquet is

Mysterious Arab Countries
神秘的阿拉伯

lucky because she will be the next to be married. Next, the couple opens the buffet for the guests, which is usually a wide variety of salads, meats, stews, and sweets. Actually the list might go on forever in some weddings. Food is considered one of the factors that reflect the wealth of the families of the bride and groom. After every guest has stuffed his or her stomach, the wedding party is over. In some weddings there may be some more entertainment. Then the bride and groom usually get a complimentary night or two at the hotel.

Modern urban weddings are obviously affected by western traditions, for example, the cutting of the cake and tossing of the bouquet. This is not the case with rural areas of Egypt. In rural areas, after the Zaffa, the wedding ceremony will usually take place in a big clearing of land where a huge Arabic tent called the Sewan is set up. Entertainment includes a belly dancer or singer and sometimes both. Drinks are passed to guests and food comes in huge plates to be served to guests. The customary food is Fattah which is pieces of lamb meat embedded in rice and bread dipped in stew. The bride and groom will leave the wedding early but the guests continue the festivities.

Whether rural or urban, weddings reflect the image of the families that have come together. Both families show off their wealth to their wedding guests. From this, it would be concluded that Egyptian weddings are not just an announcement of marriage but also an announcement of the economic positions of the families. If you visit Egypt, keep an eye out for weddings. In many seasons, there will be weddings almost every night in hotels such as the Nile Hilton. Do not hesitate to ask permission to join the wedding. I guarantee you that you will be welcomed. Sing, dance and enjoy the culture of Egypt.

New Words

assure [ə'ʃuə] v. make certain of 保证；担保
historical [hɪ'stɒrɪkl] adj. belonging to the past; having once lived or existed in the past 历史的；历史上的
ceremony ['serəmənɪ] n. a formal event performed on a special occasion 典礼；仪式；礼仪
ritual ['rɪtʃuəl] n. any customary observance or practice 仪式；惯例；礼制

Unit 11 Arabia Marriage

adj. 仪式的；例行的；礼节性的
enthusiasm [ɪn'θjuːzɪæzəm] n. a feeling of excitement 热心；热忱；热情
imposition [ˌɪmpə'zɪʃn] n. an uncalled-for burden 强加；被迫接受；税收
indicate ['ɪndɪkeɪt] v. to state or express briefly 指出；表明
register ['redʒɪstə] v. record in writing 登记；注册；记录
prestige [pre'stiː(d)ʒ] n. a high standing achieved through success or influence or wealth（由财富等而产生的）威望；声望
rural ['ruərəl] adj. relating to rural areas 农村的；乡下的
engagement [ɪn'geɪdʒmənt] n. a meeting arranged in advance 订婚；婚约；诺言
bride [braɪd] n. a woman who has recently been married 新娘
negotiate [nɪ'gəuʃɪeɪt] v. discuss the terms of an arrangement 谈判；商议 vi. 谈判；交涉
dowry ['dauərɪ] n. money or property brought by a woman to her husband at marriage 嫁妆
banquet ['bæŋkwɪt] n. a ceremonial dinner party for many people 宴会；盛宴
toss [tɔs, tɔːs] v. throw or toss with a light motion 投掷；与…掷币打赌 vi. 辗转；颠簸；掷钱币决定某事
fertility [fə'tɪlətɪ] n. the state of being fertile 多产；肥沃；丰饶
alter ['ɔːltə] v. cause to change 改变；更改
dictate [dɪk'teɪt] v. issue commands or orders for 命令；控制；指示
mosque [mɔsk] n. 清真寺
feature ['fiːtʃə] n. a prominent aspect of something 特色；特征
tuxedo [tʌk'siːdəu] n. semiformal evening dress for men 男士无尾半正式晚礼服
parade [pə'reɪd] n. a ceremonial procession including people marching 游行；检阅
decorate ['dekəreɪt] v. make more attractive by adding ornament, color 点缀；装饰
continuous [kən'tɪnjuəs] adj. continuing in time or space without interruption 连续的；延伸的
sherbet ['ʃɜːbət] n. 冰冻果子露
luxurious [lʌg'ʒuərɪəs] adj. rich and superior in quality 奢侈的；豪华的
bouquet [bu'keɪ] n. 花束
stuff [stʌf] v. fill with something until it's full or eat a lot of things 填满；吃饱

Mysterious Arab Countries
神秘的阿拉伯

complimentary [ˌkɔmpliˈmentəri] adj. conveying or resembling a compliment 赠送的；称赞的；问候的
customary [ˈkʌstəməri] adj. in accordance with convention or custom 习俗的
embed [ɪmˈbed] v. fix or set securely or deeply 把…嵌入
guarantee [ˌgærənˈtiː] v. make certain of 保证；担保

Phrases & Expressions

regard…as	把…认作
be familiar with	熟悉的
take place	发生；举行
consist of	由…组成；包括
a variety of	多种的；各种各样的
set up	建立；安排
show off	炫耀；卖弄
keep an eye out for	注意；警觉

Proper Names

Zaffa	婚礼游行
Nile Hilton [naɪl ˈhɪltən]	希尔顿饭店
Mosque [mɔsk]	清真寺
Pharaoh [ˈfeərəu]	法老（古埃及君主称号）
Islamic custom [ɪzˈlæmɪk]	伊斯兰习俗

Background Information

1. The Ancient Concept of Marriage in Egypt[①]

　　The concept of marriage in Egypt is not an easy topic. Certainly

---

① http://www. Lifes Greatest Question. com.

Egyptians seem to have taken mates in what most often appears to be lifelong monogamous (一夫一妻的) relationships. After the Third Intermediate period we begin to find ancient "marriage contracts" that incorporate the phrase *shep en shemet* (price for "marrying" a woman) and mostly set out property rights without elaborating on the act of marriage itself. More abundant are divorce records that also deal mostly with property settlements.

When examining ancient relieves and statues, it is easy to assume that the ancient Egyptians marriage was similar to today's institution, but beyond these visual clues, there is little in the way of documentation to substantiate this. Little written evidence of either true marriage ceremonies or marriages as a concept has been found. Usually there was a grand party associated with the joining of two people, but we believe it was simply a social affair and had no real religious or legal bearing.

2. The Modern Concept of Marriage in Egypt[①]

Our modern, romantic concept of marriage is a relationship based on love between partners who consent to share their lives together. But up until the 26th dynasty, relatively late in Egyptian history, the bride herself seems to have little choice in the marriage. In fact, during this time frame most marriage contracts are actually between the girl's father and future husband. The girl's father and even her mother had much more say in the matter than the bride. After the 26th dynasty, the bride appears to have had more say in her future husband, and we find phrases in marriage contracts that indicate a more defined relationship.

Among common people, polygamy may very well have existed as it obviously did in the royal class, but if so it was rare. We knew from excavations such as Deir El Medina that the housing of common people conformed more to monogamy rather than polygamy.

---

① Ditto.

Mysterious Arab Countries
神秘的阿拉伯

3. Ancient Egyptian Ideal Marriage[①]

Ancient Egyptian ideal marriage means mutually respecting and loving couples. Tomb murals that reflect this harmonious relationship between husband and wife often painted with an extremely gentle gesture — connecting hands or one arm gently resting on each other's neck or shoulders. In some painting, the couple hugged tightly, and there are many wives image side marked "his beloved" such words.

Study & Practice

I. Read Aloud and Memorize

Read the following paragraph aloud until you have learned them by heart.

Before marriage in ancient Egypt, there were many chances for men and women to meet in places such as the temples or at the common feasts. There was a custom in the Egyptian family which allowed the adult daughter to welcome guests who came to visit her parents. Even today there remains in some parts of rural Egypt a custom that the eldest daughter is to marry before the youngest. The ancient Egyptians had an engagement period in order for the couple to become familiar with each other. The groom-to-be and his parents would go to the bride's house and meet the head of the family. They would negotiate an agreement where the groom would pay a dowry and buy the bride a gift of precious stones or gold. On the day of the wedding there would be a great banquet where all the guests would eat, sing and dance. Then the bride and groom would be led to their home and on the way, green wheat would be tossed in the air as a symbol of fertility.

---

① http: //www. guil in line. com.

II. Answer the Following Questions

1. What is the most important ceremony for Egyptian females?
2. What did the ancient Egyptians regard marriage as?
3. Who was allowed to welcome guests who came to visit the parents according to the custom in the Egyptian family?
4. Although reception parties differ from place to place in Egypt, what are the common features?
5. What do the bride and the groom wear in their ceremony?
6. What does the Kosha usually consist of?
7. If a female catches the bride's bouquet, what does that imply?
8. Why do we say the Egyptian weddings are not just an announcement of marriage but also an announcement of the economic positions of the families?

III. Cloze

Complete the following passages according to your own understanding, and change the forms where necessary.

1. Guidelines for Women[①]

Muslims are conservative when it _____ (1) to dress. They do not approve _____ (2) women showing off their skin in any form. A woman's arms, legs, shoulders, and chest should all be _____ (3) A head covering, such as a scarf, should likely be worn if the wedding takes place in a mosque, as well as long, thick socks to cover the ankles; _____ (4) women are required to remove their shoes upon entering a mosque. Jewelry is acceptable, and the most appropriate outfit would be a long dress or skirt _____ (5) long sleeves and high neckline.

---

① www. en. irisegypt. com.

Mysterious Arab Countries
神秘的阿拉伯

2. Guidelines for Men

_____ (6) the many restrictions imposed on women in Islamic societies, men are freer to act and wear _____ (7) they choose. In regards to dress, men are only _____ (8) to be covered from navel to knee, so they are not nearly as limited as women are. An _____ (9) outfit for a man to wear to a Muslim wedding would be similar to what he would wear to any other wedding, such as a suit. It's _____ (10) to note that men must also remove their shoes before entering a mosque and may want to cover their feet accordingly for personal comfort, _____ (11) it is not necessary.

3. Other Considerations

Although many Muslim weddings are formal and _____ (12) there has been a movement towards westernizing them in recent years. _____ (13) attending a Muslim wedding, it is best to ask the bride or groom what type of wedding they plan _____ (14) having, and if there are any clothing requirements that you should be aware of before you choose an outfit for _____ (15) If you ask first, you will limit the risk of being embarrassed when you arrive _____ (16) to inappropriate attire. You do not want to _____ (17) your hosts, so checking with them first is the best idea.

IV. Spot Dictation

In this part, you will hear a passage three times. When the passage is read for the first time, you should listen carefully for its general idea. When the passage is read for the second time, you are required to fill in the blanks numbered from 1 to 10 with the exact words you have heard. Finally, when the passage is read for the third time, you should check what you have written.

Marriage was the _____ (1) and most desirable state for _____ (2) Egyptians of both genders and all social classes. Athenian men _____ (3) little respect or affection for women and _____ (4) marriage until well into their thirties, but most Egyptian men were eager to follow the advice of the _____ (5) literature urging them to take a wife _____ (6) still young so they could found a _____ (7) and raise a family. Most men were _____ (8) by the age of twenty to girls who _____ (9) have been as young as fifteen. There was an age _____ (10) but usually not more than two or three years.

V. Translation

Turn the following sentences into English, using as many words and phrases you have learned from the text as possible.

1. 广播员请他的听众留意逃跑的犯人。

2. 人们赞美并视为成功的生活，只不过是生活中的一种。

3. 一般而言，紫色与高贵和财富相关，因为紫色在古代中国是社会地位的一种象征。

4. 瑞士是个相当富有的国家，然而那儿的人们并不怎么炫耀自己的财富。

5. 当没有了信任，即便是双方都想和解，这些被破坏的关系几乎也是不可修补的。

6. 学习是一个漫长的过程，没有耐心和毅力是难以坚持到底的。

7. 必须想办法保证我们的孩子有一个不错的人生开端。

8. 小草象征一个坚强的人，其顽强的品格只有在危机和不幸中才能充分展现。

9. 一名大学生目击了一场暴力射杀事件，但是声称并没有因此受到影响。

10. 在这个时代，英语被看作一种比对文学、文化或历史的审美更加有价值的实用工具。

VI. Oral Practice

Find a partner or partners, and discuss with them about the following questions.

1. What's your opinion on the following picture?

图片来源：http://www.twoeggz.com/news/51394.html.

2. Make a comparison between Chinese and Western weddings. Which

one do you prefer?

3. Do you know anything about parents-arranged marriages? Talk with your partner (s) about the traditional Chinese marriage.

VII. Language Enhancement

Learning the words from *The Prophet* by heart may provide the reader with a guide to living, since the oracle (智者), Almustafa, was delivering homilies on a variety of topics central to daily life: love marriage and children, work and play, possessions, beauty, truth, joy and sorrow and death.

On Marriage[①]

Then Almitra spoke again and said, "And what of Marriage, master?"
And he answered saying:
You were born together, and together you shall be forevermore.
You shall be together when white wings of death scatter your days.
Aye, you shall be together even in the silent memory of God.
But let there be spaces in your togetherness,
And let the winds of the heavens dance between you.
Love one another but make not a bond of love:
Let it rather be a moving sea between the shores of your souls.
Fill each other's cup but drink not from one cup.
Give one another of your bread but eat not from the same loaf.
Sing and dance together and be joyous, but let each one of you be alone,
Even as the strings of a lute are alone though they quiver with the same music.
Give your hearts, but not into each other's keeping.
For only the hand of Life can contain your hearts.
And stand together, yet not too near together:
For the pillars of the temple stand apart,

---

① http://www-personal.umich.edu/~jrcole/gibran/prophet/prophet.htm#Contents. (The Chinese version of *The Prophet* can be checked out in Appendix II.)

Mysterious Arab Countries
神秘的阿拉伯

And the oak tree and the cypress grow not in each other's shadow.

On Love

Then said Almitra, "Speak to us of Love."
And he raised his head and looked upon the people, and there fell a stillness upon them. And with a great voice he said:
When love beckons to you follow him,
Though his ways are hard and steep.
And when his wings enfold you yield to him,
Though the sword hidden among his opinions may wound you.
And when he speaks to you believe in him,
Though his voice may shatter your dreams as the north windlays waste the garden.
For even as love crowns you so shall hecrucify you. Even as he is for your growth so is he for your pruning.
Even as heascends to your height and caresses your tenderest branches that quiver in the sun,
So shall he descend to your roots and shake them in their clinging to the earth. Like sheaves of corn he gathers you unto himself.
He threshes you to make you naked.
He sifts you to free you from your husks.
He grinds you to whiteness.
He kneads you until you are pliant;
And then he assigns you to his sacred fire, that you may become sacred bread for God's sacred feast.
All these things shall love do unto you that you may know the secrets of your heart, and in that knowledge become a fragment of Life's heart.
But if in your fear you would seek only love's peace and love's pleasure,
Then it is better for you that you cover your nakedness and pass out of love's threshing-floor,
Into the seasonless world where you shall laugh, but not all of your laughter, and weep, but not all of your tears.
Love gives naught but itself and takes naught but from itself.

Unit 11　Arabia Marriage

Love possesses not nor would it be possessed;
For love is sufficient unto love. When you love you should not say, "God is in my heart," but rather, I am in the heart of God.
And think not you can direct the course of love, if it finds you worthy, directs your course.
Love has no other desire but to fulfill itself.
But if you love and must needs have desires, let these be your desires:
To melt and be like a runningbrook that sings its melody to the night.
To know the pain of too much tenderness.
To be wounded by your own understanding of love;
And to bleed willingly and joyfully.
To wake at dawn with a winged heart and give thanks for another day of loving;
To rest at the noon hour and meditate love'secstasy;
To return home at eventide with gratitude;
And then to sleep with a prayer for the beloved in your heart and a song of praise upon your lips.

lute n. 鲁特琴；古琵琶	cypress n. 柏树
beckon v. 召唤；吸引	pinion n. 鸟翼；双臂
lay waste 糟蹋	ascend v. 攀登；上升
thresh v. 敲打	knead v. 揉捏
brook n. 小溪	ecstasy n. 狂喜

Mysterious Arab Countries
神秘的阿拉伯

Unit 12
Yasser Arafat

Warm-Up Questions

1. Are you interested in political news? Would you like to become a political official?
2. People in some areas are suffering from the outbreak of wars and conflicts. In your opinion, what is the root of this?
3. China has been playing a very important role in international relationships. Do you know anything about China's efforts in improving globalization?

Text

Arafat, the leader of the PLO, had devoted all his life to fulfilling his dream of establishing an independent Palestinian state, but for the dream, he would never realize completely in his lifetime. He leaves us the mixed legacy as a "terrorist" and a revolutionary.

Arafat Leaves Mixed Legacy[①]

The leader of the Palestine Liberation Organization, Yasser Arafat, died Thursday in France where he was ailing for several days. Mr. Arafat, born August 24, 1929, had devoted his life to establishing a Palestinian homeland. It was a dream he would never realize completely in his lifetime. Being the leader who was known as a terrorist and a revolutionary, the Israelis condemned him as a terrorist and then negotiated peace with him. Arab leaders sometimes treated him as a statesman, sometimes as a traitor. Palestinians viewed him as a father figure and the leader of their quest for a homeland. Yasser Arafat took a giant step toward that dream when he signed an agreement in 1993 for Palestinian self-rule in the Gaza Strip and the West Bank and then returned home to Gaza in triumph.

The next year, he won the Nobel Peace Prize for his achievement, an award he shared with Israeli Prime Minister Yitzhak Rabin and Foreign Minister Shimon Peres. The Palestinian leader spoke through a translator as he accepted the honor in Oslo, Norway. "Peace will enable us to show our identity to the world, our real identity to the world," he said. Two years later, Mr. Arafat became the first elected president of the Palestinian Authority, the closest he would come to fulfilling his dream of presiding over an independent Palestinian state. Still, he remained convinced there would be a Palestinian state with or without him. "We want achievement of the peace of courageous people to end this long suffering in order to build an independent nation having a lot of democracy and caring for its children and where laughter is heard of happy, healthy kids," he said.

Mr. Arafat had come a long way since his days as a teenager. His first combat experience against Israel was running weapons for his father and older brother in the 1948 war. Yasser Arafat made his first public demand for a Palestinian liberation movement when he was still a student in Cairo in the 1950s. Later, while living in Kuwait, he created the "Fatah" movement, which becomes the core of the Palestine Liberation Organization the PLO. He was

---

① http://www.24en.com/voa/news/2006-03-22/37511.html.

named PLO leader in 1968 and remained so until his death. In his early years, Yasser Arafat gained a reputation as a ruthless terrorist. By 1988, Mr. Arafat had begun to make the transition to diplomacy. That was when he told the United Nations the PLO would recognize Israel as a sovereign state. Mr. Arafat's transition was most evident in his approval and support for secret peace talks that led to the Oslo peace accords. He signed the interim agreement with Israeli Prime Minister Yitzhak Rabin at the White House in 1993, amid high hopes for an end to decades of conflict. Sadly, seven years later, Palestinian and Israeli hopes for peace had deteriorated into an unrelenting cycle of violence. Efforts to revive the peace process faltered.

In 2000, U. S. President Bill Clinton brought Mr. Arafat together with Israeli Prime Minister Ehud Barak at the U. S. presidential retreat Camp David for one last effort to forge a peace accord that would give the Palestinians statehood and control over the Islamic holy sites in Jerusalem. But the Palestinian leader balked at some of the details. He did not take that final step and Mr. Barak backed away from the offer. As a Palestinian uprising surged, Israel blamed Mr. Arafat for not curbing the violence and barred him from leaving his West Bank headquarters. But that final humiliation only increased his popularity among Palestinians despite their complaints about Mr. Arafat's autocratic leadership style. Palestinians have always viewed Yasser Arafat as the father of their struggle for statehood. "Be sure we will continue to be committed to the peace process, to the peace of the brave, and will continue to be, with all the peace lovers," he said. With his trademark checkered black and white kafiyah and scruffy beard, Yasser Arafat jetted around the world promoting the cause of his people. He survived assassination attempts and a plane crash and managed to bounce back after serious political and military defeats. He surprised many by his decision at the age of 62 to marry his young Christian secretary, Suha, since Mr. Arafat had always rejected marriage, saying he was married to the Palestinian cause. They had a daughter who was born in 1995. For the last several years of his life he was in failing health and rumored to have Parkinson's disease His condition worsened in October 2004. Israel agreed to allow him to be transferred to a hospital in Paris on October 29 where his wife stayed by his side. He died November 11, 2004, at age 75.

Unit 12 Yasser Arafat

For nearly half a century Arafat was the symbol of Palestinian nationalism. Though he was not a military man, he was rarely seen out of his uniform in an effort to project strength and his commitment to armed struggle. He wore his kaffiyeh in a unique fashion, draped over his shoulder in the shape of Palestine, that is, all of historic Palestine, including Israel. The high-profile terrorist attacks he directed helped gain international attention and sympathy for the Palestinian cause, but, ultimately, his unwillingness to make the psychological leap from terrorist mastermind to statesman prevented him from achieving independence for the Palestinian people, and brought them decades of suffering that could have been avoided if he had abandoned his revolutionary zeal for liberating Palestine and agreed to live in peace with Israel. Mixed?

New Words

ail [eɪl] v. cause suffering to 使受病痛；使疼痛；使烦恼；折磨

terrorist ['terərɪst] n. a radical who employs terror as apolitical weapon 恐怖主义者；恐怖分子

revolutionary [revə'lju:ʃənərɪ] n. a radical supporter of political or social revolution. 革命者

condemn [kən'dem] v. express strong disapproval of 谴责；宣判

negotiate [nɪ'gəuʃɪeɪt] v. discuss the terms of an arrangement 谈判；协商；交涉

traitor ['treɪtə] n. someone who betrays his country by committing treason 叛徒；卖国贼；背信弃义之人

figure ['fɪgə] n. the impression produced by a person 形象；人物

triumph ['traɪʌmf] n. a successful ending of a struggle or contest or victory 胜利；成就

identity [aɪ'dentɪtɪ] n. the individual characteristics by which a thing or person is recognized or known 身份；个性

preside [prɪ'zaɪd] v. be in charge of, be the president of (+ over) 主持；指挥

convince [kən'vɪns] v. make (someone) agree, or realize the truth something 说服；使明白；使确信

Mysterious Arab Countries
神秘的阿拉伯

democracy [dɪˈmɔkrəsɪ] n. a system of government in which people choose their rulers by voting for them in elections 民主政体

combat [ˈkɔmbæt] v. fight against in or as if in a battle 与…战斗；斗争 n. a battle 战斗

transition [trænˈsɪʃən] n. the act of passing from one state or place to the next 过渡；转变；转换

diplomacy [dɪˈpləuməsɪ] n. negotiation between nations 外交；外交手腕

sovereign [ˈsɔvrɪn] adj. independent and not under the authority of any other country 独立自主的

evident [eviˈdənt] adj. clearly apparent or obvious to the mind or senses 明显的；明白的

accord [əˈkɔːd] n. harmony of people's opinions or actions or characters 符合；一致；协议

interim [ˈɪntərɪm] adj. serving during an intermediate interval of time 暂时的；临时的 n. the time between one event, process, or period and another 临时协定

deteriorate [dɪˈtɪərɪəreɪt] v. become worse in some way 恶化；变坏

unrelenting [ˌʌnrɪˈlentɪŋ] adj. without caring whether to hurt or embarrass others; never ceasing 无情的；不松懈的；不屈不挠的

revive [rɪˈvaɪv] v. becomes active, popular, or successful again 使振奋；复原；使再生

falter [ˈfɔːltə] v. lose power or strength in an uneven way, or no longer make much progress 衰退

ruthless [ˈruːθlɪs] adj. harsh or cruel 残酷的

humiliation [hjuːˌmɪlɪˈeɪʃn] n. state of disgrace or loss of self-respect 丢脸；耻辱；蒙羞；谦卑

bounce [bauns] v. spring up; move up and down repeatedly 弹跳；使弹起

achievement [əˈtʃiːvm(ə)nt] n. something that someone has succeeded in doing, especially after a lot of effort 成就

courageous [kəˈreɪdʒəs] adj. showing courage and brave 勇敢的

attempt [əˈtem(p)t] v. try to do sth. hard 试图（尤指做困难的事）

reputation [repjuˈteɪʃ(ə)n] n. the state of being held in high esteem and honor 名声

gain [geɪn] v. gradually get sth. 获得

retreat [rɪˈtriːt] v. move away from something or someone. 退出；离开
surge [sɜːdʒ] n. a sudden large increase in something that has previously been steady 激增
despite [dɪˈspaɪt] prep. 尽管；不管；虽有
statehood [ˈsteɪthud] n. the condition of being an independent state or nation 独立国家地位
autocratic [ɔːtəˈkrætɪk] adj. making decisions without asking anyone else's advice. 独裁的
scruffy [ˈskrʌfɪ] adj. dirty and messy 脏乱的
political [pəˈlɪtɪkəl] adj. relating to the way power is achieved and used 政治的
military [ˈmɪlɪt(ə)rɪ] adj. relating to the armed forces of a country 军事的
checker [ˈtʃekə(r)] n. 方格图案
cause [kɔːz] n. an aim or principle which a group of people supports or is fighting for 事业；追求

Phrases & Expressions

devoted to	热衷于…的
view…as…	把…看作是
quest for	追求；探索；设法找到
take a step toward	朝着…前进
share with	与…分享
agreement with	协议
balk at	畏缩；回避
back away from	躲开；（由于恐惧或厌恶等）后退
blame for	指责；责怪
complain about	怨言；投诉
bounce back	卷土重来；受挫后恢复原状

Proper Names

Gaza Strip [ˈgeɪzə]	加沙地带（地中海岸港市）
Palestinian [pælɪsˈtɪnɪən]	巴勒斯坦人

Mysterious Arab Countries
神秘的阿拉伯

Israel [ˈɪzreɪəl] 以色列（亚洲国家）；犹太人，以色列人
Oslo [ˈuslu] 奥斯陆（挪威首都）
Cairo [ˈkaiərəu] 开罗（埃及首都）
Kuwait [kuˈweɪt] 科威特（中东国家）
Christian [ˈkristjən] 基督徒；信徒
Jerusalem [dʒəˈruːsələm] 耶路撒冷
Yasser Arafat [ˈjaːsə ˈærəfæt] 亚瑟尔·阿拉法特
Yitzhak Rabin [ˈɪzæk ˈræbɪn] 伊扎克·拉宾（以色列政治家）
Shimon Peres [ˈsɪmən ˈpɪrɪəs] 西蒙·佩雷斯（以色列政治家）

Background Information

1. Yasser Arafat (Aug. 27, 1929 – November 11, 2004)

Mohammed Yasser Abdel Rahman Abdel Raouf Arafat al-Qudwa al-Husseini (24 August 1929 – 11 November 2004), popularly known as Yasser Arafat (Arabic:) or by his kunya Abu Ammar (Arabic: 'Abū`Ammār) was a Palestinian leader. He was Chairman of the Palestine Liberation Organization (PLO), President of the Palestinian National Authority (PNA), and leader of the Fatah political party and former paramilitary（军事性的）group, which he founded in 1959. Arafat spent much of his life fighting against Israel in the name of Palestinian self-determination. Originally opposed to Israel's existence, he modified his position in 1988 when he accepted UN Security Council Resolution 242. Arafat and his movement operated from several Arab countries. In the late 1960s and early 1970s, Fatah faced off with Jordan in a brief civil war. Forced out of Jordan and into Lebanon, Arafat and Fatah were major targets of Israel's 1978 and 1982 invasions of that country.

2. The Palestine Liberation Organization (PLO) (巴勒斯坦解放组织)

It is an organization founded in 1964 with the purpose of creating an independent State of Palestine. It is recognized as the "sole legitimate representative of the Palestinian people" by over 100 states with which it holds diplomatic relations, and has enjoyed observer status at the United Nations since 1974. The PLO was considered by the United States and Israel to be a terrorist organization until the Madrid Conference in 1991. In 1993, PLO recognized Israel's right to exist in peace, accepted UN Security Council resolutions 242 and 338, and rejected "violence and terrorism"; in response, Israel officially recognized the PLO as the representative of the Palestinian people.

3. The Nobel Peace Prize (诺贝尔和平奖)

Itis one of five Nobel prizes, the selection work is responsible by the Norwegian Nobel committee, in Oslo. According to Nobel's will, the peace prize should be awarded "friendly in order to promote national unity, cancellation or reduction of standing armies and for the peace conference of the organization and propaganda to exercise the utmost effort" or the person that make the greatest contribution. By 2006, 94 persons and 19 institutions were awarded the Nobel peace prize.

4. The Oslo I Accord or Oslo I (奥斯陆协议)

Officially called the *Declaration of Principles on Interim Self-Government Arrangements or Declaration of Principles* (DOP), was an attempt in 1993 to set up a framework that would lead to the resolution of the ongoing Israeli-Palestinian conflict. It was the first face-to-face agreement between the government of Israel and the Palestine Liberation Organization (PLO).

Negotiations concerning the agreement, an outgrowth of theMadrid Conference of 1991, were conducted secretly in Oslo, Norway hosted by the Fafo institute, and completed on 20 August 1993; the Accords were subsequently officially signed at a public ceremony in Washington, D. C., on 13 September 1993 in the presence of PLO chairman Yasser Arafat, the then Israeli Prime Minister Yitzhak Rabin and U. S. President Bill Clinton.

The Accord provided for the creation of a Palestinian interimself-government, the Palestinian National Authority (PNA). The Palestinian Authority would have responsibility for the administration of the territory under its control. The Accords also called for the withdrawal of the Israel Defense Forces (IDF) from parts of the Gaza Strip and West Bank.

It was anticipated that this arrangement would last for a five-year interim period during which a permanent agreement would be negotiated (beginning no later than May 1996). Issues such as Jerusalem, Palestinian refugees, Israeli settlements, security and borders were left to future negotiations. In 1995, the Oslo I Accord was followed by Oslo II. Neither promised Palestinian statehood.

5. Presidential Retreat Camp David

It is the country retreat of the president of the United States. It is located in wooded hills about 62 miles (100 km) north of Washington, D. C., in Catoctin Mountain Parknear Thurmont, Maryland. It is officially known as Naval Support Facility Thurmont and is technically a military installation; staffing is primarily provided by the US Navy and the US Marine Corps.

First known as Hi-Catoctin, Camp David was originally built as a camp for federal government agents and their families, by theWPA, starting in 1935, opening in 1938. In 1942, it was converted to a presidential retreat by Franklin D. Roosevelt and renamed "Shangri-La" (for the fictional Himalayan paradise). Camp David received its present name from Dwight D. Eisenhower, in honor of his father and grandson, both named David. Additionally, his own middle initial "D" stands for David. Camp David is not open to the general public. Catoctin Mountain Park does not indicate the location of Camp David on its official park maps due to privacy and security concerns.

Study & Practice

I. Read Aloud and Memorize

Read the following poem aloud until you have learned them by heart.

Mr. Arafat was not in "effective control". As for the Palestinian leader's denial of any knowledge of an attempt to smuggle a boatload of weapons into Palestinian areas, Mr. Cheney said bluntly, "We don't believe him." The US administration is debating a number of options, including the severing of ties with Mr. Arafat and his administration. This is causing alarm among Arab and European officials— not because they like Yasser Arafat or consider him blameless, but because they're worried about where all this may be leading. Many believe Ariel Sharon, the Israeli prime minister, wants to topple Mr. Arafat, and fear the language coming from Washington will simply encourage him. Later this week George Bush will meet King Abdullah of Jordan. He's been in close touch with Saudi Arabia and Egypt, and will tell Mr. Bush that all three countries believe it would be highly dangerous for the US to break its ties with Mr. Arafat. They fear such a move would further radicalize opinion in the Arab and Muslim worlds. They also argue that, for all his faults, Yasser Arafat is better placed to promote peace with Israel than any possible successor would be.

II. Answer the Following Questions

1. Where did the leader of the Palestine Liberation Organization, Yasser Arafat, die?
2. What was the dream he would never realize completely in his lifetime?
3. When did he win the Nobel Peace Prize for his achievement and with whom?
4. What did Yasser Arafat say as he accepted the honor in Oslo, Norway?
5. When did Mr. Arafat become the first elected president of the Palestinian Authority?
6. What did he create when he was living in Kuwait?
7. When did he sign the interim agreement with Israeli Prime Minister Yitzhak Rabin at the White House?
8. Why had Mr. Arafat always rejected marriage before the age of 62?
9. What was his first combat experience against Israel? And with whom?
10. Whatkind of image did Yasser Arafat leave in the mind of people of

Mysterious Arab Countries
神秘的阿拉伯

Palestine?

III. Cloze

Complete the following paragraphs according to your own understanding, and change the forms where necessary.

Paragraph 1①

While George Bush _____ (1) himself with saying he was disappointed with Mr. Arafat, Dick Cheney used much blunter language. Sunday's bomb _____ (2) in Jerusalem, he said, was one more sign Mr. Arafat was not in "effective control". As for the Palestinian leader's denial of any _____ (3) of an attempt to smuggle a boatload of weapons into Palestinian areas, Mr. Cheney said bluntly, "We don't believe him." The US administration is debating a number of options, including the severing of ties with Mr. Arafat and his administration. This is _____ (4) alarm among Arab and European officials — not because they like Yasser Arafat or consider him _____ (5) but because they're worried about where all this may be leading. Many believe Ariel Sharon, the Israeli prime minister, wants to topple Mr. Arafat, and fear the language coming from Washington will simply _____ (6) him. Later this week George Bush will meet King Abdullah of Jordan. He's been in _____ (7) touch with Saudi Arabia and Egypt, and will tell Mr. Bush that all three countries believe it would be highly dangerous or the US to break its _____ (8) with Mr. Arafat. They fear such a move would further radicalize _____ (9) in the Arab and Muslim worlds. They also argue that, for all his faults, Yasser Arafat is better placed to promote peace with Israel than any _____ (10) successor would be.

Passage 2②

Panetta is in Asia promoting the U. S. plan to shift forces to the Asia-Pacific region, but his _____ (1) has been called to events in the

---

① http: //www. hjenglish. com/new/p4927/.
② http: //www. hjenglish. com/new/print/476725.

Unit 12 Yasser Arafat

Middle East. On Thursday he gave an exclusive _____ (2) on the situation in Gaza to VOA. "Anytime violence _____ (3) up in the Middle East, _____ (4) it is, it's a cause for concern because you never know quite where it's all gonna lead. I _____ (5) the reasons Israel is doing what they're doing." In the past year, Israel has been hit by nearly 800 rockets from Gaza and has _____ (6) with air strikes. In a wide-ranging interview with VOA in Bangkok, Panetta said the violence shows the need for a long-term _____ (7) to the Israeli-Palestinian _____ (8) Our hope is that, in striking back, they can minimize the civilian deaths that are likely to _____ (9) But, you know, I hope in the end that all sides recognize that this is no way to _____ (10) the problems of the Middle East. Ultimately, the hope is that we can get back to trying to negotiate a permanent peace agreement between the Israelis and the Palestinians and provide a more permanent peace in that region.

IV. Spot Dictation

In this part, you will hear a passage three times. When the passage is read for the first time, you should listen carefully for its general idea. When the passage is read for the second time, you are required to fill in the blanks numbered from 1 to 10 with the exact words you have heard. Finally, when the passage is read for the third time, you should check what you have written.

Palestinian leader Yasser Arafat says he is ready to begin peace talks with Israel but he says the other side does not seem ready. His _____ (1) came between _____ (2) with China's top leaders Friday in Beijing. China's President Jiang Zemin smiled broadly as he _____ (3) Palestinian Authority President Yasser Arafat in Beijing. In an earlier meeting, Mr. Arafat _____ (4) the head of the National People's Congress, Li Peng, who returned the _____ (5) Beijing is expected to reaffirm support for a Palestinian state and offer financial _____ (6) On Friday, China again called on the two sides, particularly Israel, to exercise "the utmost restraint" and urged both parties to resume _____ (7) In a brief television _____ (8) on Reuters Mr. Arafat was asked if the two sides were likely to _____ (9) talks. He says the Palestinians are ready "at all times" but said the Israelis "are refusing." Israel has repeatedly said Mr. Arafat needs to take steps to _____ (10) Palestinian terrorist attacks if he wants to resume peace talks.

V. Translation

Turn the following sentences into English, using as many words and phrases you have learned from the text as possible.

1. 员工在工作中应讲求实效、团结合作、自我激励和自我约束，致力于不断改进提高。

   _____

   _____

2. 中国90%的可利用天然草原都有不同程度的恶化。

   _____

   _____

3. 无论什么困难也不能阻碍我们促进合作的决心。

   _____

   _____

4. 那位以拾荒为生的老人为慈善事业做出了巨大的贡献。

   _____

   _____

5. 青少年犯罪在日益增加，然而与社会因素相比，父母有更大的责任。

   _____

   _____

6. 从长期的角度来看，法国人民对于经济的恢复很有信心。

   _____

   _____

7. 人生就像一道多项选择题，困扰你的往往是众多的选择项，而不是题目本身。

   _____

   _____

8. 畏惧经济改革的选民越多，政治家们大谈特谈价值观的情况也就会越多。

_____

9. 这个运动受到三大政党关键人物的支持。

_____

10. 每个星期一的早上，我会召集和主持部门会议。

_____

VI. Oral Practice

Find a partner or partners and discuss with them about the following questions.

1. Which is more reliable as a source of information of the world, newspaper, TV, radio or the Internet? Why?
2. Which area do you usually pay more attention to while surfing online, politics, education, entertainment, economy, sports or others?
3. Faked animal photography has been reported now and then. What's your opinion on it?

VII. Language Enhancement

Remarks on Receiving the Nobel Prize for Peace[①]
by PLO Chairman Yasser Arafat

Oslo, December 10, 1994

Your Majesties,
Chairman of Nobel Prize,

---

① http://wenku.baidu.com/view/87697629915f804d2b16c1a9.html. (Its Chinese version can be checked out in Appendix II.)

Mysterious Arab Countries
神秘的阿拉伯

Ladies and Gentlemen,

Since my people entrusted me with the hard task of searching for our lost home, I have been filled with warm faith that those who carried their keys in the Diaspora as they carry their own limbs, and that those who endured their wounds in the homeland and maintained their identity will be rewarded by return and freedom for their sacrifices. I have also been filled with faith that the arduous trek on the long path of pain will end in our home's yard.

As we celebrate together the first sight of peace, I, at this podium stare into the open eyes of the martyrs within my conscience. They ask me about the national soil and their vacant seats there. I conceal my tears from them and tell them: How true you were; your generous blood has enabled us to see the holy land and to take our first steps in a difficult battle, the battle of peace, the peace of the brave.

As we celebrate together, we invoke the powers of creativity within us to reconstruct a home destroyed by war, a home overlooking our neighbor's, where our children will play with their children and will compete in picking flowers. Now, I have a sense of national and human pride in my Palestinian Arab people's patience and sacrifice, through which they have established an uninterrupted link between the homeland, history and the people, adding to the old legends of the homeland an epic of hope. For them, for the children of those good-natured and tough people, who are made of oaks and dews, of fire and sweat, I present this Nobel Prize, which I will carry to our children, who have a promise of freedom, security and safety in a homeland not threatened by an invader from outside or an exploiter from inside.

I know, Mr. Chairman, that this highly indicative prize has not been granted to me and my partners, Israel's Prime Minister Yitzhak Rabin and Foreign Minister Shimon Peres, to crown a mission that we have fulfilled, but to encourage us to complete a path which we have started with larger strides, deeper awareness, and more honest intentions. This is so we can transfer the option of peace, the peace of the brave, from words on paper to practices on the ground, and so we will be worthy of carrying the message that both our peoples and the world and human conscience have asked us to carry. Like their Arab brethren, the Palestinians, whose cause is the guardian of the gate of the

Arab-Israeli peace, are looking forward to a comprehensive, just and durable peace on the basis of land for peace and compliance with international legitimacy and its resolutions.

Peace, to us, is a value and an interest. Peace is an absolute human value which will help man develop his humanity with freedom that cannot be limited by regional, religious or national restrictions. It restores to the Arab-Jewish relationship its innocent nature and gives the Arab conscience the opportunity to express—through absolute human terms—its understanding of the European tragedy of the Jews. It also gives the Jewish conscience the opportunity to express the suffering of the Palestinian peoples which resulted from this historical intersection and to find an echo for this suffering in the pained Jewish soul. The pained people are more capable than others of understanding the suffering of other people.

Peace is an interest because, in an atmosphere of just peace, the Palestinian people will be able to achieve their ambitions for independence and sovereignty, to develop their national and cultural existence through relations of good neighborliness, mutual respect, and cooperation with the Israeli people. Peace will enable the Israeli people to define their Middle East identity and to enjoy economic and cultural openness toward their Arab neighbors, who are eager to develop their region, which was kept by the long war from find its real position in today's world in an atmosphere of democracy, pluralism, and prosperity.

As war is an adventure, peace is also a challenge and a gamble. If we do not fortify peace to stand against storms and wind, and if we do not support it and strengthen it, the gamble will then be exposed to blackmail, perhaps to fall. Therefore, I call on my partners in peace on this high platform to expedite the peace process, achieve early withdrawal, pave the road for elections, and to move to the second stage in record time, so that peace will grow and become a firm reality.

We have started the peace process based on land for peace, on UN Resolutions 242 and 338, and on the other international resolutions calling for achieving the legitimate rights of the Palestinian people. While the peace process has not yet reached its target, the new atmosphere of confidence and the modest achievements of the first and second year of the peace process are promising. Therefore, the parties are urged to abandon their reservations, facilitate measures, and achieve the remaining goals, foremost of which are transferring powers and taking steps toward an Israeli withdrawal in the West Bank and the settlements. This will finally lead to a comprehensive withdrawal and will enable our society to build its infrastructure and utilize its status, heritage, knowledge and awareness to formulate our new world.

In this context, I call on Russia and the United States, sponsors of the peace process, to accelerate the steps of this process, to take part in its formulation and to overcome its obstacles. I urge Norway and Egypt, in their capacity as hosts to the Palestinian-Israeli agreement, to continue their good initiative, which started from Oslo and reached Washington and Cairo. I also urge all countries, foremost of which are the donor countries, to make their contributions quickly to enable the Palestinian people to overcome their economic and social problems, to rebuild themselves and to establish their infrastructure. Peace cannot grow and the peace process cannot be entrenched unless their necessary material conditions are met.

I then urge my partners in peace to view the peace process in a comprehensive and strategic way. Confidence alone cannot make peace, but only recognizing the rights, together with confidence, can make peace. Encroaching on rights generates a sense of injustice, keeps the fire under the ashes, and will push peace to a dangerous point and toward quicksand that may destroy it. We view peace as a strategic option, rather than a tactical option influenced by temporary calculations of loss and profit. The peace process is not only a political one, but also an integrated process in which national awareness and economic, scientific and technological development play an important role. The interaction of cultural, social and creative elements also play basic roles in strengthening the peace process.

I view all this as I recall the difficult peace march, in which we have covered only a short distance. We should have courage and move as far as possible to cover the greater distance based on just and comprehensive peace and to absorb the strength of creativity which is contained in the deeper lesson of peace.

As long as we have decided to coexist and live in peace, then we should coexist on a solid basis that can last through all time and that is acceptable to the future generations. In this context, full withdrawal from the West Bank and the Gaza Strip requires deep discussions about the settlements that cut through geographic and political unity, prevent free movement between the areas of the West Bank and the Strip, and create hotbeds of tension that conflict with the spirit of peace, which we want to be free of anything that spoils its purity.

As for Jerusalem, it is the spiritual home of Christians, Muslims and Jews. To Palestinians, it is the city of cities. The Jewish shrines in the city are our shrines, the same as the Islamic and Christian shrines. So let us make Jerusalem an international symbol of this spiritual harmony, this cultural brightness, and this religious heritage of humanity as a whole.

There is an urgent task that activates the peace mechanism and enables it to overcome the problem that is troubling hearts, the question of prisoners. It is important to release them so smiles can return to their children, their mothers, and their wives. Let us together protect this little baby from the winter's winds, and let us provide it with the mild and honey it deserves in the land of milk and honey in the land of Salim, Ibrahim, Ismail, and Ishaq—the holy land, the land of peace.

……

Your Majesties, ladies and gentlemen, I emphasize to you that we will discover ourselves through peace more than we did through confrontation and conflict. I am certain that Israelis will find themselves through peace more than they did in war.

Glory to God in the highest, and on Earth peace, and good will toward men.

Thank you!

Mysterious Arab Countries
神秘的阿拉伯

Unit 13
Women Writers in Arabia

Warm-Up Questions

1. Which Arabic writer do you like? Why?
2. What do you know about Arabic literature?
3. Do you like Chinese literature or the literature of Arabia? Why?

Text

Born to Wade Matar, a pioneering architect and Leila Richo, an artistic home maker, Gladys Matar grew up in an environment ideally suited for nurturing the growth of her artistic and literary talents from early age.

Gladys Matar[1]

Gladys Matar was born in Latakia in 1962. She graduated in 1984 in French literature from Tishreen University, Latakia. She has four collections of short stories and one novel and two books of essays.

Born to Wade Matar, a pioneering architect and Leila Richo, an artistic home maker, Gladys Matar grew up in an environmentideally suited for nurturing the growth of her artistic and literary talents from early age. In Latakia, the city with the distinction of being the most important port of Syria, Ms. Matar attended Les Carmelites catholic school from kindergarten through middle school, and then moved to the public school system (following legislative changes that prohibited private religious schools thereafter) . Later, she attended the foreign literature program at the University of Latakia, graduating in 1984 with a degree in French literature.

In 1982, while still in college, her short story *The Rain* won the Arab Writers Guild's first prize for a short story in Syria. In 1984 her short story *Who Would Bring Aiisha Back Her Toy* won the prestigious Arab Woman Magazine's first prize for an Arabic short story, among participants from numerous countries across the Arab World. In 1989 an article she authored entitled *Donkey's Tail* won the first prize of the Middle East newspaper from London, England. Ms. Matar was in the United States at the time, pursuing her first in-depth studies in the arts and receiving training as a professional translator.

Upon returning home she published her first book, *Awaiting the Limestone to Flourish*, with an introduction by renowned author Adel Abou-Shanab. This seminal work was republished in 1989 by Nofal Publishing House in Beirut, Lebanon. From 1989 right on through to 2006, she published in volume. Her works included *Fleeting Joy*, a collection of short stories, and *off Beat*, a collection of articles on the arts. These were followed by *Love, Sized for the World* another collection of short stories offered by Nofal Publishing House as a first in a series of books targeting middle school students. This work was

---

[1] http://www.arabwomenwriters.com/.

Mysterious Arab Countries
神秘的阿拉伯

eventually adopted as required reading by the Ministry of Education and Higher Education of Lebanon. The introduction to this book and its enriching quizzes at the end of each chapter that test a comprehension, were contributed by Antoine Toomey, PhD, one of Lebanon's top education specialists.

In 2001, publisher Ward House in Damascus, Syria produced Ms. Matar's *Velvet Revolution*, a work of fiction that was widely distributed and attracted critical acclaim. The book featured an introduction by renowned Moroccan author and thinker, Fatima Almarnisi, as a novel dealing with "how an Arab relates to his past." In 2003, Al-Hiwar House in Latakia published *Dormant Desire*, Ms. Matar's purely political work, in which she probed the strange world of the major players in the Middle East political scene.

In her *Behind The Veil of Femininity*, Ms. Matar delved into the mind of Arab women. This work, published by Ward House, is currently in production. It features an introduction by Abdel-Kabir Alminawi, Morocco's renowned author and critic.

Here is her interview:
I've been writing so long, I don't actually remember when I started! I guess since I was 10 or 12 years old or maybe way long before that. I can be completely honest andliteral in saying, without resorting to exaggeration that I was borne with a burning desire to write.

It is really thesingular dream I recall as a child: to become a writer. Later on, when I graduated high school, I wanted to go to Damascus and study acting and theater but my dad refused me permission to travel to a large metropolis like Damascus while I was still seventeen years of age.

I wrote my first story when I was an eighteen year old college student in my freshman year. It was a short story titled *The Rain*. It was published to some acclaim having received an award by the Union of Arab Writers. It is interesting that I didn't really consider myself "a writer" until I published my first novel, *Velvet Revolution* in 2000. This book created such a stir in the media and with the public that I knew that I was on the right path to success.

The great Colombian author, Gabriel García Márque, who was awarded the Nobel Prize in 1982, played an influential role with me. From the moment I first read his novel, *One Hundred Years of Solitude*, I had a strange feeling that I, myself, wrote that book! And this feeling has stayed with me up to the present. I loved the literary style of magical realism in this novel and the extensive uses of metaphors and irony. I have read this novel 15 years ago and I am still very much into it.

My father also influences me: As a highly educated person, withsolid foundations in literature and science, he was constantly reading at home, or writing, or involved in discussion with my mother about something he studied. He owned a significant number of books, an extremely valuable gift that I had the good fortune to inherit from him.

I have been asked about my writing style… I guess the most prominent is the "ironic" style when it comes to writing short stories and the "epic" style when it comes to writing novels. And when I am being a serious academic I often season my wording with a sarcastic slant.

I have also beenqueried as to my process of coming up with titles for my work: When I am into writing something I begin with the heart of my subject, and then proceed to build up chapters and sections upon that base. I allow the title to "surface" during this process.

Typically, what occurs is that I wake up, say, at four in the morning, with the title ready to go. But it can also happen the other way around, where I feel a title flying around in my head begging to get out, as it were, and then I build up a subject upon it.

This is, in fact, what happened with my book *Delaying The Sunset*:

One day I was watching a cartoon show and one of the characters, who was a princess, wanted to "delay the sunset" using her magiccrystal so that the lover could make it on time for their marriage. It was a fairytale. The moment I heard that expression I thought about the exhausting effort that that woman spent to "delay her sunset." Later, of course, I developed on this idea in a different ways.

And of course people want to know if there is one messageunderlying my work. The answer is yes, national solidarity.

New Words

collection [kə'lekʃn] n. several things grouped together or considered as a

Mysterious Arab Countries
神秘的阿拉伯

whole 收集；收藏品；募捐
ideally [aɪˈdɪəlɪ] adv. in an ideal manner 理想地；观念上地
nurture [ˈnɜːtʃə(r)] v. help develop, bring up 养育；培育
distinction [dɪsˈtɪŋkʃn] n. a discrimination between things as different and distinct 区别；差别
legislative [ˈledʒɪslətɪv] adj. of or relating to or created by legislation 立法的 n. persons who make or amend or repeal laws 立法权；立法机构
entitle [ɪnˈtaɪtl] v. give right to, give title to 给…权利；给…定书名
pursue [pəˈsjuː] v. carry out or participate in an activity; be involved in 继续；从事
in-depth [ˈɪnˈdepθ] adj. 彻底的；深入的
limestone [ˈlaɪmstəun] n. [岩] 石灰岩
renown [rɪˈnaun] n. the state or quality of being widely honored and acclaimed 声誉；名望
seminal [ˈseminl] adj. containing seeds of later development 升值的
volume [ˈvɔljuːm] n. 卷；大量；册
target [ˈtaːgɪt] n. 目标；靶子 v. intend (something) to move towards a certain goal 把…作为目标；瞄准
adopt [əˈdɔpt] v. choose and follow theories, ideas, policies, strategies or plans 采取；接受；收养
specialist [ˈspeʃəlɪst] n. an expert who is devoted to one occupation or branch of learning 专家
contribute [kənˈtrɪbjuːt] v. provide 投稿；贡献；捐赠
fiction [ˈfɪkʃən] n. a literary work based on the imagination and not necessarily on fact 小说；虚构；编造
critical [ˈkrɪtɪkəl] adj. marked by a tendency to find and call attention to errors 批评的；爱挑剔的；评论的
acclaim [əˈkleɪm] n. enthusiastic approval 欢呼；称赞 v. praise 称赞；为…喝采
feature [ˈfiːtʃə] n. a prominent aspect of something 特征；特写
probe [prəub] v. question or examine thoroughly and closely 探索；调查
femininity [ˌfeməˈnɪnətɪ] n. the trait of behaving in ways considered typical for women 女性气质；娇弱；妇女的总称
delve [delv] v. turn up, loosen, or remove earth 钻研；探究；挖

literal ['lɪtərəl] adj. without interpretation or embellishment 文字的；无夸张的
resort [rɪ'zɔ:t] n. 度假胜地；求助对象 vi. have recourse to 求助；诉诸；采取某手段或方法（…to）
singular ['sɪŋgjələ] adj. unusual or striking 单数的；单一的；非凡的
metropolis [mə'trɔpəlɪs] n. a large and densely populated urban area 大都市
stir [stə:] v. move very slightly 搅拌；激起；惹起
extensive [ɪk'stensɪv] adj. large in spatial extent or range or scope or quantity 广泛的；大量的；广阔的
metaphor ['metəfə] n. 暗喻；隐喻
irony ['aɪərənɪ] n. witty language used to convey insults or scorn 讽刺；反语；具有讽刺意味的事
ironic [aɪ'rɔnɪk] adj. 讽刺的；反话的
solid ['sɔlɪd] adj. of definite shape and volume; firm; neither liquid nor gaseous 固体的；可靠的；结实的；一致的 n. 固体；立方体
foundation [faun'deɪʃən] n. the basis on which something is grounded 基础；地基；基金会
inherit [ɪn'herɪt] v. obtain from someone after their death 继承；遗传而得
epic ['epɪk] adj. 史诗的；叙事诗的 n. 史诗；叙事诗；史诗般的作品
season ['si:zən] v. lend flavor to 给…调味；使适应
sarcastic [sɑ:'kʌztɪk] adj. expressing or expressive of ridicule that wounds 挖苦的；尖刻的；辛辣的
slant [slɑ:nt] n. a biased way of looking at or presenting something 倾斜；偏见 v. lie obliquely 使倾斜；使倾向于
query ['kwɪərɪ] v. pose a question 质疑；对…表示怀疑
crystal ['krɪstəl] n. 晶体；水晶 adj. 水晶的；透明的；清澈的
fairytale ['feərɪteɪl] n. a story about fairies 童话故事
underlying [ˌʌndə'laɪɪŋ] adj. located beneath or below 潜在的；在下面的
solidarity [ˌsɔlɪ'dærɪtɪ] n. a union of interests or purposes or sympathies among members of a group 团结；团结一致

Mysterious Arab Countries
神秘的阿拉伯

Phrases & Expressions

graduate from	从某处毕业
be suited for	适合于
be adopted as	采用
on the path to	去往…的路上
come up with	想出；提出
make it	成功；及时到达

Proper Names

Gladys Matar [ˈglædɪs ˈmɑːtə]	格拉迪斯·马塔尔
Wade Matar [ˈweɪd ˈmɑːtə]	韦德·马塔尔
Leila Richo [ˈliːlə ˈrɪtʃəu]	莱拉·里秋
Les Carmelites [ˈles ˈkɑːməlaɪts]	莱斯·加尔默罗斯
Adel Abou-Shanab [ˈədel ˈəbuːˈʃeɪnəb]	阿德尔·阿布西纳博
Fatima Almarnisi [ˈfætɪmə ɔlmɑːnɪsɪ]	法蒂玛·奥玛尼西
Abdel-Kabir Alminawi [ˈæbdel ˈkəbɪ ˈælmɪnəwə]	阿布德尔·科比阿尔米那威
Gabriel Garcia Marque [ˈgeɪbrɪəl ˈgɑːʃjə ˈmɑːk]	加布里埃尔·加西亚
Latakia [lætəˈkiə]	[地名] 拉塔基亚（叙利亚）
Syria [ˈsɪrɪəl]	叙利亚（西南亚国家）
Beirut [beɪˈruːt]	[地名] 贝鲁特（黎巴嫩首都）
Lebanon [ˈlebənən]	黎巴嫩（西南亚国家）
Damascus [dəˈmæskəs]	大马士革（叙利亚首都）

Background Information

1. *The Prophet* (1923)

The Prophet is the highest achievement of Kahill Gibran (1883~1931), a philosopher, writer and painter in Lebanon. He has lived in America for a very long time. He wrote by Arabic and English. He is called the greatest prophet of human's soul and known as famous as Tagore（泰戈尔）.

In this book, Gibran created an oracle（智者）named Almustafa who was to go back to his hometown. When he was saying goodbye to the villagers, a pious woman came to him and gave her best whishes and begged him to tell something about the Truth. Then Almustafa began to answer questions. Those questions relate to all things between birth and death and 26 aspects on life and society — love and hate, beauty and ugly, good and evil, crime and punishment, etc.. For instance, "When either your joy or your sorrow becomes great, the world becomes small".

2. Azhar Muslim University

Azhar Muslim University since ancient times cultivate talent, academic and cultural dissemination of Islamic thought and made a great contribution to the world's Muslims with lofty ideals to pursue advanced studies of the garden, it has a higher status and prestige in Islamic education and academic culture, known as "the world's beacon of Islamic learning, culture and orientation."

3. Velvet Revolution

The Velvet Revolution or Gentle Revolution was a non-violent revolution in Czechoslovakia（捷克斯洛伐克）that took place from November 16/17 to December 29, 1989. Dominated by student and other popular demonstrations against the single-party government of the Communist Party of Czechoslovakia, it saw to the collapse of the party's control of the country, and the subsequent conversion to a parliamentary republic.

The term Velvet Revolution was coined by Rita Klímová, the English translator who later became the new non-Communist regime's ambassador to the United States. The term was used internationally to describe the revolution, although the Czech side also used the term internally. After the dissolution of Czechoslovakia in 1993, Slovakia used the term Gentle Revolution, the term that Slovaks used for the revolution from the beginning. The Czech Republic

Mysterious Arab Countries
神秘的阿拉伯

continues to refer to the event as the Velvet Revolution.

Study & Practice

I. Read Aloud and Memorize

Read the following paragraph aloud until you have learned them by heart.

I've been writing so long, I don't actually remember when I started! I guess since I was 10 or 12 years old or maybe way long before that. I can be completely honest and literal in saying, without resorting to exaggeration that I was borne with a burning desire to write.

It is really the singular dream I recall as a child: to become a writer. Later on, when I graduated from high school, I wanted to go to Damascus and study acting and theater but my dad refused me permission to travel to a large metropolis like Damascus while I was still seventeen years of age.

II. Answer the Following Questions

1. What environment did she grow up in?
2. What happened in her life in 1982?
3. When did Gladys Matar win her first prize? What prize?
4. When is the most productive phase of her?
5. What is her childhood dream?
6. Which writer has the deepest influence on her?
7. What is her writing style?
8. What is the core message expressed in her work?

III. Cloze

Complete the following passages according to your own understanding, and change the forms where necessary.

Unit 13 Women Writers in Arabia

Kahlil Gibran[①]

He was _____ (1) in the town of Bsharri in the north of modern-day Lebanon , as a young man he immigrated with his family to the United States, where he _____ (2) art and began his literary career, writing in both English and Arabic. In the Arab world, Gibran is _____ (3) as a literary and political rebel. His romantic style was at the _____ (4) of a renaissance in modern Arabic literature, _____ (5) prose poetry, breaking _____ (6) from the classical school. In Lebanon, he is still celebrated as a literary hero.

His first book for the _____ (7) company Alfred A. Knopf, in 1918, was *The Madman*, Gibran's best-known work is *The Prophet*, a book composed of twenty-six poetic essays. Its popularity grew markedly _____ (8) the 1960s with the American counterculture and then with the flowering of the New Age movements. It has remained popular with these and with the wider population to this day. _____ (9) it was first published in 1923, *The Prophet* has never been out of print. Having been _____ (10) into more than forty languages, it was one of the best-selling books of the twentieth century in the United States.

Outside Views of Arabic Literature[②]

Literature in Arabic has been largely influential outside the Islamic world. One of the first important _____ (1) of Arabic literature was Robert of Ketton's translation of the *Quran* in the 12th century but it would not be _____ (2) the early 18th century that much of Arabic's diverse literature would be recognized, largely _____ (3) to Arabists such as Forster Fitzgerald Arbuthnot and his books such as *Arabic Authors: A Manual of Arabian History and Literature*.

Antoine Galland's translation of the *Thousand and One Nights* was the first major work in Arabic _____ (4) found great success outside the Muslim world. Other significant translators were Friedrich Rückert and Richard Burton,

---

① http://en.wikepedia.org/wiki/Kahlil_Gibran.
② http://en.wikipedia.org/wiki/Arabic_literature.

Mysterious Arab Countries
神秘的阿拉伯

_____ (5) with many working at Fort William, India. The Arabic works and many more in other eastern _____ (6) fuelled a fascination in Orientalism within Europe. Works of dubious "foreign" morals were _____ (7) popular but even these were censored for content, _____ (8) as homosexual references, which were not permitted in Victorian society. Most of the works _____ (9) for translation helped confirm the stereotypes of the audiences with many more still untranslated. Few modern Arabic _____ (10) have been translated into other languages.

IV. Spot Dictation

In this part, you will hear a passage three times. When the passage is read for the first time, you should listen carefully for its general idea. When the passage is read for the second time, you are required to fill in the blanks numbered from 1 to 10 with the exact words you have heard. Finally, when the passage is read for the third time, you should check what you have written.

Taha Hussein[①]

Taha Hussein was born in 1889 during the period of _____ (1) which _____ (2) the failure of the Arab revolution and the British _____ (3) of Egypt in 1882. He was born and lived his _____ (4) in a small community in the Governorate of Minya in the south of the country. In this _____ (5), poverty and ignorance, disease and destitution were endemic, and there was no _____ (6) whatever of preventive medicine or medical care. For this, Taha Hussein would pay dearly, _____ (7) his sight at the age of 6, His father, a _____ (8) civil servant weighed down by the _____ (9) of keeping a large family, could do nothing but enroll him in the village school to learn the Koran. There the child mingled with graduates from al-Azhar and _____ (10) popular culture by listening to storytellers recounting the lives of Antar bin Shadad, Sayf bin Dhi Yazan and other Arab folk heroes. Despite all the _____ (11) facing him, an intense desire arose in the boy to travel to Cairo and study at al-Azhar.

---

① http://www.touregypt.net/tahamuseum.htm.

V. Translation

Turn the following sentences into English, using as many words and phrases you have learned from the text as possible.

1. 这本集子是由诗、散文和短篇小说三部分组合而成的。

2. 麦克奈尔高中在新泽西州连续多年被评为排名第一的公立高中。它的学生几乎都升入大学深造,其中包括美国最有名望的几所大学。

3. 他的行政职务使他享有某种极少给予别人的礼遇。

4. 那家诊所让病人从一个又一个专科医生那里接受不必要的检查,因而受到责难。

5. 一种欲望一旦被满足,就会被另一种欲望代替。

6. 本杂志中的各篇文章未经特殊许可一律不得转载。

7. 从儿童时期起,你所吃的食物和饮用的饮料对骨骼中的钙含量都是非常关键的。(Calcium)

8. 在实习的过程中这个优势却并不突出,这都是因为我的专业水平有待提高。

Mysterious Arab Countries
神秘的阿拉伯

9. 一个适合教学的实验平台可以让学生更加深刻地了解实验的内容。

10. 另一组科学家提出了相反的证据。

VI. Oral Practice

Find a partner or partners and discuss with them about the following questions.

1. Why can Gladays Matar become a famous writer?
2. Do you have any singular dreams since your childhood?
3. What do you think can contribute mostly to success, nature or nurture?

VII. Broaden Your Horizon

Women writers play an irreplaceable role in the Arabic literature. Their stories articulate the female experience from across the Arab world. They speak of old values, new needs, marriage, childbearing, love, education, work, and freedom. The intimate and vividly crafted portrait of the Arab woman that emerges from these narratives is not only touching and fascinating but endlessly thought-provoking.

The Woman of My Dreams[1]
Fadila al-Faruq

I like to call him "philosopher," for the simple reason that he really is a philosopher. Life, in his opinion, is an egg, and the egg resembles the world, and the world is a point, and he's a point, and I'm the most important point in his life. That's what he tells me anyway. Sometimes he calls me "Egg." When I ask him flirtatiously what an egg means to him, he replies without hesitation, "Life is an egg, Egg." We've known each other for five years.

---

[1] http://www.docin.com/p-405288016.html.

Now the time has come to choose a direction for our relationship.

He teaches philosophy, which is lost in the jelly of this "egg," in a secondary school, and I teach chemistry, which means nothing to my students except for the process of making a bomb. My troublemaker student, Umar Hassun, constantly asks, "When are we going to make ourselves a bomb, teacher?" In fact, I don't know when we will have an opportunity to make a bomb together, and even the philosopher fails to give me a concrete answer to this question. He stares at me, as if he has lost something in my features, and doesn't utter a word for an entire hour. Instead, he keeps rubbing his beard, which he hasn't shaved for a long time.

He's a philosopher, and it's his right to behave in an eccentric manner, so long as I'm not yet his wife. I want to whisper this simple truth to him because I've been thinking about it for a while. But Umar Hassun's question silences the words on the tip of my tongue.

Recently, I've decided to present this question to him again: "When can we make a bomb, my ugly philosopher?" This is not a lie that I've fabricated against him one day, because he is rather unattractive. His eyeballs are protruding from so much contemplation, and his long teeth resemble the great Chinese wall. As for his hair, it's been hanging loose over his shoulders since he was a university student. I still can't understand the physical attraction, because he's really ugly, although there are times that I never tire of looking at him.

He prefers to discuss matters in the order of their importance. He classifies them, invents strange names for things we know, and poses many questions about what we consider self-evident. He's different.

He's still gazing at me, while I'm waiting for an answer with which to satisfy Umar Hassun the troublemaker. It's my chance to delve beyond his eyes into his innermost thoughts. I wonder whether he'll make up his mind today and set a date for our engagement, a date for our wedding, a date for ending all our secret meetings in the Studio of Lights. Will he make up his mind today?

"Are you thinking about our marriage, philosopher?"

"Egg, darling, when you talk about marriage you appear to be as stupid as all the other women who allow the idea of marriage to dominate their thoughts."

"But marriage is the true relationship between—"

He cuts me short: "We're unable to make a bomb because we always think about establishing true relations between us. We think⋯think⋯"

What is this crazy man saying? He fills me with anxiety. In the twinkling of an eye he changes my identity to a prostitute—according to the customs and conventions of our society.

"But I love you. I love you," he declares. "I want to continue my life with you. Can't you understand? It's difficult for me to stop at this point, which doesn't represent the proper ending to what I've begun with you⋯"

"Why can't you be an unconventional woman? Why can't you be an extraordinary woman who doesn't change with the purchase of a document that supposedly confers respectability? Why can't you be a dream woman, one who plays a big role in my research and studies, as well as in history? Yes, I want you to be the woman of my dreams, Egg. I want you to remain vibrant forever. I don't want you to be a wife whose concerns revolve around food, children, tantrums, and dinner invitations—a woman for others. I don't want you like that."

All men lie. They lie in general. Even the philosopher, a year after this speech, married another woman and had children by her, while granting me the permanent label of fallen woman as a result of my relationship with him in the Studio of Lights. I didn't find a husband to help rid me of the complexes that the philosopher bequeathed to me, so I returned to him to be a woman for his dreams.

Oddly enough, after his marriage, I could no longer bear Umar Hassun's question, "When can we make a bomb?" It seemed to me that he was asking, "When will you establish a true relationship with your lover? When will you get married?" I began to hate his question, hate his face, hate his presence. So I gave him a recipe for making a traditional bomb, and put an end to his question. Later, I forgot him completely, when I became merely a woman of dreams.

Appendix I
Keys to Post-Reading Exercises

Unit One   History of Saudi Arabia

II. Answer the Following Questions.

1. Over the centuries, the peninsula has played an important role in history as an ancient trade center and as the birthplace of Islam, one of the world's major monotheistic religions.
2. Because of the climate change: the European ice cap melted during the last Ice Age, some 15,000 years ago, the climate in the peninsula became dry. Vast plains once covered with lush grasslands gave way to scrubland and deserts, and wild animals vanished. River systems also disappeared.
3. The Arabian Peninsula located between the two great centers of civilization, the Nile River Valley and Mesopotamia.
4. Their goods and services were in great demand regardless of which power was dominant at the moment; In addition, the peninsula's great expanse of desert formed a natural barrier that protected it from invasion by powerful neighbors.
5. A Muslim scholar named Shaikh Muhammad bin Abdul Wahhab began advocating a return to the original form of Islam.
6. In 1902, Abdulaziz, — accompanied by only 40 followers — staged a daring night march into Riyadh to retake the city garrison, known as the Masmak Fortress. This legendary event marks the beginning of the formation of the modern Saudi state.

Mysterious Arab Countries
神秘的阿拉伯

7. Oil industry provided the funds to build the basic infrastructure of roads, airports, seaports, schools and hospitals. And the modern oil industry plays an equally important role in the development of the non-oil industrial sector by providing the raw materials and feedstock that facilitates this growth.

8. The objectives are to diversify the economy away from oil into other fields and to build a modern economy capable of producing consumer and industrial goods that previously had been imported. The first phase is to establish an infrastructure. The next is to develop the human resources necessary to help bring about the planned economic transformation. Finally, the focus could shift to economic diversification.

III. Cloze

Passage 1:

(1) producer   (2) reserves   (3) located
(4) production (5) role   (6) impact
(7) committed   (8) crisis   (9) fluctuations
(10) increases

Paragraph 2:

(1) discovered (2) part   (3) virtual
(4) nation   (5) what   (6) money
(7) brought   (8) extensive   (9) practically
(10) into

IV. Spot Dictation

Agriculture in Saudi Arabia

At its founding, the country inherited (1) the simple, tribal economy of Arabia. Many of the people were nomads, engaged in raising (2) camels, sheep, and goats. Agricultural production was localized (3) and subsistent. Two major constraints (4) on cultivation are poor water supply and poor soil.

Less than 2 percent of the total land area is used for crops. Of the cultivated land, about half consists of rain-fed dry farming, two-fifths is in tree crops, and the remainder is irrigated. The kingdom's development plans have given domestic (5) food production special attention, and the government has made subsidies and generous incentives (6) available to the agriculture sector. Concrete (7) and earth-filled dams have been built, primarily in the southwest, to store water for irrigation and as a means of flood control. Agricultural expansion (8) has been great in irrigated areas, while the amount of land given to rain-fed farming has decreased. Substantial (9) resources of subterranean water have been discovered in the central and eastern parts of the country and exploited for agriculture.

The kingdom has achieved self-sufficiency (10) in the production of wheat, eggs, and milk, among other commodities, though it still imports the bulk of its food needs.

V. Translation

1. The company is a professional company dedicating to managing modernized office furniture.
2. A serious deficiency of iodine occurs, therefore, mainly in populations living off the land in remote and isolated regions.
3. The president concluded that he must give way to a younger, more decisive candidate.
4. Many Americans, including President Barack Obama and his predecessors, have said the United States must stop depending on importing oil from foreign countries, which is crucial to the national safety.
5. Prince Abdullah has promised to make every effort to ensure equilibrium in the oil markets and to stabilize prices.
6. Police warned the public to be on the alert for suspected terrorists.
7. After a month's fight, the colonists succeeded in taking over some important military positions in Arabism.
8. The House of Wisdom was said to have been built about hundreds of years ago.

Mysterious Arab Countries

神秘的阿拉伯

Unit Two   Arabia Geography

II. Answer the Following Questions:

1. It has been said that not only institutions but geography, climate, and many other conditions unite to form the influences which acting through successive generations, shape up the character of individuals and nations, and character plays a vital role in shaping up their history.
2. It's a stern, grim and inhospitable land and his survival in it depended upon his ability to come to terms with it.
3. Though most of the surface of the desert is bleak and desolate, Arabia has many parts which are highly photogenic. They possess a peculiar and haunting beauty. If the desert has many faces, it also has many moods, and most of them are unpredictable.
4. Its presence or absence has shaped its history to a great extent.
5. Settlers were attracted to the site of Makkah in Hijaz by the presence of the spring Zamzam. Assured by the availability of its waters in all seasons, they built the city of Makkah around it. The hydrosphere of the region consists of wells, torrents and flash-floods.
6. Then came oil and everything changed. Within a few years, annual revenues from petroleum exceeded $1 million. Life was transformed—spectacular fortunes, rapid economic development, the arrival of foreign labor, international clout. The oil wealth is changing the face of the land in numerous parts of Saudi Arabia and the Gulf sheikdoms.
7. For example: to draw water from great depths or to convert sea water through desalination, and to bring barren lands under cultivation by using it for irrigation. Reclamation of land for farming.
8. Because the camel was indispensable for survival in the desert before. The milk of the camel formed an important part of the diet of the desert Arabs, and camel hair was used by them to make their tents.

Appendix I

III. Cloze:

Passage 1:
(1) determines (2) located (3) important
(4) population (5) provide (6) on
(7) education (8) helpful (9) rate
(10) reflect

Passage 2:
(1) nature (2) Considering (3) divided
(4) plains (5) second (6) includes
(7) coastal (8) which (9) rich
(10) resources

IV. Spot Dictation

Physical Geography

Physical geography is the study of natural features and phenomena on the planet's surface and our interactions (1) with them. These features include vegetation (2), climate, the local water cycle, and land formations. As humans have migrated (3) across the planet, they have had to adjust themselves to all the changing conditions they were exposed (4) to. For an instance, Arctic-dwelling Inuit adapted by storing more body fat and increasing metabolic (5) rates, due to the climatic influence, which is the pattern of variation in temperature, humidity (6) and pressure over an area for long periods of time. All humans need water to survive, so people tend to settle (7) near bodies of water. For example, nearly the entire population of Egypt is concentrated (8) around the delta of the Nile River because the rest of the country is an arid desert, making it difficult to sustain plants and prevent massive (9) loss of life. Soil carries out several functions that profoundly (10) impact human activity. Soil recycles nutrients, regulates water quality, sustains life, and provides structural support for buildings. Without healthy soil, a previously fertile area turns into a desert.

V. Translation

1. The Nile valley extends approximately 800 km from Aswan to the outskirts of Cairo.
2. The Nile Valley and Delta, the most extensive oasis on earth, was created by the world's longest river and its seemingly inexhaustible sources.
3. The Western Desert covers an area of some 700,000 km^2, which accounts for around two-thirds of Egypt's total land area.
4. It has taken Arthur a long time to come to terms with his disability.
5. Saudi Arabia is bounded by seven countries and three bodies of water.
6. Modern technology has located and increased the availability of much of the underground water.
7. Change, or the ability to adapt oneself to a changing environment, is essential to evolution.
8. We shouldn't be deceived by these outer expressions that are in fact devoid of true intellectual development.

Unit There   Media in Arab World

II. Answer the Following Questions.

1. Prior to the Islamic Era, poetry was regarded as the main means of communication on the Arabian Peninsula.
2. Before the introduction of the printing press Muslims obtained most of their news from the Imams at the Mosque, friends or in the marketplace.
3. Don't know for sure, because there is debate over when the first Arabic language newspaper was published
4. In most Arab countries, newspapers cannot be published without a government-issued license. Most Arab countries also have press laws, which impose boundaries on what can and cannot be said in print.

5. The desire for political influence is probably the biggest factor driving television channel growth.
6. Regimes have attempted to curtail what people are able to read, but the Internet is a medium not as easily manipulated as telling a newspaper what it can or cannot publish.
7. It can not be stopped just like a snowball effect, now that the snowball is rolling, it can no longer be stopped. Getting bigger and stronger, it is bound to crush down all obstacles.
8. Whatever the major media mentioned above are, the Arab media values strictly revolve around political news putting the human interest stories to the side.
9. The power of news as political tool was discovered in the early 19th century, with the purchase of shares from Le Temps a French newspaper by Ismail the grandson of Muhammad Ali.
10. Media researchers stress that the moral and social responsibility of media people dictates that they should not agitate public opinion, but rather should keep the status quo.

III. Cloze

Passage 1:
  (1) estimated   (2) case   (3) mobile
  (4) account   (5) terms   (6) highlighted/stressed
  (7) issue   (8) worth   (9) efforts
  (10) increase

Passage 2:
  (1) behind   (2) adopting   (3) difficulty
  (4) cost   (5) access   (6) respectively
  (7) least   (8) average   (9) growth
  (10) accepted   (11) control   (12) based
  (13) traditional   (14) opted   (15) while

Mysterious Arab Countries
神秘的阿拉伯

IV. Spot Dictation

Digital Revolution Marks the Beginning of Information Era

The present age is known to be the information era. Another term which refers to this phenomenon is the so-called the third industrial revolution. People begin to realize the power and the importance of information and knowledge. Information is what <u>stimulates</u> (1) people to develop and utilize all their talents and abilities to create advanced <u>features</u> (2) tools, and instruments. In the information era, technology has been becoming the central axis and speedily <u>redefining</u> (3) globalization. This progress eventually leads to the larger transition of <u>telecommunications</u> (4) which can build <u>innovative</u> (5) and efficient ways of working and socializing. The third industrial revolution has powerfully transformed the way information <u>disperses</u> (6) across various sectors in a worldwide range such as providing grounds for businesses to move beyond the national markets to the international markets and <u>uplifting</u> (7) the interconnectedness of the world. <u>Nonetheless</u> (8) there are people having a negative impression on this great revolution. They see this atmosphere just as a merely <u>devastating</u> (9) progress. They say that it <u>diminishes</u> (10) personal privacy, it lessens the professionalism of journalists and it does make people find themselves in difficulty to distinguish between personal and professional life.

V. Translation

1. The government's bottom line with regard to the trade issue has not changed.
2. They employed an expert to lay out the grounds of the mansion.
3. All the arrangements should have been completed prior to our departure.
4. This section of the road is so narrow that there is bound to have traffic jams now and then.

Appendix I

5. Birds cry plaintively before they die, men speak kindly in the presence of death.
6. From a strategic perspective, one false move can be very costly.
7. We're trying to raise awareness about the environment in general and air pollution in particular.
8. If we have to offer a discount to these cars, we aren't to make a profit.

Unit Four Economic Crisis in Egypt

II. Answer the Following Questions

1. Because he was annoyed at being skinned in a Cairo bazaar.
2. It has been trying to extend a generous package of aid to Egypt.
3. No, the current one, dominated by the Muslim Brotherhood, is no exception.
4. Because the government is fearful of imposing austerity ahead of a general election due later this year.
5. It has not stemmed the slide.
6. Because the value of Egypt's currency eroding since December.
7. It shied for more than a decade from tackling a system that provides ungrateful consumers with such items as bread at the equivalent of less than an American cent a loaf.
8. Nearly half the subsidy bill.
9. Because the state oil monopoly has had to export more crude oil to pay off pressing debts and Egyptians were in desperate need of it.
10. Because the local wheat harvest accounts for barely half of consumption.

III. Cloze

Passage 1:
(1) less than   (2) accounts   (3) private
(4) reckon   (5) annual   (6) Arab
(7) means

Mysterious Arab Countries
神秘的阿拉伯

Passage 2:
(1) published   (2) underdeveloped (3) benefited
(4) advantage   (5) between   (6) widening
(7) with   (8) infrastructure (9) doubt
(10) negligence (11) repercussions

IV. Spot Dictation

Egypt is the biggest of the nations hit by recent protests (1) in North Africa and the Middle East. One of the causes of this spreading wave of popular dissatisfaction (2) is a lack of economic progress.

Egypt is not a major oil exporter (3) and its economy is not big enough to affect world economic growth. But important pipelines (4) cross Egypt. And Egypt controls the Suez Canal. About eight percent of world shipping passes through this link between Europe and Asia. That includes two million barrels (5) of oil each day, mainly to Europe.

Many experts say they expect the canal (6) to remain open. Still, concerns (7) about the Suez have pushed oil prices to their highest levels since two thousand and eight.

Fariborz Ghadar heads the Center for Global Business Studies at Penn State University. He says poverty (8) in Egypt remains high — up to forty percent in some areas.

Yet Egypt is not alone. Foreign investors (9) worry about corruption (10) mismanagement and security problems across North Africa and the Middle East.

Every year millions of young people enter the job market. Populations are young and fast growing. In Egypt, the economy grew about five percent last year— too little growth to create enough jobs.

V. Translation

1. I can't seem to get it home to my son that extra time spent studying now will pay off in the future.
2. During the economic recession the factory terminated a large number

Appendix I

of workers.
3. When dad lost his job, we had to cut back on entertainment expenses.
4. The report pointed out that tourism is an important sector of the economy for a number of Arab countries, and is highly vulnerable to climate change.
5. Without the reform of the economic management system our industry will go from bad to worse.
6. They had to stimulate their domestic economy by inflation.
7. The financial crisis devitalized the economy of the Asian countries.
8. But I believe that it is quite natural for the two sides to exchange views on the situation of world economy, especially the trend of the Asian economy.

Unit Five   Education in Egypt

II. Answer the following questions:

1. Egypt aims to increase access in early childhood to care and education and the inclusion of ICT at all levels of education, especially at the tertiary level.
2. There is no a highly centralized system to offering more autonomy to individual institutions.
3. The second tier of basic compulsory education is the preparatory stage or lower secondary which is three years long. Completion of this tier grants students the Basic Education Completion Certificate. The importance of completion of this level of education is to safeguard students against illiteracy as early drop outs at this stage easily recede into illiteracy and eventually poverty.
4. In Egypt, the Ministry of Education coordinates the preschool education. In 1999 – 2000 the total enrollment rate of pre-primary students was 16 percent and that increased to 24 percent in 2009. Irrespective of private or state run, all preschool institutions come under Ministry of Education.
5. Do not take the thing as extremely difficult to do, as long as you wish,

you can use all available resources.
6. Students must pass a national exam which is given at end of the secondary stage and take the Certificate of General Secondary Education take the Certificate of General Secondary Education. Because the far efforts enable students to gain certification in practical skills needed in the job market.
7. "It" means "introduce broad vocational skills in the curricula of general secondary schools." The control of the MoE causes the enrollments from MoE's general secondary schools or technical schools and have much smaller enrollment numbers.
8. Because the bulk of the curriculum consists of religious subjects as described below. All the students are Muslims, and males and females are separated in the prep and secondary stages.
9. Because public education is not capable of providing quality education and is hardly providing any education with the shortage in facilities, lack of trained educators and inflation in classes. Private is still incapable of reform for the lack of interest, shortage in trained educators, defective curricula, commercialization of education.

III. Cloze

Paragraph 1:
- (1) increase
- (2) quality
- (3) private
- (4) obligation
- (5) In addition
- (6) common
- (7) shortage
- (8) abundance
- (9) primarily
- (10) necessary

Paragraph 2:
- (1) faces
- (2) ethnography
- (3) lack
- (4) conflict
- (5) attracts
- (6) conducted
- (7) less
- (8) with
- (9) brought
- (10) protested

Appendix I

IV. Spot Dictation

Ancient Egyptian Education

In Ancient Egypt the child's <u>world</u> (1) was not as clearly separated from the adult's as it tends to be in modern Western society. As the years went by childish pastimes would give way to <u>imitations</u> (2) of grown-up behavior. Children would more and more <u>frequently</u> (3) be found lending a hand with the less onerous tasks and gradually <u>acquiring</u> (4) practical skills and knowledge from their elders.

By precept and example, parents would <u>instill</u> (5) into them various educational principles, moral attitudes and views of life. Thus from a tender age they would <u>receive</u> (6) their basic education in the bosom of the family. For girls, this was usually all the schooling they would get, but for boys it would be <u>supplemented</u> (7) by proper training in whatever line they chose, or was chosen for them. Education, of course, covers both the general <u>upbringing</u> (8) of a child and its training for a particular vocation. The upbringing of boys was left largely in the hands of their fathers, that of girls was entrusted to their mothers. Parents <u>familiarized</u> (9) their children with their ideas about the world, with their religious outlook, with their ethical principles, with correct behavior toward others and toward the super-natural beings in whom everyone believed. They taught them about <u>folk</u> (10) rituals and so forth.

V. Translation

1. Egypt also has a shortage of skilled and semi-skilled workforce.
2. The Egyptian government has a responsibility to provide free education at all levels of education, such as elementary school, junior high school, high school and college.
3. Egypt has the largest overall education system in the Middle East and North Africa and it has grown rapidly since the early 1990s.
4. Technical and vocational secondary education Technical education, which is

provided in three-year and four-year programs, includes schools in three different fields: industrial, commercial and agricultural.
5. Do not think this thing is very difficult to do, as long as you wish, you can use all resources available.
6. There were a few attempts to make a positive impact and educational reform from the civil community in Egypt but those efforts remained very limited on their impact on the educational process.

Unit Six   Travel in Dubai

II. Answer the following questions:

1. There is one word to describe Dubai, and it's "ostentatious".
2. No. It isn't. Because the author expected the infinite blue sky, the intense, unrelenting heat, the way the city sprawl would stop abruptly to make way for rolling, barren dunes. But in real life Dubai is the luxury, the slick modernity.
3. The function of the example is to show the Dubai's ostentatious.
4. Though this sentence, we can know clearly how the luxury and cash-splashing Dubai is.
5. The Palm, The Palm 2, Seven-star hotel, The soon-to-be-built house an entirely underwater hotel, a Disney world-style theme park, the world's biggest shopping mall, and the soon-to-be-built world's biggest indoor ski slope.
6. It is not, because it is the part of a very shrewd plan for sustainability hatched by its ruler, Sheik Mohamed, and his family.
7. It has cleverly secured its future by positioning itself as a business and finance hub.
8. Because during the daylight hours, the desert temperatures top 50 degrees centigrade, at night, the temperature drops to a positively chilly 30 degrees.
9. The author think Dubai is an exciting destination and a city of fascinating contrasts. But there's a pervading sense that in five or 10 years, when cranes no longer dominate the skyline and it's possible to see and touch

Appendix I

all these fledgling developments. Dubai will be truly breathtaking.
10. Use your own word to answer this question. The answer should be reasonable.

III. Cloze:

Paragraph 1:
- (1) higher
- (2) nothing
- (3) probably
- (4) fleet
- (5) arrival
- (6) search
- (7) book
- (8) larger
- (9) before
- (10) where

Paragraph 2:
- (1) most
- (2) which
- (3) varying
- (4) least
- (5) that
- (6) afford
- (7) Unless
- (8) meantime
- (9) number
- (10) entire

IV. Spot Dictation

The Traditional Dubai

While vast swaths of the city have been demolished in the relentless <u>drive</u> (1) toward the future, one neighborhood harks back to the quiet fishing village once was. The Bastakia Quarter, <u>which</u> (2) squeezes itself between the Dubai Creek and the buzzing Bur Dubai district, is a mini maze of wind-towered buildings, a clutch of which have been <u>transformed</u> (3) into art galleries and cafés. Start your tour at XVA Gallery, which <u>specializes</u> (4) in contemporary art from across the Gulf region. Continue your appreciation of Middle Eastern art at the Majlis Gallery before lunching on <u>hearty</u> (5) salads and a refreshing mint-and-lime juice in the neighboring Basta Art Cafe's sun-dappled courtyard.

Once <u>refreshed</u> (6) weave through the textile souk — where you'll find magnificent bolts of fabric, <u>along</u> (7) with less inspiring tat — and on to the Creek where you can either join the commuters for a ride across the water or hire your own boat for a scenic (8) tour of the waterway. Back in port, head to the small but interesting Dubai Museum to see how oil and ambition (9) mixed to make this modern oasis. If you get hungry again, check out Bastakiah Nights, an atmospheric Lebanese restaurant with a great rooftop (10) area.

V. Translation:

1. Weariness pervaded his whole body.
2. Many monster high-rise buildings spring up all over the city.
3. Theoretically, a line can extend into infinity.
4. Moral beauty ought to be ranked above all other beauty.
5. Only if you throw down did you learn how to stand.
6. Cloudy skies hang over the whole city before a rainstorm.
7. During the war, they laid an embargo on commerce with enemy countries.
8. City workers and volunteers are working feverishly to remove the heavy snow from the roofs of homes.

Unit Seven Belly Dance

II. Answer the following questions:

1. Most of the dancing that goes on in the Arab world happens at weddings and other celebrations.
2. Arabic dance choreography varies much from country to country. Many of the traditional dance forms in the Arab world focus on movements of the hips, shoulders, arms and feet. Many forms involve using props or an artistic manipulation of the costume.
3. The term "Arabic dance" is often associated with the style of belly dance. Though this is an inaccurate label.
4. Many experts say belly dancing is the oldest form of dance, having roots in all ancient cultures from the orient to India to the mid-East. It is at least 6,000 years old dating back to Mesopotamia time.
5. Probably the greatest misconception about belly dancing is that it is intended to entertain men.

6. The exact origin of this dance form is actively debated among dance enthusiasts, especially given the limited academic research on the topic.
7. Egyptian belly dance is one of the most elegant dance styles of belly dance. It is a slow and sensual style with a lot of isolations, shimmies and layering.
8. When you dance Egyptian everything from your toes to the top of your head should be dancing. This means that you must actually feel the music, and you must dance with it.
9. Limit your spins and kicks when dancing Egyptian. It's okay to do a few, but if you get excessive with it then you are more than likely going to look like a Turkish dancer.
10. In America, belly dancing enjoyed its first significant renown when the famous dancer Little Egypt performed at the Chicago World's Fair in 1893.

III. Cloze

Passage 1:
  (1) entertain   (2) Despite   (3) won
  (4) Therefore   (5) that   (6) communicates
  (7) sounds   (8) being   (9) limited
  (10) dance

Paragraph 2:
  (1) benefits   (2) work out   (3) on
  (4) suitable   (5) it   (6) consult
  (7) what   (8) geared   (9) as well as
  (10) comes with

IV. Spot Dictation

Belly Dance

During the course of history many of the dances we associate (1) with

Mysterious Arab Countries
神秘的阿拉伯

belly dance today were performed (2) as separate dances; men for men, women for women. There are few depictions (3) of co-ed dances. For many years this made it so that a "good" woman would not be seen dancing by any but her husband, her close family or the women she was with at a get-together. This extended (4) to separate the musicians so that only female musicians could perform (5) for female dancers. This custom continues in much of the Middle East, depending (6) on which country you are in. In some areas the professional (7) dancer will go to a woman gatherings (8) with the musicians, get the women up and dancing then go to the men's portion (9) of the house and perform for the male guests at a function (10).

V. Translation

1. Despite the heat, he wore a dark business suit complete with vest.
2. He planned to participate in the parade, but then he got cold feet.
3. I don't want my son to be involved with bad guys.
4. He felt that medicine was the most important cause to which he could dedicate himself.
5. Such a proposal may give rise to a research field of interest.
6. These ideas descend from those of the famous anthropologist.
7. The plot of the novel is intricate and fascinating.
8. Boldness and arrogance will be equivalent to frustrations and failures in near future.

Unit Eight　Arabic Music

II. Answer the Following Questions:

1. In the ninth century.
2. The basis of Arabic music is the maqam or mode.
3. Arabic music measure itself in terms of the degree of intensity and emotion in the tone, feeling, ornamentation, performance and singing.
4. The Waslat.
5. The key starting point for Arabic music is song.

Appendix I

6. A singer's career is usually characterized by a thorough training in Koran recitation according to the traditional rules of song.
7. In European music the smallest interval is the semitone.
8. Because the musically modulated performance of the suras is part of the cultural heritage of classical Arabic music.
9. The traditional orchestra for classical music, called al tacht, consists of three main instruments: the oud, the qanoun and the nay.
10. Arabic music does not measure itself in terms of technical perfection, but by the degree of intensity and emotion in the tone, feeling, ornamentation, performance and singing.

III. Cloze

Paragraph 1:
(1) popular (2) began (3) musicians
(4) elements (5) into (6) made
(7) pioneered (8) which (9) and
(10) from

Paragraph 2:
(1) around (2) exception (3) along
(4) instruments (5) attention (6) bands
(7) gaining (8) especially (9) an
(10) fusion

IV. Spot Dictation

Arabic music is also known as Arab music which includes several styles and genres of music that <u>ranges</u> (1) from pop music to classical (Arabic) and also from secular to sacred music. Though Arab music will be very independent and also <u>livelier</u> (2), they have a very good <u>interaction</u> (3) with other music genres and styles.

Arabic music has <u>evolved</u> (4) through the ages and several people are now <u>familiar</u> (5) in this genre of Arabic music. It has been around for several years now but the main tweak in the sounds of Arabic music came when Ahmad

Mysterious Arab Countries
神秘的阿拉伯

Baba Rachid blended (6) traditional music with pop sounds to create a new type of sound. Male singers of the Arabic music genre are called as cheb or cheba for female (7) singers. There are several different styles of Rai Arabic music styles present and singers specialize (8) in them to ensure popularity. There is no doubt about the fact that Arabic music surely sounds a far lot different than any form of Western music. A distinctly (9) clear drum beat is heard most of the times in the sound without any particular musical or vocal accompaniment (10) Descriptions about Arabic music often are attached with a lot of technicalities.

V. Translation

1. Undoubtedly, this can be difficult for students who are accustomed to getting the right answers.
2. The Arabic Music as is known today is the product of an evolutionary art form that may have started as far back as the Greek civilization.
3. He could not dwell on anything else but her words, telling of her passionate love.
4. Marwa is considered is one of the most famous Arabic pop music artist in the Middle East, characterized by a sweet voice.
5. Every weekend, we would have parties at home, filled with traditional Arabic food and music and roaring conversations, mostly in Arabic.
6. His attitude with regard to her, though it was contemplative and critical, was not judicial.
7. Birdsong may have more in common with human speech than we realize.
8. The differences in the children's achievements were not wholly explicable in terms of their social backgrounds.
9. The music of Irving Berlin is scarcely comparable to that of Beethoven.
10. If we memorized a few verses each day, by the time we finished high school we would have memorized the entire classic work. What a special honor!

Unit Nine Egyptian Clothing

II. Answer the Following Questions.

1. Light clothing made from plant fibers, predominantly linen and occasionally cotton. Wool was used to a lesser extent, small amounts of silk were found in Egyptian tombs.
2. They reaped the plants and by beating and combing the plants they extracted fibers from them, which could be spun into thread.
3. Many garments consisted simply of pieces of cloth draped around the body and held together by a belt. But the cloth was often hemmed to prevent fraying, with either simple, or rolled and whipped hems.
4. Tunics, shirts, kilts, aprons and sashes, socks, head-dresses, caps, scarves, gauntlets and gloves…Underwear in the form of a triangular loincloth was also found.
5. Men doing physical labor wore a loin cloth, wide galabiyeh-like robes or, if they were working in the water, nothing at all.
6. Its color was generally whitish, in contrast to the colorful clothes foreigners wore in Egyptian depictions, although dyed cloth was not unknown.
7. The robes worn by both sexes in Egypt were called kalasiris by Herodotus.
8. They were sewn from a rectangular piece of cloth twice the desired garment length. An opening for the head was cut at the centre of the cloth, which was then folded in half. The lower parts of the sides were stitched together leaving openings for the arms.
9. They used it to stick sheets of papyrus together.
10. The depictions did not it very clearly, so it is quite unsure whether the Egyptians wear any headdress as a rule.

III. Cloze

Passage 1:
　　(1) decorated　　(2) bride　　(3) dresses

Mysterious Arab Countries
神秘的阿拉伯

  (4) reasons   (5) touch   (6) provide
  (7) bridal   (8) Muslim   (9) countries
  (10) weddings

Passage 2:
  (1) variety   (2) faces   (3) hair
  (4) conservative   (5) shoulders   (6) without
  (7) As well   (8) never   (9) mixture
  (10) skirts

IV. Spot Dictation

  Ancient Egyptian clothing (1) is quite different from the ancient Mediterranean type. The Egyptians usually worn tunics (2) that were sewn to fit them. These were like a long T-shirt that reached the knees (3) in case of men or up to the ankles in case of women. The material was generally linen and has white color. The heads were left bare. The feet were also bare and occasionally (4) leather sandals were worn. Those men who worked outside adorned (5) short skirts rather than tunics. A piece of cloth was covered around the waist (6) and legs. Men and women wore blue and green eyeshadow (7) and black kohl eyeliner when it was aimed to dress up fancy. Men kept their hair short and did not prefer retaining (8) beards and mustaches (9). Women grew their hair so that they reached the shoulders. As for their affordability, individuals (10) of either sexes used gold jewelry.

V. Translation

  1. In social life, the division of labor between men and women is often different.
  2. We studied the ancient Egyptians contemporary costumes and archaeological data mostly from books and document.
  3. We can make do with the present facilities for the next two or three years.
  4. A wide variety of clothing in Tutankhamun's tomb reflects the unparalleled wisdom of the ancient Egyptians.

Appendix I

5. How to realize mutual supplement with each other's advantages between the network and the traditional education is a great challenge to us.
6. Costume design is an interesting and lengthy process, on the one hand, it is constantly studying to explore and develop your spirit, on the other hand, it is a test of your perseverance.
7. In fact, people dresswith big differences on different occasions.
8. If confidence is a prerequisite for success, then tireless effortsare the only way to success.

Unit Ten　Cuisine in Arabia

II. Answer the Following Questions.

1. Wheat and rice are the major and preferred sources of staple foods.
2. Bread is a universal staple in the region.
3. Varieties of thyme are common in Syria, Lebanon, and Palestine.
4. The most common are the cubed cuts on skewers, known as shish kebab in most places.
5. Vegetables and pulses are the predominant everyday food of the great majority of the people of the Middle East.
6. Tomato is the most ubiquitous ingredient in Middle Eastern cookery. It is used fresh in a variety of salads, cooked in almost every stew and broth, and grilled with kebab.
7. They are commonly called dolma, the Turkish word meaning "stuffed".
8. In the 1980s, instant coffee became popular.
9. The alcoholic drink "arak" is most famous for its potency and milky-white color when water is added, producing the drink nicknamed "the milk of lions".
10. Share your own opinion.

III. Cloze

Passage 1:
　　(1) that　　(2) for example　　(3) like

Mysterious Arab Countries
神秘的阿拉伯

    (4) relies   (5) heavier   (6) Unlike
    (7) which   (8) emphasis   (9) appreciated
    (10) available

Passage 2:
    (1) forbid   (2) alcoholic   (3) butchered
    (4) importer   (5) mutton   (6) served
    (7) hospitality   (8) fast   (9) nourishes
    (10) perform

IV. Spot Dictation

Middle Eastern food first came and became popular in the 1990s and the heart-healthy (1) Mediterranean Diet. According to the Mayo Clinic, the benefits (2) included a reduced risk of heart disease, a reduced risk of Alzheimer's disease, and a reduced risk of cancer. Coupled (3) with the rising obesity (4) rates, restaurants have become increasingly health conscious (5), and Middle Eastern food is exactly what so many are trying to incorporate (6) into their menus. For example, Freekeh is a whole grain that has four times the fiber of brown rice, which helps keep blood sugar low. It also has more powerful vision protectors (7) than other grains and helps increase healthy bacteria (8) in the digestive tract. Healthfulness and freshness (9) are central to the Middle Eastern diet, and these qualities (10) are becoming part of a change going on in the American diet as well.

V. Translation

1. Varieties of these crops have been collected from all around the district.
2. Poor diet and excess smoking will seriously damage the health of your body.
3. There are its own traditional dress, cuisine, folklore and handicrafts in this village.
4. The street slept in darkness, aside from the occasional twinkling of lights from two or three windows.

5. Every visitor to Georgia is overwhelmed by the kindness, charm and hospitality of the people.
6. In these places, one can wander at leisure and learn about the country's rich artistic heritage.
7. The first ingredient of an economic system is the natural resources from which goods are produced.
8. Occupational safety training programs must place special emphasis on the interaction between humans and technology.

Unit Eleven   Arabia Marriage

II. Answer the Following Questions.

1. The Egyptian wedding is the most important ceremony for Egyptian females.
2. The ancient Egyptians were the first civilization to regard marriage as a legal relationship.
3. The adult daughter was allowed to welcome guests who came to visit her parents according to custom in the Egyptian family.
4. Common features include singing, dancing, a banquet and a lot of guests.
5. The bride wears an ordinary bridal dress and the groom wears a black suit or a tuxedo in their ceremony.
6. The Kosha usually consists of two comfortable seats in front of the guests where the bride and groom reign as though king and queen.
7. It means that who ever catches the bouquet will marry the bride after that.
8. Food is considered one of the factors that reflect the wealth of the families of the bride and groom. Whether in rural or urban, weddings reflect the image of the families that have come together. Both families show off their wealth to their wedding guests.

Mysterious Arab Countries
神秘的阿拉伯

III. Cloze

Paragraph 1:
    (1) comes   (2) of   (3) covered
    (4) with   (5) Unlike

Paragraph 2:
    (6) Unlike   (7) what   (8) required
    (9) appropriate   (10) important   (11) though

Paragraph 3:
    (12) traditional   (13) Before   (14) on
    (15) yourself   (16) due   (17) offend

IV. Spot Dictation

Marriage was the <u>normal</u> (1) and most desirable state for <u>ancient</u> (2) Egyptians of both genders and all social classes. Athenian men <u>evinced</u> (3) little respect or affection for women and <u>delayed</u> (4) marriage until well into their thirties, but most Egyptian men were eager to follow the advice of the <u>wisdom</u> (5) literature urging them to take a wife <u>while</u> (6) still young so they could found a <u>household</u> (7) and raise a family. Most men were <u>married</u> (8) by the age of twenty to girls who <u>might</u> (9) have been as young as fifteen. There was an age <u>difference</u> (10) but usually not more than two or three years.

V. Translation

1. The announcer told his listeners to keep an eye out for the escaped criminal.
2. The life which men praise and regard as successful is but one kind.
3. Typically, purple is associated with royalty and wealth, because it was used as a symbol of status in society in ancient China.
4. Switzerland is a very wealthy country, but they don't really show off their wealth.

Appendix I

5. These relationships can be next to impossible to mend after the trust is broken, even when both parties want to reconcile.
6. As we know, learning is a long process which requires a lot of patience and endurance to be carried on.
7. Ways must be found to assure our children a decent start in life.
8. Here it is a symbol of strong man, whose character is revealed in crisis and adversity.
9. A college student witnesses a violent shooting but claims not to be affected by it.
10. In this age, where English as a practical tool is considered of more worth than an aesthetic appreciation of literature, culture or history.

Unit Twelve   Yasser Arafat

II. Answer the Following Questions.

1. The leader of the Palestine Liberation Organization, Yasser Arafat, died Thursday in France where he was ailing for several days.
2. Had devoted his life to establishing a Palestinian homeland.
3. He shared with Israeli Prime Minister Yitzhak Rabin and Foreign Minister Shimon Peres.
4. "Peace will enable us to show our identity to the world, our real identity to the world," he said.
5. In the year of 1996.
6. While living in Kuwait, he created the 'Fatah' movement.
7. He signed the interim agreement with Israeli Prime Minister Yitzhak Rabin at the White House in 1993.
8. Because Mr. Arafat had always saying he was married to the Palestinian cause.
9. His first combat experience against Israel was running weapons for his father and older brother in the 1948 war. With his father and older brother.
10. Palestinians viewed him as a father figure and the leader of their quest for a homeland.

Mysterious Arab Countries
神秘的阿拉伯

III. Cloze

Passage 1:
  (1) contented   (2) attack   (3) knowledge
  (4) Causing   (5) blameless   (6) encourage
  (7) close   (8) ties   (9) opinion
  (10) possible

Passage 2:
  (1) attention   (2) interview   (3) springs
  (4) wherever   (5) understand   (6) responded
  (7) solution   (8) conflict   (9) occur
  (10) solve

IV. Spot Dictation

  Palestinian leader Yasser Arafat says he is ready to begin peace talks with Israel but he says the other side does not seem ready. His <u>comments</u> (1) came between <u>meeting</u> (2) with China's top leaders Friday in Beijing. China's President Jiang Zemin smiled broadly as he <u>greeted</u> (3) Palestinian Authority President Yasser Arafat in Beijing. In an earlier meeting, Mr. Arafat <u>embraced</u> (4) the head of the National People's Congress, Li Peng, who returned the <u>gesture</u> (5) Beijing is expected to reaffirm support for a Palestinian state and offer financial <u>assistance</u> (6) On Friday, China again called on the two sides, particularly Israel, to exercise "the utmost restraint" and urged both parties to resume <u>negotiations</u> (7) In a brief television <u>interview</u> (8) on Reuters Mr. Arafat was asked if the two sides were likely to <u>restart</u> (9) talks. He says the Palestinians are ready "at all times" but said the Israelis "are refusing." Israel has repeatedly said Mr. Arafat needs to take steps to <u>halt</u> (10) Palestinian terrorist attacks if he wants to resume peace talks.

V. Translation

  1. The employeesare required to be efficient in work, be operative and

team-spirited, self-motivated, self-disciplined and committed to continuous improvement.
2. Ninety percentage of the usable natural grasslands have deteriorated to various certain extents in China.
3. Whatever difficulties can not hold back our determination to take a giant step toward cooperation.
4. The old man who lives on rag-picking has made great contribution to the cause of charity.
5. Juvenile crime is rising, parents, however, are more to blame for compared with social factors.
6. In the long run, the French people can have confidence that their economy will bounce back.
7. Life is like a multiple choice question. Sometimes, the choices but not the question itself confuses you.
8. The more voters balk at economic reform, the more politicians keep on talking about values.
9. The movement is supported by key figures in the three main political parties.
10. Every Monday morning I would convene and preside over our department meeting.

Unit Thirteen   Women Writers in Arabia

II. Answer the Following Questions.

1. Gladys Matar grew up in an environment ideally suited for nurturing the growth of her artistic and literary talents from early age, since her father is a pioneering architect and her mother an artistic home maker.
2. In 1982, while still in college, her short story "*The Rain*" won the Arab Writers Guild's first prize for a short story in Syria.
3. In 1984 her short story "*Who Would Bring Aiisha Back Her Toy*" won the prestigious Arab Woman Magazine's first prize for an Arabic short story, among participants from numerous countries across the Arab World.

4. From 1989 right on through to 2006, she published in volume.
5. It is really the singular dream her recall as a child: to become a writer.
6. The great Colombian author, Gabriel García Márque, who was awarded the Nobel Prize in 1982, played an influential role with her.
7. The "ironic" style and the "epic" style.
8. The core message expressed in her work is national solidarity.

III. Cloze

Passage 1:
- (1) born
- (2) studied
- (3) regarded
- (4) heart
- (5) especially
- (6) away
- (7) publishing
- (8) during
- (9) Since
- (10) translated

Passage 2:
- (1) translations
- (2) until
- (3) due
- (4) which
- (5) along
- (6) other
- (7) particularly
- (8) such
- (9) chosen
- (10) works

IV. Spot Dictation

Taha Hussein

Taha Hussein was born in 1889 during the period of demoralization (1) which followed (2) the failure of the Arab revolution and the British occupation (3) of Egypt in 1882. He was born and lived his childhood (4) in a small community in the Governorate of Minya in the south of the country. In this environment (5) poverty and ignorance, disease and destitution were endemic, and there was no provision (6) whatever of preventive medicine or medical care. For this, Taha Hussein would pay dearly, losing (7) his sight at the age of 6, His father, a minor (8) civil servant weighed down by the burdens (9) of keeping a large family, could do nothing but enrol him in the village school to learn the Koran. There the child mingled with graduates from al-Azhar and acquired (10) popular culture by listening to storytellers recounting the lives of Antar bin Shadad, Sayf bin Dhi Yazan and other Arab folk heroes. Despite all the difficulties (11) facing him, an intense desire arose in the boy to travel to Cairo and study at al-Azhar.

V. Translation

1. This collection is made up of three parts: poems, essays and short stories.
2. McNair consistently ranks as the top public high school in the state, and virtually all its students go on to college, including to some of the most prestigious institutions in the United States.
3. His executive position entitled him to certain courtesies rarely accorded others.
4. The clinic was accused of ping-ponging patients from one specialist to another.
5. As soon as a desire is requited, it is always replaced by another.
6. It is forbidden to reprint any article from this magazine without special permission.
7. What you eat and drink, from childhood on, is critical to the amount of calcium in your bones
8. In the process of practice the advantage is not prominent, which proves that I should improve my professional level.
9. A good experimental platform must be suited for teaching and it should make students understand the content of the experiment.
10. Another team of scientists has come up with conflicting evidence.

Appendix II
Chinese Version of "Broadening Your Horizon"

　　前三篇课外阅读材料选自黎巴嫩诗人哈里利·纪伯伦的散文诗集《先知》和阿拉伯民间故事集《一千零一夜》。散文诗集中关于"婚姻"与"爱"的章节，语言优美绝伦，意境高深，赋人启迪。《驼背的故事》通过朴素的现实描绘与浪漫的幻想互相交织的表现手法，生动地反映了广大人民群众对于美好生活的憧憬。课外阅读材料可进一步拓宽读者的视野，激发读者对阿拉伯世界的研究兴趣。

婚姻①

　　艾尔梅特拉又开口问道：婚姻又是怎样的呢，大师？
　　他回答道：
　　你们一同降生，你们将永远相依。
　　当死神的白色羽翼驱散你们的日子，你们也应在一起。
　　的确，你们始终相守，即使在上帝的记忆中。
　　但在聚守中你们要保留空间，
　　让空中的风在你们之间飞舞。
　　彼此相爱，但不要让爱成为束缚；
　　让爱成为奔流于你们灵魂海岸间的大海。
　　盛满彼此的杯盏，但不要只从一只杯盏中取饮。
　　彼此互赠面包，但不要只向一块面包取食。

---

① All the Chinese translation of the words quoted from *The Prophet* are from http://www.doc88.com/p-531467468438.html.

一起欢歌曼舞，但要保持各自的独立。

鲁特琴的琴弦也彼此分开，即使它们为同一首乐曲震颤。

奉献你们的心，但不要让对方保管。

因为只有生命之手才能接纳你们的心。

站立在一起，但不要靠得太近；

因为殿宇的支柱总是彼此分立的，

橡树和松柏也不在彼此的阴影下生长。

爱

于是艾尔梅特拉说，请给我们谈谈爱吧。

他抬头望着众人，人群一片寂静。他用洪亮的声音说道：

当爱挥手召唤你们时，跟随着他，

尽管他的道路艰难而险峻。

当他展翼拥抱你们时，依顺着他，

尽管他羽翼中的利刃会伤害你们。

当他对你们说话时，要相信他，

尽管他的声音会击碎你的梦，像狂风尽扫园中的花。

爱虽可为你们加冕，也能将你们钉上十字架。他虽可助你们成长，也能将你们削砍剪刈。

他会攀至你们的高处，轻抚你们在阳光下颤动的最柔嫩的枝条，

他也会降至你们的根柢，动摇你们紧紧依附着大地的根须。

爱把你们像麦捆般聚拢在身边。

他将你们脱粒，使你们赤裸。

他将你们筛选，使你们摆脱麸糠。

他碾磨你们，直至你们清白。

他揉捏你们，直至你们柔顺。

尔后，他把你们交予圣火，让你们成为上帝圣宴上的圣饼。

这一切都是爱为你们所做，使你们或许能从中领悟自己心中的秘密，从而成为生命之心的一小部分。

但是如果你们出于畏惧只去寻求爱的和美与爱的欢乐，

那你们最好掩起自己的赤裸，离开爱的打谷场，

踏入那没有季节的世界，在那里，你会开怀，但不是尽情欢笑；你会哭泣，但不是尽抛泪水。

爱除了自身别无所予，除了自身别无所取。
爱不占有，也不被占有；
因为爱有了自己就足够了。
当你爱了，你不应说"上帝在我心中"，而应说"我在上帝心中"。
别以为你可以指引爱的方向，因为爱，如果他认为你配，将指引你的方向。
爱别无他求，只求成全自己。
但如果你爱了，又必定有所渴求，那就让这些成为你的所求吧：
融化为一道奔流的溪水，在夜晚吟唱自己的清曲。
体会太多温柔带来的痛苦。
被自己对爱的体会所伤害。
心甘情愿地淌血。
清晨，带着一颗生翼的心醒来，感谢又一个充满爱的日子；
午休，沉思爱的心醉神怡；
黄昏，带着感激归家；
睡前，为你心中的挚爱祈祷，唇间吟诵着赞美诗。

驼背的故事[①]

在都市里住着一个裁缝，他性情快活，喜好嬉戏。一天他碰到一个驼背。这驼背给人滑稽的感觉，他的言谈举止使人一下子忘记了苦闷，情不自禁地快乐起来。裁缝夫妇兴致勃勃地打量一番驼背，一时高兴，便约他一道回家，大家好一块儿吃饭玩乐。

驼背一请便动，到裁缝家时，天已快黑。裁缝马上到市上去买了煎鱼、馍馍、柠檬和葡萄，以丰盛的晚餐款待驼背。他们围着餐席开怀大吃。裁缝的老婆拿了块很大的鱼肉塞进驼背嘴里，开玩笑似的捂住他的嘴，说道："你肯定能整块吞下这鱼肉，不许你嚼，快吞吧，快吞吧。"

驼背果然遵命一咽，一根带肉的大鱼刺一下勾住他的喉管，噎得他喘不上气来，只一会，他就被鲠死了。裁缝惊呆了，不由叹道："这个可怜虫，早不死，迟不死，为什么偏偏死在我们手里！"

"你可不能就这样坐着不动呀？"老婆焦急地埋怨裁缝，"我们可是坐

[①] http://www.tom61.com/ertongwenxue/yiqianlingyiyegushi/2007 - 05 - 14/506.html.

在熊熊的火焰上了。"

"那该怎么办呢？"

"来吧，你来抱住他的身子，我在他的脸上蒙上一张丝帕，然后我先出去，你再跟在我后面，趁黑夜我们把他弄出去，在街上，你一边走，一边要不停地说：'孩子，我和你妈妈这就带你看医生去。'"

裁缝按老婆的吩咐，抱着驼背的身体，跟在老婆后面出去，老婆在前面一边走一边嚷："哟！我的儿啊，你快好起来吧。真让我痛苦呀！不过我知道，这样的天花，确实是到处都很容易染上的哪。"

夫妇俩一路走着，说着，沿街向人打听医生的住处，以便让全街的人都知道他们的孩子病了。最后，他们终于找到犹太医生的家。

医生的黑女仆听到他们敲门，为他俩开门。看见裁缝夫妇，她以为他们抱着的是他们的孩子，问道："有什么事吗？"

"我们带孩子来看病，"裁缝的老婆说："这是一枚四分之一的金币，请拿去给你的主人，让他下来为我们的孩子看病吧。这孩子病重哪。"

女仆转身上楼时，裁缝夫妇趁机闯进医生的家门。

"快把驼背放下，"裁缝的老婆说，"我们快脱身。"

裁缝匆忙放下驼背，让他靠着楼梯，两人一溜烟跑掉了。

女仆回到楼上，对医生说："门前有一对夫妇来看病，他们说把这个四分之一的金币给你，请你去替他们的孩子看病。"

医生见了金币，非常高兴，立刻起身，匆匆下楼来看病人。下楼时，一脚踢在死了的驼背身上，给绊得跌了一跤，驼背滚下楼去。医生爬起身，叫道："啊！我怎么会踢到这个病人，使他滚下去，一下子跌死了。我对这个死在家中的尸体可怎么办呀！"

医生战战兢兢地驼着驼背的尸体到楼上，把刚才发生的事情告诉老婆。

"你怎么还不想办法呢？"老婆说，"你要是坐着不动，等到天亮，我们就完了，我和你会把命送掉的！来呀，我们把他抬上平台，放到隔壁那家中去吧。"

原来医生的邻居是王宫里的厨房总管，他经常把王宫里的肉带到家中，惹得猫和老鼠去偷吃，而且他家没人时，连狗也会爬过墙头，下去偷吃，因此糟蹋了不少的肉。这时医生夫妇两人，一个提着驼背的双手，一个抬着他的双脚，沿墙边把他慢慢地放了下去，让他靠着屋角。做完这一切后，他们悄悄地潜回自己家里。

驼背被放下去时，那个总管刚好回家。他打开门，拿着蜡烛走进屋，立刻发现有人站在屋角。

他嚷起来:"好啊!原来偷我那么多肉的是人呀!你偷了我的肉,我还一直错怪是猫和狗,以致巷中许多猫和狗都遭了殃,却原来是你从屋顶上爬下来偷的呀!"他嚷着,马上去拿起一柄大锤,朝驼背胸部打了几锤。

驼背被打倒在地,一动不动,总管这才惊惶失措起来,既忧愁又苦闷。他想到事情关系着自己的性命,骂道:"这些讨厌的肉啊!这个人的生命难道就这样断送在我手里吗?"

他仔细一看,原来是个驼背。

"你生为驼背做孽还不够吗?"他说,"定要做贼来偷油偷肉吗?"于是总管负着驼背,趁夜一直摸索到街拐角处,偷偷放他下来,让驼背的身体靠在一家店铺门前,然后拔脚开溜。

这时,一个喝得酩酊大醉的基督教商人,东倒西歪着,正要去澡堂洗澡。他念叨说:"快了!快到澡堂了!"他摇摇晃晃地走到驼背面前,坐下去解鞋带,猛见身旁立着一个人,便一骨碌爬起来,以为这人是想来偷他的缠头的。原来昨天夜里,他的缠头刚被人偷了,他正为此愤愤不平。于是他猛地一拳打在驼背脖子上,驼背马上倒了下去。这个商人醉得厉害,一面大声喊叫"捉贼",一面趁势扑在驼背身上,两手紧紧掐着驼背的脖子不放。巡察闻声赶到,正看见这个商人骑在驼背身上乱捶乱打。

"为什么打人?"巡察问。

"这个人要抢我的缠头。"

"起来!"

基督教商人站了起来。巡察走过去一看,人已被打死了。"好了!"巡察说,"基督教徒打死人了。"于是绑起基督教徒,带往衙门。

"基督呀!圣母玛利亚呀!"基督教商人忿恨地嚷叫:"我怎么会打死人呢?我只打了一拳,他怎么会死?他死得多快呀!"

之后,基督教商人酒醒了过来,恢复了理智,悲哀地和驼背在监狱里过了一夜。

次日,法官在处决杀人犯之前,掌刑官宣布了基督教商人的罪状,把他带到绞刑架下。当绞绳套上他的脖子,快行刑时,那个厨房总管却忽然赶了来。他从人群中挤进去,见基督教商人就要被绞死,便使出全身力量挤到掌刑官面前,大声说道:"别绞他,这个人是我杀的。"

"你为什么杀人?"法官问。

"昨夜我回家时,他正从屋顶上爬下来,要偷我的东西,我一气之下,用大铁锤打中了他的胸部,打死了他。由于害怕,我背起他到大街上,把他扶靠在一家铺子门前。可是现在我想,我已经杀了一个人,可不能再让这个基督教徒死于非命,现在请拿我偿命,绞死我吧。"

听了总管的自首,法官宣布基督教商人无罪,释放了他。"绞这个人吧。"法官指着厨房总管,吩咐掌刑官。

掌刑官按法官的命令,从基督教商人脖子上取下绞绳,套在总管脖子上,牵他到绞刑架下,准备动手开绞。这时,那个犹太医生挤开人群,叫喊着冲到绞架下,说道:"你不能绞他,杀人的不是他,而是我。是这样的:昨天我在家中,有一男一女来求医,他们带着这个驼背,叫女仆把一个四分之一的金币给我,说是给他治病。那一男一女进入我家,让他靠着楼梯休息,两人便走了。我摸索着下楼去看病人,黑夜里看不清,一脚踢在了他身上,他跌倒下去,立刻摔死了。老婆和我把尸体抬到平台上,设法将它放到总管家里,因为他是我们的邻居。总管回去发现驼背在他家中,以为是贼,用锤把他打倒,还以为是自己打死了他。我无意间杀死了一个人,可不愿有意地害了另一个人的生命!"

由于犹太医生的自首,法官便吩咐掌刑官:"放掉总管,绞犹太人偿命好了。"

掌刑官又将绞绳套在犹太医生脖子上,刚要动手开绞,那个裁缝又突然挤开人群,奔到绞刑架下,对掌刑官说:"别绞他,杀人的不是他,而是我。是这样的:昨天清晨我出门散完步,午后回家的时候,碰到这个喝得醉醺醺的驼背。他敲着小鼓,哼着小曲。我当时邀他到我家,用煎鱼招待他。我妻子拿了块鱼肉请吃,塞在他嘴里,他一咽便鲠死了。我妻子和我把他抱到犹太医生家里,他的女仆来开门,我对她说:'告诉你的主人,请他快下来,给我们的孩子看病。'当时,我给了她一枚四分之一的金币。她上楼去通知主人的时候,我把驼背放在楼梯上,然后带着老婆悄悄溜走。医生下楼踢在他身上,便认为是自己杀死的。"

"这是事实吧?"他问犹太医生。

"对,真是这样。"医生回答。

"放掉犹太人吧,"裁缝望着法官,"让我来偿命好了。"

"这真是一件可以记录下来当史料的怪事。"法官听了裁缝的自首,感到非常惊讶,随即吩咐掌刑官:"放掉犹太人,根据裁缝的自首,绞他好了。"

掌刑官一边把绞绳套在裁缝脖子上，一边说道："麻烦极了！一会儿要绞那个一会儿要绞这个，结果，谁也死不了！"

那个驼背本是供皇帝逗笑取乐的一个侏儒，随时随地侍奉皇帝。他喝醉酒，溜出王宫后，一连两天也不见回宫。皇帝便吩咐打听他的下落。侍臣出去打听了情况，回宫禀报国王："启禀主上，驼背已死了，尸体被人送到衙门里。法官要绞死杀人犯。可非常奇怪，每当他宣布了罪状，快要行刑开绞时，总有人出来自首，承认是自己杀人，已有好几个人自首了，每人都讲了杀人的原委。"

于是，皇帝吩咐侍卫："你快去法场传法官进宫，要他带全部犯人来见我。"

侍卫到法场时，掌刑官刚准备好，就要开绞裁缝了。

"且慢！"侍臣制止了掌刑官，向法官传达了皇帝的旨意，随即命人抬着驼背的尸体，并将裁缝、犹太医生、基督教商人和总管一齐带进宫去。法官见到皇帝，跪下去吻了地面，把事件经过一五一十报告了皇帝。皇帝听了，又惊奇又激动。

这时，一个刚进宫的理发匠站了出来，看了这场面。他到很奇怪。

"陛下！"理发匠说："为什么这个裁缝、基督教商人、犹太医生、总管和死了的驼背都在这儿呢？这是怎么一回事呀？"

皇帝笑着说："来吧，把驼背昨天吃晚饭时的情形，以及基督教商人、犹太医生、总管和裁缝所谈的一切经过，全都讲给理发匠听吧。"

理发匠听了这一切，说："这可是奇事中的奇事了！"接着他摇着头说："让我看一看驼背吧。"于是他靠近驼背坐下，把他的头挪在自己的腿上，仔细打量一番，突然哈哈大笑，笑得差一点倒在地上，他说："每个人的死都是有原因的，驼背之死尤其值得记载呢。"

他的言行使得所有的人都莫名其妙，皇帝也一样摸不着头脑。

"陛下，以你的恩惠起誓，这个驼背并没有死，他还在喘气呢。"理发匠说着，从袋里拿了一个罐子出来，打开，从中取出一个眼药瓶，拿瓶中的油质抹在驼背脖子上，接着又掏出一只铁夹子，小心地把铁夹子伸进驼背的喉管，挟出一块裹着血丝、带着骨片的鱼肉。驼背突然打了一个喷嚏，一骨碌爬了起来，神气十足，伸手抹一抹嘴脸。

皇帝和所有的人惊奇之余，全笑得死去活来。

皇帝说："这可真是奇事，没有比这更稀奇古怪的事了，臣民们。"他接着说："难道你们曾见过死了又活回来的人吗？若不是这个理发匠，这驼背一定假死变成真死呢。"

人们齐声说："这真算得是万中仅一的奇事了。"

皇帝惊讶之余，一面吩咐宫中的人记录驼背的故事，作为历史文献保存；一面赏赐犹太医生、基督教商人和总管每人一套名贵衣服，然后让他们全都回家，裁缝、驼背和理发匠也各得到了皇帝赏给的一套名贵衣服。从那以后，裁缝在宫中做起缝纫活，按月领取薪俸；驼背仍然陪伴皇帝，谈笑取乐，得到了很高的俸禄；理发匠却成为皇帝的随身陪侍，替皇帝理发。

他们各得一份差事，舒适愉快地生活着。

阿拉法特在领取和平奖时的发言①

哈拉尔德国王陛下，
索尼娅王后陛下，
诺贝尔委员会主席希杰斯特德教授，
女士们，先生们：

自从信任我的人民把寻找失去家园这一艰巨的任务交给我的那一刻起，我就坚信：那些漂流异乡的人们会像爱惜自己不可分割的肢体一样珍藏着自己家园的钥匙，那些留守在故乡的人们也忍受着各种痛苦和创伤，我坚信他们所做的这些牺牲必将换来返回家园和获得自由的回报。我还坚信，这条充满荆棘的艰难之旅必将通往幸福的家园。

今天，当我们欢聚一堂庆祝和平出现的时候，当我站在这个讲台的时候，我看到了那些永不瞑目的殉难者，他们的容貌已深深刻在了我的脑海中。他们向我询问他们的家园和已经空荡荡的故土。我强忍着泪水对他们说："你们非常了不起，你们的浴血奋战使我们守住了神圣的家园，使我们在这场为了争取和平的艰苦战争中跨出了第一步。"

今天，我们庆祝我们恢复了创造力，并开始重建一个被战争摧毁的家园，一个可以俯瞰四邻的家园，我们的孩子可以在一起竞相采花、玩耍。我们巴勒斯坦阿拉伯人民的忍耐力和奉献精神以及在国家、历史和人民之间建立起来永不分割的纽带的伟大力量，让我拥有了民主自豪感和做人的尊严。同时也为我们国家古老的传奇掀开了新的篇章，增添了希望的史诗。

---

① http://blog.donews.com/ynews/archive/2004/11/12/167799.aspx.

为了他们，为了那些坚韧不屈的经历了战火和汗水洗礼的国家的儿女们，我将把这诺贝尔奖赠予那些渴望祖国不受外来侵略和内战的伤害，并对自己的国家拥有自由、安全充满憧憬的孩子们。

主席先生，我完全明白这种最高荣誉的授予并不是由于我和我的同伴——以色列总理伊扎克·拉宾和以色列外交部长西蒙·佩雷斯所取得的成就，更重要的是激励我们以更快的步伐、更高的觉悟和更坚定的信念继续沿着这条和平之路前进，这样我们就可以将我们选择的和平、勇敢者的和平由口号变为现实，这是我们两国人民对我们的信任，也是全人类道义责任的要求，我们应无愧于此。

以保卫"阿以和平"之路为己任的巴勒斯坦人民同他们的阿拉伯兄弟一样，期望在"土地换和平"的原则上，在遵循国际法和有关规定的基础上，实现广泛、公正和持久的和平。和平对我们来说是一种财富，是我们的利益所在。和平能够使个人自由发展其个性，而不受地域、宗教和种族的限制。和平将恢复阿以关系纯洁的本质。它将使阿拉伯人通过纯粹的人类感情来表达他们对欧洲地区犹太人的悲惨遭遇的深刻理解。同样，也使得犹太人能够对巴勒斯坦人民因多种历史原因所遭受的苦难表示无限的同情。只有受过苦难的人才能真正了解那些正在承受苦难的人。

和平是我们的利益所在：因为只有在公正和平的氛围中，巴勒斯坦人民才能实现其国家独立和恢复主权的正当愿望，才能够在享有同以色列人民友好睦邻、互相尊重、团结合作的同时，发展自己的民族和文化。同样，和平也能够使以色列人民明确中东局势，向其阿拉伯邻邦开放经济和文化交流。长年的战争已经使得阿拉伯地区失去了在当今世界中的地位，在现在民主、多元和繁荣的环境里，阿拉伯人民热切盼望本地区的繁荣发展。

正如战争是一场冒险，和平同样也是一种挑战和赌注，如果我们运用各种手段也没有使和平经受住风暴中的动乱，如果我们没有维护好和平，这种冒险就会升级。因此，在这里我呼吁我的同伴们加快推进和平进程，早日实现裁军，以便选举能够顺利进行，快速进入和平进程的下一阶段。只有这样，和平才能得到维护，并成为稳固的现实。

在"土地换和平"的原则基础上，根据联合国 242 号和 338 号决议以及其他未实现巴勒斯坦人民合法权益签署的国际协议，我们开始了和平进程。尽管和平进程还没有实现其全部目标，但是和平进程的第一年和第二年所取得的成果和营造的信任环境却使和平充满了希望，因此我呼吁各方消除顾虑，简化程序。我们必须实现尚未完成的目标，尤其是完成权利的交接，进一步推进以色列西岸和居民区的裁军，最终实现彻底裁军。这将给我们一个重建社会的机会，用我们的文化、知识和技能为创造新世界做出贡献。

因此，我们呼吁和平进程的共同发起人——俄罗斯和美国参与到这一进程中来，消除障碍，大力推进和平进程。我呼吁东道国挪威和埃及继续努力，这种努力已经达成了奥斯陆、华盛顿、开罗等协议，奥斯陆这一光辉的名字同那些支持多边谈判的国家一样伴随着和平进程。

我呼吁我的和平同伴从全面的战略角度考虑和平进程。

仅仅靠信任不会取得和平，只有将信任和承认相互合法，权利二者相结合才能缔造和平，不承认这些权利，就会产生不公平，就像灰烬掩盖下的火焰，它将会把和平推向可能摧毁它的流沙之处，点燃即将引爆的导火索。

我们认为和平是一种具有历史意义的战略选择，而不是急于战士利益得失的权宜之计。和平进程不仅仅是政治进程，它还包括发挥重要作用的民族意识、经济、科学和科技发展在内的一体化进程。此外，文化社会和创新的一体化在巩固和平的进程中也发挥着重要作用。

回顾往昔，我想起了我们所走过的短暂却很艰难的和平之路。我们必须鼓起勇气武装自己，在吸取以往深刻教训的基础上，向着公正、广泛的和平勇敢地走完前面的路。

一旦我们决定与和平共生存，我们就必须将和平置于一个坚实的基础之上，这个基础应该经受得起时间的考验，甚至是几代人的考验。从西岸和加沙地带全面裁军，需要深入考虑居民点的问题，这些居民点割裂了地理与政治的统一，阻碍了西岸各地区和加沙地带之间的自由沟通，是造成紧张局势的焦点，与我们追求的和平进程相违背，破坏了原有的安详。至于伊斯兰教徒、基督教徒和犹太教徒的精神归宿——耶路撒冷，不仅是巴勒斯坦人和犹太人的圣地，也是所有伊斯兰教徒和基督教徒的圣地，所以让我们把耶路撒冷建成一个协调各种信仰、发扬人类文化和宗教遗产的世界性典范城市。目前一个非常紧迫的任务就是使和平机制运转起来，解决一些根深蒂固的问题，也就是释放被关押的巴勒斯坦人的问题。释放这些人很重要，它会使这些人的母亲、妻子和孩子重新绽放笑容。

让我们一起在严冬的寒风中呵护这个新生的幼儿，让我们用这块土地所产的乳汁和蜂蜜来哺育这个孩子吧。因为这是萨利姆、亚伯拉罕、伊斯梅尔和以扎克曾生活的土地，因为这是神圣的土地，这是和平的土地。

最后，我祝贺我的和平伙伴——以色列总理伊扎克·拉宾和以色列外交部长西蒙·佩雷斯荣获诺贝尔和平奖。

同时，我也向主办这次颁奖大会的东道主国家——挪威以及友好热烈的挪威人民表示感谢。女士们，先生们，我相信比起战争和对抗，我们在和平中更能了解自身，就像我相信以色列人民同样会在和平中更能找回自己一样。

和平降临大地

祝福全世界人民

谢谢！

Appendix III
Glossary

A

a variety of 多种的；各种各样的　　　　　　　　　　　　Unit 11
above all 首先　　　　　　　　　　　　　　　　　　　Unit 6
abruptly [əˈbrʌptlɪ] adv. quickly and without warning 突然地；唐突地
　　　　　　　　　　　　　　　　　　　　　　　　Unit 6
access [ˈækses] v. reach or gain access to 接近；进入　　Unit 3
accompany [əˈkʌmpənɪ] v. be associated with 陪伴；陪同　Unit 8
acclaim [əˈkleɪm] n. enthusiastic approval 欢呼；称赞 v. praise 称赞；为…喝采　　　　　　　　　　　　　　　　　　　　Unit 13
achievement [əˈtʃiːvm(ə)nt] n. 成就　　　　　　　　　Unit 12
accent [ˈæksənt] v. to stress, single out as important 强调；重读　Unit 7
accessory [əkˈsesərɪ] n. clothing that is worn or carried, but not part of your main clothing 配件　　　　　　　　　　　　　　Unit 7
accord [əˈkɔːd] v. allow to have 给予　　　　　　　　　Unit 5
accord [əˈkɔːd] n. 符合；一致；协议　　　　　　　　　Unit 12
account for（比例）占　　　　　　　　　　　　　　Unit 5
account [əˈkaunt] n. a record or narrative description of past events 描述；解释　　　　　　　　　　　　　　　　　　　　　Unit 3
accountability [əˌkauntəˈbɪlɪtɪ] n. 负有责任；应作解释　　Unit 5
accreditation [əˈkredɪˈteɪʃən] n. 鉴定合格；信任　　　　Unit 5
achievement [əˈtʃiːvmənt] n. the action of accomplishing something 成就；成绩　　　　　　　　　　　　　　　　　　　　Unit 3
acknowledge [əkˈnɔlɪdʒ] v. accept or admit that sth. exists, is true, or is real 承认　　　　　　　　　　　　　　　　　　　　　Unit 3

Mysterious Arab Countries
神秘的阿拉伯

adaptone selves to 调整以适应	Unit 2
address [əˈdres] v. be busy with or work on 从事；忙于	Unit 5
adopt [əˈdɔpt] v. 采取；接受；收养	Unit 13
advocate [ˈædvəkeɪt] v. push for something 提倡；主张 n. 拥护者；提倡者；	Unit 1
adorned [əˈdɒːnd] adj. 被修饰的	Unit 9
agency [ˈeɪdʒənsɪ] n. an administrative Unit of government 代理；中介	Unit 5
agitate [ˈædʒɪteɪt] v. 激烈争论；激怒	Unit 3
agreement with 协议	Unit 12
ail [eɪl] v. cause suffering to 使受病痛；使疼痛；使烦恼；折磨	Unit 12
aim to 旨在；目的是	Unit 6
align [əˈlaɪn] v. place in a line or arrange so as to be parallel or straight 使结盟；匹配	Unit 5
alter [ˈɔːltə] v. cause to change 改变；更改	Unit 11
annual [ˈænjuəl] adj. yearly or once every year 每年的；一年的	Unit 2
anonymity [ænəˈmɪnɪtɪ] n. the state of being anonymous 匿名；笔者不详	Unit 3
anthropologist [ænθrəˈpɔlədʒɪst] n. 人类学家	Unit 7
anticipate [ænˈtɪsɪpeɪt] v. regard something as probable or likely 预期；期望；盼望	Unit 6
appear to 出现；似乎	Unit 6
arak [əˈraːk] n. 亚力酒；麦芽糖化槽酒（等于arrack）	Unit 10
arena [əˈriːnə] n. place or scene of activity or conflict 活动场所；竞技场	Unit 3
aromatic [ˌærəˈmætɪk] n. 芳族植物；芳香剂	Unit 1
artery [ˈɑːtərɪ] n. a major thoroughfare that bears important traffic 动脉	Unit 1
artillery [ɑːˈtɪlərɪ] n. 炮，大炮；炮兵部队	Unit 1
as well as 也；和…一样	Unit 10
as a means of 作为一种手段	Unit 6
as we know 就我们所知	Unit 6
ascribe [əˈskraɪb] v. attribute or credit to 归因于；归咎于	Unit 8

Appendix III

aside from 除…以外 Unit 10
assessment [əˈsesmənt] n. the act of judging 评定；估价 Unit 5
assuage [əˈsweɪdʒ] v. provide physical relief, as from pain 缓解；减轻
　　Unit 6
assume [əˈsjuːm] v. take on a certain form or show 呈现 Unit 2
assure [əˈʃuə] v. make certain of 保证；担保 Unit 11
at leisure 空闲地；悠闲地 Unit 10
atmosphere [ˈætməsfɪə] n. 气氛；大气 Unit 10
attempt [əˈtem(p)t] vt. try to do sth. hard 试图（尤指做困难的事）
　　Unit 12
austerity [ɔːˈsterətɪ] n. 节衣缩食 Unit 4
autocratic [ɔːtəˈkrætɪk] adj. 独裁的 Unit 12
automatically [ɔːtəˈmætɪkəlɪ] adv. in the mechanical manner 自动地；机械地 Unit 5
awesome [ˈɔːsəm] adj. very impressive and often frightening 令人敬畏的；可怕的 Unit 2

B

backdrop [ˈbækdrɔp] n. background 背景 Unit 2
back away from 受支持的 Unit 12
balk at 畏缩；回避 Unit 12
banquet [ˈbæŋkwɪt] n. a ceremonial dinner party for many people 宴会；盛宴 Unit 10
barley [ˈbaːlɪ] n. 大麦 Unit 10
barren [ˈbærən] adj. dry and bare 贫瘠的；荒芜的；空的 Unit 2
be accustomed to 习惯于 Unit 8
be adopted as 领养；采用 Unit 13
be bound to 注定 Unit 3
be characterized by …的特点在于；…的特点是 Unit 8
becomparable with 可比较的；比得上的；可同…比较 Unit 8
be crucial to 对…是至关重要的 Unit 1
be determined to 下决心；决心做 Unit 1
be devoid of 缺乏 Unit 2
be familiar with 熟悉的；有好的 Unit 11

Mysterious Arab Countries
神秘的阿拉伯

be in place of 代替 Unit 10
be involved with 涉及；与…有关联 Unit 9
be part of 成为…的一部分 Unit 8
be prohibited 被禁止的 Unit 10
be stitched on 被缝上 Unit 9
be suited for 适合于 Unit 13
be used in 适用于；被用于 Unit 10
bear［beə］（bore, borne/born）v. have or put up with 忍受；具有；支撑 Unit 8
belt［belt］n. 腰带 Unit 9
benign［bɪˈnaɪn］adj. kind, gentle and harmless 温和的；善良的 Unit 2
beseech［bɪˈsiːtʃ］v. ask for or request earnestly 恳求；请求 Unit 4
besiege［bɪˈsiːdʒ］v. surround so as to force to give up 围困；包围 Unit 1
blade［bleɪd］n. 刀片；刀锋；剑 Unit 9
blame for 指责；责怪 Unit 13
blossom［ˈblɒsəm］v. develop or come to a promising stage 成长 Unit 3
bounce［baʊns］v. spring up; move up and down repeatedly 弹跳；使弹起 Unit 12
bounce back 卷土重来；受挫后恢复原状 Unit 12
boundary［ˈbaʊndrɪ］n. a line determining the limits of an area 边界；分界线 Unit 3
bouquet［buˈkeɪ］n. 花束 Unit 11
branch［brɑːntʃ］v. grow and send out branches or branch-like structures 分支；分叉 Unit 3
break up into 分解为 Unit 1
bride［braɪd］n. a woman who has recently been married 新娘 Unit 11
brochure［ˈbrəʊʃə］n. a small book usually having a paper cover 印刷资料（或广告）手册；小册子 Unit 6
broiling［ˈbrɔɪlɪŋ］adj. very hot 炙热的 Unit 2

C

cabaret［ˈkæbəreɪ］n. 卡巴莱歌舞表演 Unit 7
candelabra［kændəˈlɑːbrə］n. 枝状大烛台 Unit 7
capacity［kəˈpæsɪtɪ］n. ability to perform or produce 能力；资格 Unit 5

Appendix III

caravan ['kærəvæn] n. （穿过沙漠地带的）旅行队（如商队）；拖车
　　　　　　　　　　　　　　　　　　　　　　　　　　　　Unit 2
carnival ['ka:nɪv(ə)l] n. 狂欢节；嘉年华会　　　　　　　Unit 10
category ['kætəgərɪ] v. a collection of things sharing a common attribute 种类；类别　　　　　　　　　　　　　　　　　　　　　Unit 3
cause [kɔ:z] n. 事业；追求　　　　　　　　　　　　　　Unit 12
centigrade ['sentɪgreɪd] n. a temperature scale on 摄氏温度　Unit 6
centralized [sentrəlaɪzd] adj. 集中的；中央集权的　　　Unit 5
ceremonial [ˌserɪ'məunɪəl] n. 仪式；礼节　　　　　　　Unit 9
cereal ['sɪərɪəl] n. 谷物；谷类植物　　　　　　　　　　Unit 10
ceremony ['serəmənɪ] n. 典礼；仪式；礼仪　　　　　　Unit 11
certificate [sə'tɪfɪkeɪt] n. 证书；执照；文凭　　　　　　Unit 5
checker ['tʃekə(r)] n. 方格图案　　　　　　　　　　　Unit 12
cheese [tʃi:z] n. a solid food prepared from the pressed curd of milk 奶酪；干酪　　　　　　　　　　　　　　　　　　　　　　Unit 10
chilly ['tʃɪlɪ] adj. uncomfortably cool 寒冷的；怕冷的　　Unit 6
choir ['kwaɪə] n. a chorus that sings as part of a religious ceremony 唱诗班；合唱队　　　　　　　　　　　　　　　　　　　Unit 8
choreography [kɔrɪ'ɔgrəfɪ] n. 舞蹈艺术　　　　　　　Unit 7
circular ['sə:kjulə] n. 通知；传单 adj. 循环的；圆形的；间接的 Unit 9
clarify ['klærɪfaɪ] v. make clear and (more) comprehensible 澄清；阐明
　　　　　　　　　　　　　　　　　　　　　　　　　Unit 10
closure ['kləuʒə] n. （永久的）停业；关闭；倒闭　　　Unit 4
coastal ['kəustl] adj. of or relating to a coast 沿海的；海岸的　Unit 10
coherent [kəu'hɪərənt] adj. logical and well organized 合乎逻辑的；有条理的　　　　　　　　　　　　　　　　　　　　　　　Unit 4
collection [kə'lekʃn] n. 收集；收藏品；募捐　　　　　Unit 13
colonial [kə'ləunɪəl] adj. 殖民地的　　　　　　　　　Unit 3
combat ['kɔmbæt] vi. fight against in or as if in a battle 与…战斗；斗争
　　　　　　　　　　　　　　　　　　　　　　　　　Unit 12
come to terms with 与…达成协议；忍受　　　　　　　Unit 2
come up with 想…；提出　　　　　　　　　　　　　Unit 13
commentary ['kɔmentərɪ] n. 评论；说明　　　　　　　Unit 7
commerce ['kɔmə:s] n. 商业；贸易　　　　　　　　　Unit 6

Mysterious Arab Countries
神秘的阿拉伯

commercialization [kəˌmɔːʃəlaɪˈzeɪʃən] n. 商业化；商品化	Unit 5
complain about 怨言；投诉	Unit 12
complete with 包括；连同	Unit 7
compliment [ˈkɔmplɪm(ə)nt] n. 恭维；称赞；问候；道贺	Unit 10
component [kəmˈpəunənt] n. an abstract part of something 成分；组件	Unit 2
compulsory [kəmˈpʌlsərɪ] adj. required by rule 义务的；必修的	Unit 5
concession [kənˈseʃən] n. 特许（权）	Unit 2
concrete [ˈkɔŋkriːt] adj. 实在的；具体的	Unit 1
condemn [kənˈdem] v. express strong disapproval of 谴责；宣判	Unit 12
configuration [kənˌfɪgəˈreɪʃn] n. an arrangement of a group of things 结构	Unit 2
conflation [kənˈfleɪʃn] n. 合并	Unit 7
considerable [conˈsɪdərəbl] adj. 相当多（大）的	Unit 2
consist of 由⋯组成；包括	Unit 11
continuous [kənˈtɪnjuəs] adj. 连续的；延伸的	Unit 11
contour [ˈkɔntuə] n. a line drawn on a map connecting points of equal height 轮廓	Unit 2
contrary to 与⋯相反	Unit 2
contribute [kənˈtrɪbjuːt] v. provide 投稿；贡献；捐赠	Unit 13
contribute to 有助于；为⋯出力	Unit 5
convention [kənˈvenʃn] n. 惯例；习俗；规矩	Unit 2
convince [kənˈvɪns] v. 说服；使明白；使确信	Unit 12
coordinate [kəuˈɔːdɪnɪt] v. bring order and organization to 协调；调整；整合	Unit 5
cornerstone [ˈkɔːnəstəun] n. 奠基石	Unit 3
corruption [kəˈrʌpʃn] n. 贪污；堕落	Unit 3
costume [ˈkɔstjuːm] n. the attire worn in a play or at a fancy dress ball 服装；装束	Unit 7
cough up 掏出；勉强说出（某事）	Unit 4
counterpart [ˈkauntəpaːt] n. 副本；配对物；相对物	Unit 8
courageous [kəˈreɪdʒəs] adj. showing courage and brave 勇敢的	Unit 12
couscous [kuskus] n. 粟（俗称小米、谷子）	Unit 10
coverage [ˈkʌvərɪdʒ] n. 新闻报道；覆盖范围	Unit 3

crack ［kræk］ v. break on the surface only; make a sharp sound 破裂；发沙哑声 Unit 10
cradle ［kreɪdl］ n. 摇篮；发源地 Unit 2
crane ［kreɪn］ n. 起重机 Unit 6
crescent ［ˈkresənt］ adj. 新月形的 n. 新月（形） Unit 2
critic ［ˈkrɪtɪk］ n. 批评家, 评论家 Unit 4
critical ［ˈkrɪtɪkəl］ adj. 批评的；爱挑剔的；评论的 Unit 13
crucial ［ˈkru:ʃ（ə）l］ adj. of extreme importance; vital 重要的；决定性的；决断的 Unit 10
crunch ［ˈkrʌntʃ］ n. an important and often unpleasant situation 紧要关头；困境 Unit 4
crush down 压倒；碾碎 Unit 3
crystal ［ˈkrɪstəl］ n. 晶体；水晶 adj. 水晶的；透明的；清澈的 Unit 13
culminate ［ˈkʌlmɪneɪt］ v. 到绝顶；达到顶点；使结束 Unit 8
current ［ˈkʌrənt］ adj. occurring in or belonging to the present time 现在的；流通的 Unit 3
curricula ［kəˈrɪkjulə］ n. an integrated course of academic studies 课程 Unit 5
curtail ［kəːˈteɪl］ v. place restrictions on 削减；缩减 Unit 3
cut back on 削减 Unit 4
cymbal ［ˈsɪmbəl］ n. （乐器）铙钹 Unit 7

D

deceptively ［dɪˈseptɪvlɪ］ adv. in a misleading way 迷惑地；欺诈地 Unit 2
decorate ［ˈdekəreɪt］ v. 点缀；装饰 Unit 11
decorative ［ˈdekərətɪv］ adj. 装饰性的；装潢用的 Unit 9
dedicate oneself to doing 专心致力于；献身于 Unit 1
defective ［dɪˈfektɪv］ adj. having a defect or not working properly 有缺陷的；不完美的 Unit 5
delegation ［delɪˈgeɪʃən］ n. 代表团 Unit 4
deliberate ［dɪˈlɪb（ə）rət］ adj. 深思熟虑的 Unit 1
delve ［delv］ v. turn up, loosen, or remove earth 钻研；探究；挖 Unit 13
democracy ［dɪˈmɒkrəsɪ］ n. 民主政体 Unit 12
demographic ［ˌdeməˈgræfɪk］ adj. of or relating to demography 人口统计学

Mysterious Arab Countries
神秘的阿拉伯

的 Unit 2
deposit [dɪ'pɒzɪt] n. money 定金；定钱 Unit 4
depend upon 依赖于 Unit 2
desalination [di:ˌsælɪ'neɪʃən] n. 脱盐作用；减少盐分 Unit 2
descend [dɪ'send] v. come from 下降；遗传 Unit 7
designate ['dezɪgneɪt] v. assign a name or title to 指定；指派；标出；把…定名为 Unit 8
desolate ['desələt] adj. empty and lacking in comfort 荒凉的；无人烟的 Unit 2
despite [dɪ'spaɪt] prep. 尽管；不管；虽有 Unit 12
destination [destɪ'neɪʃən] n. the place designated as the end 目的地；终点 Unit 6
determinism [dɪ'tɜ:mɪnɪzm] n. 宿命论；决定性要素 Unit 2
deteriorate [dɪ'tɪərɪəreɪt] v. become worse in some way 恶化；变坏 Unit 12
devise [dɪ'vaɪz] v. to invent sth new or a new way of doing sth 发明；设计；想出 Unit 4
devoid [dɪ'vɔɪd] adj. completely lacking 缺乏 Unit 2
devoted to 热衷于…的 Unit 12
devour [dɪ'vauə(r)] v. destroy completely or eat eagerly 吞没；毁灭 Unit 2
dictate [dɪk'teɪt] v. issue commands or orders for 命令；控制；指示 Unit 11
differ in 不同在；在…方面存在不同 Unit 8
dilemma [dɪ'lemə] n. 困境；进退两难 Unit 3
dilute [daɪ'lu:t] v. lessen the strength or flavor of a solution or mixture 稀释 Unit 10
dip [dɪp] v. to go downwards or to a lower level （使）下降；下沉 Unit 4
dip into 动用 Unit 4
diplomacy [dɪ'pləʊməsɪ] n. negotiation between nations 外交；外交手腕 Unit 12
dispatch [dɪs'pætʃ] v. send away towards a designated goal 派遣；调度 Unit 1
disseminate [dɪ'semɪneɪt] v. cause to become widely known 散播；公开；

Appendix III

宣传	Unit 3
distinctive [dɪˈstɪŋktɪv] adj. 有特色的；与众不同的	Unit 7
distinction [dɪsˈtɪŋkʃn] n. 区别；差别	Unit 13
distinctive [dɪˈstɪŋtɪv] adj. 有特色的；与众不同的	Unit 10
distribute [dɪˈstrɪbjuːt] v. give out and make available 分配；散布	Unit 5
diversify [daɪˈvəːsɪtɪ] n. the state of being diverse 差异；多样性	Unit 1
domestic [dəˈmestɪk] adj. 国内的；家庭的；驯养的	Unit 10
domesticate [dəˈmestɪkeɪt] v. 驯服的；驯养的	Unit 1
domestication [dəuˌmestɪkeɪʃən] n. 驯养；教化	Unit 2
dowry [ˈdauərɪ] n. 嫁妆	Unit 11
dramatically [drəˈmætɪkəlɪ] adv. in a very impressive manner 戏剧地；引人注目地	Unit 10
drape around 将松松地披在…上；周围悬挂	Unit 9
drift [drɪft] n. a general tendency to change (as of opinion) 趋势；动向	Unit 2
dromedary [ˈdrɒmədərɪ] n. 单峰驼	Unit 2
drop out 退出；退学	Unit 5
dropout [ˈdrɒpaut] n. someone who quits school before graduation 辍学学生	Unit 5
dual [ˈdjuːəl] adj. consisting of two parts 双重的；双倍的	Unit 5
dune [djuːn] n. （由风吹积成的）沙丘	Unit 2
dwell on/upon 老是想着；详述	Unit 8
duty [ˈdjuːtɪ] n. 税收	Unit 4

E

ecclesiastical [ɪˌkliːzɪˈæstɪkl] adj. 教会的；神职的；基督教的	Unit 8
eerily [ˈɪərɪlɪ] adv. strangely, mysteriously, frighteningly 怪异地；神秘地；恐怖地	Unit 4
eligible [ˈelɪdʒəbl] adj. qualified for or allowed or worthy of being chosen 合格的；符合条件的	Unit 5
emanate [ˈeməneɪt] v. give out (breath or an odor) 发散；发出	Unit 7
embed [ɪmˈbed] v. fix or set securely or deeply 把…嵌入	Unit 11
embrace [ɪmˈbreɪs] v. include; contain 包括；拥抱	Unit 3
emerge [ɪˈməːdʒ] v. to come into view 新兴；出现	Unit 6

Mysterious Arab Countries
神秘的阿拉伯

endorse [ɪnˈdɔːs] v. give support or one's approval to 赞同；支持　　Unit 3
emerge [ɪˈməːdʒ] v. come out of, become known or apparent 浮现；显现出来　　Unit 3
emergence [ɪˈməːdʒəns] n. the gradual beginning or coming forth 出现；发生　　Unit 1
engage [ɪnˈgeɪdʒ] v. take part in; busy oneself with; get the right to use 从事于；忙于；吸引　　Unit 3
engagement [ɪnˈgeɪdʒmənt] n. a meeting arranged in advance 订婚；婚约；诺言　　Unit 11
enhance [ɪnˈhaːns] v. increase 提高；增强　　Unit 3
enlist [ɪnˈlɪst] v. hire for work or help or support in doing something 取得（帮助）；支持　　Unit 2
ensemble [aːnˈzaːmbl] n. a group of musicians playing or singing together 全体；总效果；合奏组　　Unit 8
entertain [entəˈteɪn] v. amuse, interest or give sb. Pleasure 招待；娱乐　　Unit 7
enhancement [ɪnˈhaːnsmənt] n. improvement that makes something more agreeable 增加；放大　　Unit 5
enthusiasm [ɪnˈθjuːzɪæzəm] n. a feeling of excitement 热心；热忱；热情　　Unit 11
enthusiast [ɪnˈθjuːzɪæst] n. a person having a strong liking for something 狂热者　　Unit 7
entrepreneurship [ˌantrəprəˈnəːʃɪp] n. 企业家精神　　Unit 5
epic [ˈepɪk] adj. 史诗的；叙事诗的　n. 史诗；叙事诗；史诗般的作品　　Unit 13
equivalent [ɪˈkwɪvələnt] adj.（价值、数量、意义等）相等的；相同的　　Unit 4
erode [ɪˈrəud] v. gradually destroy or remove 逐渐毁坏；削弱；损害　　Unit 4
establish [ɪˈstæblɪʃ] v. bring about or set up or accept 制定；建立　　Unit 5
estimate [ˈestɪmeɪt] v. judge to be probable 估计；判断　　Unit 5
exceed [ɪkˈsiːd] v. go beyond 超过；超越　　Unit 2
excessively [ekˈsesɪvlɪ] adv. to an excessive degree 过分地；极度　　Unit 7
exotic [ɪgˈzɔtɪk] adj. 外国的；有异国情调的　　Unit 7

expatriate [eks'pætrɪeɪt] n. 侨居者；移居国外者　　　　　　　Unit 6
expeditionary [ˌekspɪ'dɪʃənerɪ] adj. 探险的；出征的（尤指军事上）
　　　　　　　　　　　　　　　　　　　　　　　　　　　　Unit 1
expose [ɪk'spəʊs] n. lay open; uncover; disclose; make known 显露；揭露；
　暴露　　　　　　　　　　　　　　　　　　　　　　　　　Unit 3
extend [ɪk'stend] v. to make sth. longer or larger 使伸长；扩大；扩展
　　　　　　　　　　　　　　　　　　　　　　　　　　　　Unit 4
extensive [ɪk'stensɪv] adj. large in spatial extent or range 广泛的；大量的；
　广阔的　　　　　　　　　　　　　　　　　　　　　　　　Unit 8
evident [evi'dənt] adj. clearly apparent or obvious to the mind or senses 明
　显的；明白的　　　　　　　　　　　　　　　　　　　　　Unit 12
evolve [ɪ'vɒlv] v. gradually change and develop 发展；使进化　Unit 2

F

Fahrenheit ['færənˌhaɪt] n. 华氏的（冰点为 32 度，沸点为 212 度）
　　　　　　　　　　　　　　　　　　　　　　　　　　　　Unit 2
fairytale ['feərɪteɪl] n. a story about fairies 童话故事　　　　　Unit 13
fall to 下降到　　　　　　　　　　　　　　　　　　　　　　Unit 4
falter ['fɔːltə] v. lose power or strength in an uneven way, or no longer make
　much progress 衰退　　　　　　　　　　　　　　　　　　Unit 12
fascinate ['fæsɪneɪt] v. cause to be interested or curious 使着迷　Unit 7
favored ['feɪvəd] adj. 受到优待的；得到宠爱的；有天赋的　　Unit 9
fava ['fɑːvə] n. (fava bean) 蚕豆　　　　　　　　　　　　　Unit 10
feast [fiːst] v. 享受；款待；宴请 n. a ceremonial dinner party for many
　people 筵席；宴会　　　　　　　　　　　　　　　　　　Unit 10
feature ['fiːtʃə] n. a prominent aspect of something 特色；特征　Unit 11
feedstock ['fiːdstɒk] n. 原料；给料　　　　　　　　　　　　Unit 1
feminine ['femɪnɪn] adj. being related to or are considered typical of women
　女性的；阴柔的　　　　　　　　　　　　　　　　　　　　Unit 7
femininity [ˌfemə'nɪnətɪ] n. 女性气质；娇弱；妇女的总称　　Unit 13
fertility [fə'tɪlətɪ] n. the state of being fertile 多产；肥沃；丰饶　Unit 11
feverish ['fiːvərɪʃ] adj. marked by intense agitation or emotion 极度兴奋的
　　　　　　　　　　　　　　　　　　　　　　　　　　　　Unit 6
fiber ['faɪbə] n. a slender and greatly elongated solid substance 纤维；光纤

Mysterious Arab Countries
神秘的阿拉伯

fiction ['fikʃən] n. 小说；虚构；编造 Unit 13
figure ['figə] n. the impression produced by a person 形象；人物 Unit 12
fiscal [fɪskəl] adj. connected with government or public money, especially taxes 财政的；国库的 Unit 4
fisticuff ['fɪstɪkʌf] n. a fight in which people hit each other with their fists 拳斗；互殴 Unit 4
fledgling ['fledʒlɪŋ] adj. young and inexperienced 初出茅庐的；无经验的 Unit 6
flinty ['flɪntɪ] adj. harsh and without emotion 坚硬的；冷峻的 Unit 2
flourish ['flʌrɪʃ] v. grow vigorously 茂盛；繁荣；活跃 Unit 1
formative ['fɔ:mətɪv] adj. forming or capable of forming or molding or fashioning 形成的；发展的 Unit 5
foundation [faun'deɪʃən] n. the basis on which something is grounded 基础；地基；基金会 Unit 13
formidable ['fɔ:mɪdəbl] adj. very great or impressive 强大的；令人生畏的 Unit 2
fortune ['fɔ:tʃu:n] n. a large amount of wealth; luck 财富；命运；运气 Unit 2
frankincense ['fræŋkɪnsens] n. 乳香 Unit 1
friable [fraɪbl] adj. easily broken 易碎的 Unit 2
from a… perspective 从某种角度来讲 Unit 3
fundamentally [ˌfʌndə'mentəlɪ] adv. 根本地；从根本上；基础地 Unit 9
fusion ['fju:ʒən] n. an occurrence that involves the production of a union 融合 Unit 7

G

gain [geɪn] v. gradually get sth. 获得 Unit 12
garrison ['gærɪsn] n. 守备队；驻地；要塞 Unit 1
gazelle [gə'zel] n. 瞪羚 Unit 6
generate ['dʒenəreɪt] v. produce; bring into existence 产生；生成 Unit 1
geopolitics [ˌdʒi:əu'pɒlətɪks] n. 地缘政治学 Unit 2
get support from 从…得到支持 Unit 5
give way to 让步 Unit 1

Appendix III

give rise to 使发生；引起 Unit 7
given ['gɪvən] prep. 考虑到 Unit 7
glamorous ['glæmərəs] adj. having an air of allure, romance and excitement 迷人的；有魅力的 Unit 7
go from bad to worse 江河日下 Unit 4
go by 判断 Unit 9
graduate from 从某处毕业 Unit 13
grant [grænt] v. let or allow to have 授予；承认；允许 Unit 5
grill [grɪl] v. cook over a grill 烧；烤 Unit 10
grim [grɪm] adj. unpleasant and depressing 令人不快的；令人沮丧的 Unit 4
groan [grəun] n. an utterance expressing pain or disapproval 呻吟；叹息 Unit 8
guarantee [ˌgærən'tiː] v. make certain of 保证；担保 Unit 11
guest [gest] n. a visitor to whom hospitality is extended 客人；来宾 Unit 6
gulch [gʌltʃ] n. 峡谷 Unit 2

H

haggle ['hægl] v. argue about the price 讨价还价；争论（价格） Unit 6
harsh ['hɑːʃ] adj. cruel, severe and unkind 残酷的；严厉的 Unit 4
hatch [hætʃ] v. devise or invent 策划 Unit 6
haunting ['hɔːntɪŋ] adj. remaining in one's mind 萦绕心头的；难以忘怀的 Unit 2
headdresses ['heddres] n. 头巾；头饰 Unit 9
headquarter ['hed'kwɔːtə] n. 总部；司令部 Unit 1
hefty ['heftɪ] adj. of considerable weight and size 重的；肌肉发达的；强有力地 Unit 6
hem [hem] v. fold over and sew together to provide with a hem 缝边；包围；约束 n. 褶边 Unit 9
henna ['henə] n. a reddish brown dye used especially on hair 指甲花；红褐色 Unit 6
herb [həːb] n. aromatic potherb used in cookery for its savory qualities 药草 Unit 10
historical [hɪ'stɔrɪkl] adj. 历史的；历史上的 Unit 11

historically [hɪˈstɔrɪklɪ] adv. throughout history 历史上地；从历史观点上说 Unit 10
homesickness [ˈhəumsɪknɪs] n. a longing to return home 乡愁 Unit 6
horizontal looms 横织机 Unit 9
hospitality [ˌhɔspɪˈtæləti] n. kindness in welcoming guests or strangers 热情；好客；款待 Unit 10
humiliation [hjuːˌmɪlɪˈeiʃn] n. state of disgrace or loss of self-respect 丢脸；耻辱；蒙羞；谦卑 Unit 12
hydrosphere [ˈhaɪdrəusfɪə] n. 水界；水圈；水气 Unit 2

I

ideally [aɪˈdɪəlɪ] adv. in an ideal manner 理想地；观念上地 Unit 13
identity [aɪˈdentɪtɪ] n. 身份；个性 Unit 12
idyll [ˈaɪdɪl] n. 田园生活 Unit 6
ignite [ɪgˈnaɪt] v. cause to start burning or arouse 点燃；激起 Unit 4
illiteracy [ɪˈlɪtərəsɪ] n. ignorance resulting from not reading 文盲；无知 Unit 5
immature [ɪməˈtjuə(r)] adj. characteristic of a lack of maturity 不成熟的；未成熟的 Unit 10
imitation [ɪmɪˈteɪʃn] n. copying someone else's actions 模仿 Unit 7
immense [ɪˈmens] adj. unusually great in size or amount or degree 巨大的；广大的；无边无际的 Unit 6
implementation [ɪmplɪmenˈteɪʃ(ə)n] n. 实施；执行 Unit 1
impose [ɪmˈpəuz] v. compel to behave in a certain way 强加；强迫 Unit 3
imposition [ˌɪmpəˈzɪʃn] n. an uncalled-for burden 强加；被迫接受；税收 Unit 11
in common 共同的；共有的 Unit 8
in earnest 认真地；坚定不移地 Unit 1
in fact 事实上；其实 Unit 6
in most cases 大部分情况下 Unit 7
in motion 在开动中；在运转中 Unit 2
in parallel with 与…平行；与…同时 Unit 5
in particular 尤其 Unit 3
in terms of 就…而言；根据 Unit 8

in the shape of …的形状 Unit 6
in the form of 以…形式 Unit 10
in the hands of 由…照管 Unit 1
in the presence of 当着某人；有某人在场 Unit 3
in turn 反之；反过来；依次；轮流； Unit 1
inability [ˌɪnəˈbɪlətɪ] n. the fact of not being able to do sth 无能；无力 Unit 4
incarcerate [ɪnˈkɑːsəreɪt] v. lock up or confine, in or as in a jail 监禁；幽闭 Unit 3
incredibly [ɪnˈkredəblɪ] adv. not easy to believe 难以置信地；非常地 Unit 2
in-depth [ˈɪnˈdepθ] adj. 彻底的；深入的 Unit 13
index [ˈɪndeks] n. 指标；指数；索引 Unit 9
indicate [ˈɪndɪkeɪt] v. to state or express briefly 指出；表明 Unit 11
indispensable [ˌɪndɪsˈpensəbl] adj. not to be dispensed with; essential 不可缺少的；绝对必要的 Unit 2
individual [ˌɪndɪˈvɪdju(ə)l] adj. 个人的；个别的 n. a human being 个人 Unit 10
indulge [ɪnˈdʌldʒ] v. give free rein to 满足；沉迷于 Unit 6
industrial [ɪnˈdʌstrɪəl] adj. of or relating to or resulting from industry 工业的；产业的 Unit 5
infinite [ˈɪnfɪnət] adj. 无限的；无穷的 Unit 6
infinity [ɪnˈfɪnətɪ] n. time without end 无穷；无限大；无限距 Unit 6
inflation [ɪnˈfleɪʃən] n. a general and progressive increase 膨胀 Unit 5
infrastructure [ˈɪnfrəstrʌktʃə] n. 基础设施 Unit 1
ingredient [ɪnˈgriːdɪənt] n. 原料；组成部分 adj. 构成组成部分 Unit 10
inherit [ɪnˈherɪt] v. obtain from someone after their death 继承；遗传而得 Unit 13
inhospitable [ˌɪnhɔˈspɪtəbl] adj. unfavorable to life or growth 不适于居住的 Unit 2
innovative [ˈɪnəvətɪv] adj. ahead of the times 革新的；创新的 Unit 6
institution [ˌɪnstɪˈtjuːʃn] n. 习俗；制度；机构 Unit 2
integrity [ɪnˈtegrətɪ] n. 正直；诚恳，诚实 Unit 3
intellectual [ˌɪntəˈlektʃuəl] adj. 智力的；有才智的 n. 知识分子；有极高

Mysterious Arab Countries
神秘的阿拉伯

  才智的人   Unit 3
intend to 打算做；想要   Unit 7
intense [ɪnˈtens] adj. in an extreme degree 强烈的；紧张的；非常的
  Unit 6
intensity [ɪnˈtensətɪ] n. the property of being intense 强度；强烈   Unit 8
intensive [ɪnˈtensɪv] adj. tending to give force or emphasis 密集的；彻底的；精细的   Unit 1
intensively [ɪnˈtensɪvlɪ] adv. in an intensive manner 强烈地；集中地 Unit 7
interim [ˈɪntərɪm] adj. 暂时的；临时的 n. 临时协定   Unit 12
interior [ɪnˈtɪərɪə] n. the region that is inside of something 内部；本质
  Unit 6
interval [ˈɪntəvəl] n. 间隔；间距；幕间休息   Unit 8
intimate [ˈɪntɪmət] adj. having or fostering a warm or friendly and close relationship 亲密的   Unit 7
intoxication [ɪnˌtɔksɪˈkeɪʃn] n. 陶醉   Unit 8
intricate [ˈɪntrɪkət] adj. 复杂的；难懂的   Unit 9
invasion [ɪnˈveɪʒn] n. any entry into an area not previously occupied 侵略；侵入   Unit 1
irony [ˈaɪərənɪ] n. 讽刺；反语；具有讽刺意味的事   Unit 13
ironic [aɪˈrɔnɪk] adj. 讽刺的；反话的   Unit 13
ironically [aɪˈrɔnɪklɪ] adv. contrary to plan or expectation 讽刺地；说反话地   Unit 6
irrevocable [ɪrɪˈvəukəbl] adj. 不可改变的；不能取消的；不能挽回的
  Unit 5
irrespective of 不论；不考虑   Unit 5
irrigation [ɪrɪˈgeɪʃən] n. 灌溉渠   Unit 4
isolate [ˈaɪsəleɪt] v. place or set apart; set apart from others 孤立；隔离
  Unit 7

J

K

kebab [kɪˈbæb] n. 烤肉串   Unit 10
keep an eye out for 注意；警觉   Unit 11

kibbeh [kɪb] n. 碎羊肉面饼 　　　　　　　　　　　　Unit 10
kofta [ˈkɔftə] n. 肉丸 　　　　　　　　　　　　　　Unit 10

L

labor [ˈleɪbə] n. 劳动力；人工 　　　　　　　　　　Unit 9
laugh at 嘲笑 　　　　　　　　　　　　　　　　　　Unit 2
lay out 制定；起草 　　　　　　　　　　　　　　　Unit 3
legendary [ˈledʒəndrɪ] adj. celebrated in fable or legend 传说的；传奇的；著名的 　　　　　　　　　　　　　　　　　　　　Unit 1
legislation [ledʒɪsˈleɪʃən] n. law 法规；法律 　　　　Unit 4
legislative [ˈledʒɪslətɪv] adj. 立法的 n. 立法权；立法机构 　Unit 13
leopard [ˈlepəd] n. the pelt of a leopard 豹；美洲豹 　　Unit 9
limestone [ˈlaɪmstəun] n. [岩] 石灰岩 　　　　　　Unit 13
linen [ˈlɪnɪn] n. a fabric woven with fibers from the flax plan 亚麻布；亚麻线；亚麻制品 　　　　　　　　　　　　　　Unit 9
literal [ˈlɪtərəl] adj. without interpretation or embellishment 文字的；无夸张的 　　　　　　　　　　　　　　　　　　　　Unit 13
live off 依赖…生活 　　　　　　　　　　　　　　　Unit 1
live [laɪv] adj. in current use or ready for use 现场的；直播的 　Unit 3
loincloth [ˈlɔɪnklɔθ] n. a garment that provides covering for the loins 缠腰带；腰布 　　　　　　　　　　　　　　　　　Unit 9
look like 像 　　　　　　　　　　　　　　　　　　Unit 6
luxurious [lʌgˈʒuərɪəs] adj. rich and superior in quality 奢侈的；豪华的 　　　　　　　　　　　　　　　　　　　　　　　Unit 11
luxury [ˈlʌkʃərɪ] n. something that is an indulgence rather than a necessity 奢侈；奢华；奢侈品 　　　　　　　　　　　Unit 6

M

maid-servants n. 女仆 　　　　　　　　　　　　　Unit 9
maize [meɪz] adj. a strong yellow color 玉米色的 n. 玉米；玉米色 　　　　　　　　　　　　　　　　　　　　　　Unit 10
majority [məˈdʒɔrɪtɪ] n. 多数 　　　　　　　　　　Unit 10
make a profit 赚钱 　　　　　　　　　　　　　　　Unit 4
make do 将就着使用；凑合着用 　　　　　　　　　Unit 9

Mysterious Arab Countries
神秘的阿拉伯

make it 成功；及时到达	Unit 13
make way for 让路	Unit 6
manipulate [mə'nɪpjuleɪt] v. 操纵；控制	Unit 3
manipulation [mənɪpju'leɪʃn] n. 操作；处理	Unit 7
massifs [mæ'si:f] n. 山丘	Unit 2
mediterranean [ˌmedɪtə'reɪnɪən] n. 地中海	Unit 9
medieval [ˌmedɪ'i:vəl] adj. 中世纪的（公元 1000 年到 1450 年）	Unit 4
megalomania [megələu'meɪnɪə] n. 狂妄自大	Unit 6
melodic [mə'lɔdɪk] adj. containing or characterized by pleasing melody 有旋律的；音调优美的	Unit 8
mesmerize ['mezməraɪz] (mesmerize) v. 使⋯入迷；使⋯目瞪口呆	Unit 8
metaphor ['metəfə] n. 暗喻；隐喻	Unit 13
metropolis [mə'trɔpəlɪs] n. a large and densely populated urban area 大都市	Unit 13
meze [mez] n. 开胃菜；前菜	Unit 10
millennia [mɪ'lenIE] n. 千年期	Unit 6
millennium [mɪ'lenIEm] n. a span of 1000 years 千禧年；一千年；千年纪念	Unit 9
millimeter ['mɪlɪˌmi:tə] n. a metric Unit of length equal to one thousandth of a meter 毫米；公厘	Unit 9
military ['mɪlɪt(ə)rɪ] adj. relating to the armed forces of a country 军事的	Unit 12
modernity [mə'də:nətɪ] n. the quality of being current or of the present 现代性；现代作风	Unit 3
modify ['mɔdɪfaɪ] v. cause to change, make different 修改；修饰；更改	Unit 8
modulate ['mɔdjuleɪt] v. 调节；（信号）调制；调整	Unit 8
mold [məuld] v. 形成；制作模具	Unit 3
monotheistic [ˌmɔnəuθɪ'ɪstɪk] adj. believing that there is only one god 一神论的	Unit 1
mosque [mɔsk] n. 清真寺	Unit 11
mourn ['mɔ:n] vi. feel sadness 哀痛；服丧	Unit 8
multilateral [mʌltɪ'læt(ə)r(ə)l] adj. 多边的；多国的	Unit 4
multi-millionaire ['mʌltɪ mɪljə'neə] n. 千万富翁	Unit 6

Appendix III

myrrh [mə:(r)] n. 没药（一种树胶树脂） Unit 1

N

negotiate [nɪˈgəʊʃɪeɪt] v. discuss the terms of an arrangement 谈判；商议
Unit 11
Neolithic [ˌniːəʊˈlɪθɪk] adj. [古] 新石器时代的；早先的 Unit 9
no longer 不再 Unit 6
nomad [ˈnəʊmæd] n. 游牧民 Unit 2
nomadic [nəʊˈmædɪk] adj. tending to travel 游牧的；流浪的；游动的
Unit 6
nominally [ˈnɒmɪnəlɪ] adv. in name only 名义上地 Unit 5
nothing at all 一无所有；什么都不是 Unit 9
notion [ˈnəʊʃn] n. an idea or belief about something 概念；观念 Unit 2
numerous [ˈnjuːmərəs] adj. amounting to do a large indefinite number 许多的；很多的
Unit 2
nurture [ˈnɜːtʃə(r)] v. help develop, bring up 养育；培育 Unit 13
nutritionist [njuːˈtrɪʃənɪst] n. 营养学家 Unit 4

O

oases [əʊˈeɪsɪːz] n. a fertile tract in a desert 绿洲；避风港；名词 oasis 的复数形式
Unit 1
obligation [ˌɒblɪˈgeɪʃ(ə)n] n. 义务；职责 Unit 10
obliterate [əˈblɪtəreɪt] v. rub off or make cancelling 擦掉；使消失 Unit 2
oblivious [əˈblɪvɪəs] adj. being unaware of 不知道的；不清楚的 Unit 4
obsolete [ˈɒbsəliːt] adj. old, no longer in use or valid 废弃的；老式的
Unit 2
obtrusion [əbˈtruːʒən] n. 闯入；闯入的东西 Unit 2
occasionally [əˈkeɪʒnəlɪ] adv. now and then or here and there 偶尔；间或
Unit 10
on a large scale 在很大范围内 Unit 3
opponent [əˈpəʊnənt] n. a person that you are playing against 对手；竞争者
Unit 4
opt for 选择；抉择 Unit 5
optimistic [ˌɒptɪˈmɪstɪk] adj. 乐观的；抱乐观看法的 Unit 4

Mysterious Arab Countries
神秘的阿拉伯

optimize ['ɔptɪmaɪz] v. 优化 Unit 1
opulence ['ɔpjuləns] n. wealth as evidenced by sumptuous living 富裕；丰富 Unit 6
orchestral [ɔː'kestrəl] adj. relating to or composed for an orchestra 管弦乐的；管弦乐队的 Unit 8
orient ['ɔːrɪənt] n. 东方；东方国家 Unit 7
orientation [ˌɔːrɪən'teɪʃn] n. a position or direction 方向；目标 Unit 3
ornament ['ɔːnəmənt] n. 装饰；装饰物；教堂用品 Unit 9
ornamentation [ˌɔːnmen'teɪʃn] n. 装饰物 Unit 8
oryx ['ɔrɪks] n. 大羚羊 Unit 6
ostentatious [ˌɔsten'teɪʃəs] adj. 招摇的；夸耀的；惹人注目的 Unit 6
outlet ['autlet] n. an opening that permits escape or release 出路；出口 Unit 3
overhaul ['əuvəhɔːl] v. 分解检查；追上并超过 Unit 5
overlook [ˌəuvə'luk] v. fail to notice 忽略 Unit 7
overwhelming [ˌəuvə'welmɪŋ] adj. 强大的；势不可挡的 Unit 2
overthrow ['əuvəθrəu] v. cause the downfall of rulers 推翻 Unit 4
overture ['əuvetʃue (r)] n. orchestral music played at the beginning of an opera 前奏曲；序幕 Unit 8

P

pagan ['peɪɡən] n. 异教徒；非基督教徒 Unit 1
palm [pɔːm] n. 棕榈树 Unit 6
parade [pə'reɪd] n. a ceremonial procession including people marching 游行；检阅 Unit 11
parallel ['pærəlel] adj. 平行的 Unit 1
paralysis [pə'rælɪsɪs] n. 麻痹；瘫痪 Unit 4
parasite ['pærəsaɪt] n. 依赖他人为生；寄生 Unit 2
participate [paː'tɪsɪpeɪt] v. be involved in; share in something 参与；分享 Unit 7
partisan ['paːtɪzn] adj. devoted to a cause or party 党派的；偏袒的 Unit 3
patrimony ['pætrɪməni] n. 遗产；教会财产 Unit 1
pay off 付清；偿清 Unit 4
perennial [pə'reniəl] adj. lasting three seasons or more 常年的；四季不断

Appendix III

的 Unit 2
perspective [pə'spektɪv] n. point of view; future 观点；想法；前景 Unit 3
pervading [pə:'veɪdɪŋ] adj. spreading through 普遍的 Unit 6
pharaoh ['feərəu] n. the title of the ancient Egyptian kings 法老；暴君
　　Unit 9
pharmacy ['fa:məsɪ] n. a shop that sells medicines and drugs 药房；药店
　　Unit 4
photogenic [ˌfəutəu'dʒenɪk] adj. 易上镜的 Unit 2
pilgrim ['pɪlgrɪm] n. 朝圣者 Unit 1
pitch [pɪtʃ] v. to throw sb./sth. with force 用力扔；投；抛 Unit 4
pitch [pɪtʃ] n. the property of sound that varies with variation in the frequency of vibration 音高 Unit 8
platform ['plætfɔ:m] n. a raised horizontal surface 平台；讲台 Unit 3
plausible ['plɔ:zəbl] adj. reasonable and likely to be true 有道理的；可信的
　　Unit 4
play an important role in 在…中起重要作用 Unit 1
plethora ['pleθərə] n. an amount that is greater than is needed 过多；过剩
　　Unit 4
political [pə'lɪtɪkəl] adj. relating to the way power is achieved and used 政治的 Unit 12
polyphony [pə'lɪfənɪ] n. 复调；复调音乐；多音 Unit 8
positively ['pɒzətɪvlɪ] adv. extremely 肯定地；明确地；断然地 Unit 6
potency ['pəutnsɪ] n. capacity to produce strong physiological or chemical effects 效能；力量；潜力 Unit 10
pottery ['pɒtərɪ] n. the craft of making earthenware 陶器 Unit 1
practically ['præktɪk(ə)l] adv. almost; nearly 实际地；几乎；事实上
　　Unit 10
predominance [prɪ'dɒmɪnəns] n. 优势；主导地位 Unit 8
predominant [prɪ'dɒmɪnənt] adj. most frequent or common 主要的；卓越的
　　Unit 10
predominantly [prɪ'dɒmɪnəntlɪ] adv. much greater in number or influence 主要地；显著地 Unit 9
prejudice ['predʒudɪs] n. 偏见；歧视 Unit 7
prescribe [prɪ'skraɪb] v. issue commands or orders for 指定；规定　vi. 建

Mysterious Arab Countries
神秘的阿拉伯

立规定；开处方 Unit 8

presence ['prezəns] n. the state of being present, current existence 存在；出席 Unit 2

present ['prezənt] adj. being or existing in a specified place 出席的；在场的 Unit 7

presentation [prezn'teɪʃn] n. 报告；外观 Unit 3

preservation [prezə'veʃn] n. the activity of protecting something from loss or danger 保存；保留 Unit 7

preside [prɪ'zaɪd] vi. be in charge of, be the president of (+ over) 主持；指挥 Unit 12

prestige [pre'sti:(d)ʒ] n. 威望；声望 Unit 11

prevalent ['prev(ə)l(ə)nt] adj. 流行的；普遍的；广传的 Unit 10

prior to 早于；优先于 Unit 3

priority [praɪ'ɔrətɪ] n. 优先权；优先考虑的事情 Unit 3

privatization [ˌpraɪvətaɪ'zeɪʃn] n. 私有化 Unit 4

probe [prəub] v. question or examine thoroughly and closely 探索；调查 Unit 13

professional [prə'feʃnl] adj. 职业的；专业的 Unit 3

proffer ['prɔfə] v. offer or give 提供；供给 Unit 4

proficiency [prə'fɪʃnsɪ] n. 熟练；精通 Unit 3

prominent ['prɔmɪnənt] adj. 突出的；显著的；杰出的 Unit 10

propaganda [prɔpə'gændə] n. 宣传；宣传内容 Unit 3

prophesy ['prɔfɪsaɪ] v. predict or reveal through; deliver a sermon 预言；预告 Unit 2

proportion [prə'pɔʃən] n. a part or share of a whole 部分；份额 Unit 4

props [prɔps] n. 小道具 Unit 7

provide with 提供；供应 Unit 4

proxy ['prɔksɪ] adj. 代理的 Unit 3

purchase ['pə:tʃəs] v. buy 购买 Unit 3

pursue [pə'sju:] v. carry out or participate in an activity; be involved in 继续；从事 Unit 13

push up 推升 Unit 4

put… to the side 把…放在一边 Unit 3

pyramidal [pɪ'ræmɪdəl] adj. 金字塔形的；锥形的 Unit 2

Q

query ['kwɪərɪ] v. pose a question 质疑；对⋯表示怀疑　　Unit 13
quest for 追求；探索；设法找到　　Unit 12
queue ['kju:] n. 队，行列　　Unit 4
quintile ['kwɪntail] n. 五分之一　　Unit 5

R

radically ['rædɪkəlɪ] adv. very important and great in degree 根本地；彻底地　　Unit 2
raise [reɪz] v. cause to be heard or known; express or utter 提出；引起　　Unit 3
rascally ['ræskəlɪ] adj. 无赖的；坏蛋的　　Unit 4
ration ['ræʃn] v. restrict the consumption of a relatively scarce commodity 限量供应；配给供应　　Unit 4
reap [ri:p] v. gather, as of natural products 收获；获得；收割　　Unit 9
recede [rɪ'si:d] v. pull back or move away or backward 后退；减弱　　Unit 5
recede into 后退；衰退　　Unit 5
regard⋯as 把⋯认作　　Unit 11
regime [reɪ'ʒi:m] n. a particular system of government 政治制度；政权；政体　　Unit 3
region ['ri:dʒ(ə)n] n. the extended spatial location of something 地区；区域　　Unit 10
register ['redʒɪstə] v. record in writing 登记；注册；记录　　Unit 11
regulate ['reɡjuleɪt] v. adjust, shape or influence; give direction to 调整；管理；控制　　Unit 3
renown [rɪ'naʊn] n. the state or quality of being widely honored and acclaimed 声誉；名望　　Unit 13
repertoire ['repətwa:] n. 全部节目　　Unit 8
replace [rɪ'pleɪs] v. take the place or move into the position of 取代；代替　　Unit 3
represent [,reprɪ'zent] v. be representative or typical for 变现；表示；代表　　Unit 3
reputation [repju'teɪʃ(ə)n] n. the state of being held in high esteem and

Mysterious Arab Countries
神秘的阿拉伯

honor 名声　　　　　　　　　　　　　　　　　　　　　Unit 12
resort [rɪˈzɔːt] n. 度假胜地；求助对象　　　　　　　　　Unit 13
vi. have recourse to 求助；诉诸；采取某手段或方法（…to） Unit 13
retain [reˈteɪn] v. keep or remember 保持；记住　　　　Unit 8
retreat [rɪˈtriːt] v. move away from something or someone. 退出；离开
　　　　　　　　　　　　　　　　　　　　　　　　　　Unit 12
retroactively [retrəuˈæktɪvlɪ] adv. 追溯地；逆动地　　　Unit 4
respective [rɪˈspektɪv] adj. considered individually 分别的；各自的 Unit 3
reservoir [ˈrezəvwaː] n. a large or extra supply of something 水库；蓄水池
　　　　　　　　　　　　　　　　　　　　　　　　　　Unit 2
restriction [rɪˈstrɪkʃn] n. a principle that limits the extent of something 限
　　制；约束　　　　　　　　　　　　　　　　　　　　Unit 3
revenue [ˈrevənjuː] n. government income （国家的）岁入；税收 Unit 1
revive [rɪˈvaɪv] v. becomes active, popular, or successful again 使振奋；复
　　原；使再生　　　　　　　　　　　　　　　　　　　Unit 12
revolve around 围绕　　　　　　　　　　　　　　　　Unit 3
revolutionary [revəˈljuːʃənrɪ] n. a radical supporter of political or social
　　revolution 革命者　　　　　　　　　　　　　　　　Unit 12
rippling [ˈrɪplɪŋ] adj. having a small wave on the surface of a liquid 使起涟
　　漪；呈波状起伏　　　　　　　　　　　　　　　　　Unit 6
rise to 上升到；升迁　　　　　　　　　　　　　　　　Unit 5
ritual [ˈrɪtʃuəl] n. any customary observance or practice 仪式；惯例；礼制
　　　　　　　　　　　　　　　　　　　　　　　　　　Unit 11
ritualized [ˈrɪtjuəlaɪzd] adj. making or evolving into a ritual rather than
　　natural 仪式化的　　　　　　　　　　　　　　　　 Unit 7
roam [rəum] v. walk about without any fixed plan or purpose 漫游；闲逛；
　　徜徉　　　　　　　　　　　　　　　　　　　　　　Unit 1
roiling [ˈrɔɪlɪŋ] adj. rough and confused 不安的；混乱的　Unit 2
ruthless [ˈruːθlɪs] adj. harsh or cruel 残酷的　　　　　　Unit 12
rural [ˈruərəl] adj. relating to rural areas 农村的；乡下的　Unit 11

S

sacrifice [ˈsækrɪfaɪs] v. endure the loss of 牺牲；献祭　n. a loss entailed
　　by giving up 牺牲；祭品　　　　　　　　　　　　　Unit 10

safari [səˈfɑːrɪ] n. an overland journey by hunters (especially in Africa) 旅行队 　　Unit 6
safeguard against 防范；预防 　　Unit 5
salient [ˈseɪlɪənt] adj. the most important or outstanding 最突出的 　　Unit 2
sarcastic [sɑːˈkʌztɪk] adj. 挖苦的；尖刻的；辛辣的 　　Unit 13
satellite [ˈsætlaɪt] n. 卫星；人造卫星 　　Unit 3
savage [ˈsævɪdʒ] adj. extremely cruel, violent, and uncontrolled 野蛮的；凶猛的 　　Unit 2
scanty [ˈskæntɪ] adj. lacking in quantity 不足的；勉强够的 　　Unit 2
scarf [skɑːf] n. 围巾；嵌接；头巾领巾 　　Unit 9
scrubland [ˈskrʌblənd] n. an uncultivated region covered with scrub vegetation 灌木丛林地 　　Unit 1
scruffy [ˈskrʌfɪ] adj. dirty and messy 脏乱的 　　Unit 12
season [ˈsiːzən] v. lend flavor to 给…调味；使适应 　　Unit 13
seek after 寻求；追求 　　Unit 1
seminal [ˈseminl] adj. containing seeds of later development 升值的 　　Unit 13
seminar [ˈsemɪnɑː] n. 进修班；研讨会 　　Unit 7
semitone [ˈsemɪtɔn] n. 半音程；半级音 　　Unit 8
sensuous [ˈsensjuəs] adj. 感觉上的；给人快感的 　　Unit 7
separate [ˈsepəreɪt] adj. independent; not United or joint 单独的；分开的 　　Unit 6
set up 建立；安排 　　Unit 11
settlement [ˈsetlmənt] n. a commUnity of people smaller than a town 定居点 　　Unit 1
settler [ˈsetlə] n. a person who settles in a new place or moves into new country 移居者；定居者 　　Unit 2
share with 共享 　　Unit 12
shape up 开始形成；顺利发展 　　Unit 2
sheikh [ʃeɪk] n. 族长；酋长 　　Unit 1
sheikdom [ˈʃeɪkdəm] n. （阿拉伯）酋长统辖的领土；酋长国 　　Unit 2
sherbet [ˈʃɔːbət] n. 冰冻果子露 　　Unit 11
shimmy [ˈʃɪmɪ] n. lively dancing with much shaking of the shoulders and hips 摇动 　　Unit 7

Mysterious Arab Countries
神秘的阿拉伯

ship [ʃɪp] v. transport commercially; go on board 装运；（用船）运送
Unit 1
show off 炫耀；卖弄 Unit 11
shrewd [ʃru:d] adj. 精明的；机灵的 Unit 6
significance [sɪɡ'nɪfɪkəns] n. the quality of being significant 意义；重要性
Unit 2
singular ['sɪŋɡjələ] adj. 单数的；单一的；非凡的 v. lie obliquely 使倾斜；使倾向于 Unit 13
skin [skɪn] v. to take the skin off an animal, a fruit or a vegetable; cheat 剥皮；欺骗 Unit 4
skyline ['skaɪlaɪn] n. the outline of objects seen against the sky 地平线；空中轮廓线 Unit 6
slant [slɑ:nt] n. a biased way of looking at or presenting something 倾斜；偏见 Unit 13
slash [slæʃ] v. to reduce sth by a large amount 大幅度削减；大大降低
Unit 4
slick [slɪk] adj. having a smooth, gleaming surface 光滑的；华而不实的
Unit 6
smuggling ['smʌɡlɪŋ] n. 走私（罪） Unit 4
snap ['snæp] v. to grasp hastily or eagerly 抓 Unit 6
snap up 抢购；抢先弄到手 Unit 6
so as to 以便；为了 Unit 5
solid ['sɔlɪd] adj. 固体的；可靠的；结实的；一致的 Unit 13
solidarity [ˌsɔlɪ'dærɪtɪ] n. 团结；团结一致 Unit 12
sophisticated [sə'fɪstɪkeɪtɪd] adj. 老练的；精密的；世故的 Unit 1
sovereign ['sɔvrɪn] adj. independent and not under the authority of any other country 独立自主的 Unit 12
sparse [spɑ:s] adj. small in number or amount, not dense 稀疏的；稀少的
Unit 2
sparsely [spɑ:slɪ] adv. in a sparse manner 稀少地；贫乏地 Unit 1
specialist ['speʃəlɪst] n. an expert who is devoted to one occupation or branch of learning 专家 Unit 13
specialty [speʃətɪ] n. an asset of special worth or utility 专长；特性
Unit 10

spectacular [spekˈtækjulə] adj. sensational in appearance or thrilling in effect 壮观的；惊人的　　　　　　　　　　　　　　　Unit 2
spice [spaɪs] n. 调味品；香料　　　　　　　　　　　Unit 1
sprawl [sprɔ:l] n. a continuous network of urban commUnities 蔓延；伸开手足躺；无计划地扩展　　　　　　　　　　　　　　　Unit 6
spring up 如雨后春笋般涌现　　　　　　　　　　　Unit 6
sprout [ˈspraut] v. put forth and grow sprouts or shoots 萌芽；迅速成长
　　　　　　　　　　　　　　　　　　　　　　　　Unit 3
sprout up 突然出现　　　　　　　　　　　　　　　Unit 3
spun into 纺成　　　　　　　　　　　　　　　　　Unit 9
staple [steɪpl] n. 主要的（食物、活动）　　　　　Unit 10
starch [sta:tʃ] n. 淀粉　　　　　　　　　　　　　Unit 9
statehood [ˈsteɪthud] n. the condition of being an independent state or nation 独立国家地位　　　　　　　　　　　　　　　　　Unit 12
status quo [ˌstətɪsˈkwəu] n. the existing state of affairs 现状　　Unit 3
stem [stem] v. to stop sth that is flowing from spreading or increasing 阻止；遏止　　　　　　　　　　　　　　　　　　　Unit 4
stern [stə:n] adj. severe 严厉的；严峻的　　　　　Unit 2
stew [stju:] v. be in a huff, be silent or sullen 炖；炖汤；焖　Unit 10
stick to 坚持　　　　　　　　　　　　　　　　　Unit 8
stir [stə:] v. move very slightly 搅拌；激起；惹起　Unit 13
stretch [stretʃ] v. extend to a greater or the full length 伸展；张开　Unit 7
stringent [ˈstrɪndʒənt] v. severe or strictly controlled 严格的；迫切的
　　　　　　　　　　　　　　　　　　　　　　　　Unit 4
stuff [stʌf] v. fill with something until it's full or eat a lot of things 填满；吃饱　　　　　　　　　　　　　　　　　　　Unit 11
stump up 掏腰包；付清　　　　　　　　　　　　　Unit 4
stylistically [staɪˈlɪstɪklɪ] adv. in a rhetorically stylistic manner 在文体上
　　　　　　　　　　　　　　　　　　　　　　　　Unit 8
submarine [ˈsʌbməri:n] n. 潜水艇　　　　　　　　Unit 6
subscribe [səbˈskraɪb] v. adopt as a belief 赞成；签署　Unit 7
subsequently [ˈsʌbsɪkwəntlɪ] adv. 随后；其后；后来　Unit 8
subsidiary [səbˈsɪdɪərɪ] n. furnishing added support 子公司；辅助者　Unit 6
subsidy [ˈsʌbsədɪ] n. 津贴；补助　　　　　　　　　Unit 4

substantial [sʌbˈstæʃl] adj. fairly large or essential 大量的；重大的
Unit 10
successive [səkˈsesɪv] adj. in regular succession without gaps 连续的；相继的
Unit 2
suite [swiːt] n. a musical composition of several movements only loosely connected 组曲；套件
Unit 8
summative [ˈsʌmətɪv] adj. of or relating to a summation 总结的；总结性的
Unit 5
sumptuous [ˈsʌmptjuəs] adj. rich and superior in quality 华丽的；奢侈的
Unit 8
supervise [ˈsjuːpəvaɪz] v. watch and direct 监督；指导；管理
Unit 5
supplement with 用…增补
Unit 9
supreme [sjuˈpriːm] adj. greatest in status or authority or power 最高的；至高的
Unit 5
suras [vsuərə] n. one of the sections (or chapters) in the Koran 节；章
Unit 8
surge [səːdʒ] n. a sudden large increase in something that has previously been steady 激增
Unit 12
surmount [səˈmaunt] v. get on top of; deal with successfully 克服；越过；战胜
Unit 8
surrealistic [səˌrɪəˈlɪstɪk] adj. 超现实主义的
Unit 2
suspicion [səˈspɪʃn] n. doubt about someone's honesty 猜疑；怀疑 Unit 1
sustainability [səˈsteɪnəbɪlətɪ] n. the property of being sustainable 持久性；持续
Unit 6
swamp [swɔmp] v. fill up with water; be hard to deal with 使淹没；使疲于应对
Unit 4
sympathy [ˈsɪmpəθɪ] n. (capacity for) sharing the feelings of others 同情；同情心
Unit 3

T

tabbouleh [təˈbuːl] n. 塔博勒色拉（一种黎巴嫩生菜） Unit 10
tackle [ˈtækl] v. to deal with a difficult problem or situation 应付；处理；解决（难题或局面）
Unit 4
tackle with 处理；解决
Unit 5

Appendix III

tactic ['tæktɪk] n. a plan or measure for attaining a particular goal 策略；手段 Unit 4
take a step toward 朝着…前进 Unit 12
take…for example 以…为例 Unit 6
take interest in 对…感兴趣 Unit 3
take the place of 代替 Unit 2
take over 接管；被接手 Unit 1
take place 发生；举行 Unit 11
take shape 形成；成型 Unit 1
talk up 热烈讨论 Unit 4
target ['tɑ:gɪt] n. 目标，靶子 v. 把…作为目标；瞄准 Unit 13
tattooist [tə'tu:ɪst] n. 有纹身的人 Unit 6
temperament ['tempərəmənt] n. 性情；性格 Unit 8
temperature ['tempərɪtʃə] n. the somatic sensation of cold or heat 温度 Unit 6
terrain [te'reɪn] n. a piece of ground having specific characteristics 地形；地势；领域 Unit 2
terrorist ['terərɪst] n. a radical who employs terror as a political weapon 恐怖主义者；恐怖分子 Unit 12
tertiary ['tə:ʃərɪ] n. 第三纪；第三修道会会员 Unit 5
textured ['tekstʃəd] adj. 有织纹的 Unit 2
the rest of 其余的；剩下的 Unit 6
theatrical [θɪ'ætrɪkl] adj. 1. of or relating to the theater 戏剧性的 Unit 7
throttle ['θrɒtl] v. 扼死；勒死 Unit 4
throughout [θru:'aʊt] adv. from first to last 自始至终；到处；全部 Unit 10
throw down 丢下 Unit 6
thwart [θwɔ:t] v. hinder or prevent (the efforts, plans, or desires) of 反对；阻碍 Unit 3
thyme [taɪm] n.（用以调味的）百里香（草） Unit 10
tier [tɪə] n. a relative position or degree 等级；层；列 Unit 5
toil [tɔɪl] v. work hard 辛苦工作；费力地做 Unit 6
tomb [tu:m] n. 坟墓；死亡 Unit 9
torrent ['tɒrənt] n. a heavy rain or a fast stream of water 奔流；急流 Unit 2

Mysterious Arab Countries
神秘的阿拉伯

tonal ['təunəl] adj. 音调的 　　　　　　　　　　　　　　Unit 8
torso ['tɔ:səu] n. 躯干 　　　　　　　　　　　　　　　　Unit 7
toss [tɔs, tɔ:s] v. throw or toss with a light motion 投掷；与…掷币打赌
　　　　　　　　　　　　　　　　　　　　　　　　　　　Unit 11
traitor ['treɪtə] n. 叛徒；卖国贼；背信弃义人 　　　　　　Unit 12
treacherous ['tretʃərəs] adj. dangerous and unpredictable 变化无常的；危险的 　　　　　　　　　　　　　　　　　　　　　　　　Unit 2
Trad [træd] n. traditional jazz as revived in the 1950s 传统主义　Unit 9
trace [treɪs] v. to go back over again 追溯（由来）；上溯；回溯　Unit 1
trace [treɪs] n. a just detectable amount 痕迹；踪迹；微量 　Unit 9
tranquil ['træŋkwɪl] adj. calm and peaceful 安静的；宁静的 　Unit 2
transition [træn'siʃən] n. the act of passing from one state or place to the next 过渡；转变；转换 　　　　　　　　　　　　Unit 12
trek [trek] v. make a long and difficult journey 艰苦跋涉 　Unit 6
tremendous [trɪ'mendəs] adj. extraordinarily large 极大的；巨大的　Unit 2
triangular [traɪ'æɡjulə] adj. 三角的；[数] 三角形的 　　　Unit 9
triumph ['traɪʌmf] n. a successful ending of a struggle or contest or victory 胜利；成就 　　　　　　　　　　　　　　　　　Unit 12
tropical ['trɔpɪkl] adj. 热带的 　　　　　　　　　　　　　Unit 2
troupe [tru:p] n. 剧团 　　　　　　　　　　　　　　　　　Unit 7
turmoil ['tə:mɔɪl] n. a violent disturbance 混乱；骚动 　　Unit 1
turbulent ['tə:bjələnt] adj. characterized by unrest or disorder 汹涌的；湍急的 　　　　　　　　　　　　　　　　　　　　　　　Unit 2
turmoil ['tə:mɔɪl] n. a state of great anxiety and confusion 动乱；骚动；混乱 　　　　　　　　　　　　　　　　　　　　　　　　Unit 4
tumble [tʌmbl] v. fall down as if collapsing 使跌倒；暴跌　Unit 4
tuxedo [tʌk'si:dəu] n. semiformal evening dress for men 男士无尾半正式晚礼服 　　　　　　　　　　　　　　　　　　　　　　Unit 11

U

ubiquitous [ju:'bɪkwɪtəs] adj. being present everywhere at once 普遍存在的；无所不在的 　　　　　　　　　　　　　　　　　Unit 10
unabashed [ʌnə'bæʃt] adj. not embarrassed 不害羞的；不畏惧的　Unit 6

Appendix III

underlying [ˌʌndəˈlaɪɪŋ] adj. located beneath or below 潜在的；在下面的
Unit 13

undulation [ˌʌndjuˈleɪʃn] n. a gentle rising and falling in the manner of waves 波动；起伏
Unit 7

uninhabitable [ˌʌnɪnˈhæbɪtəbl] adj. not fit for people to live 不适宜居住的
Unit 1

universal [ˌjuːnɪˈvɜːsl] adj. of worldwide scope or applicability 普遍的；全世界的
Unit 10

unpredictable [ˌʌnˈprɪdɪktəbl] adj. impossible to foretell or unknown in advance 不可预测的
Unit 2

unrelenting [ˌʌnrɪˈlentɪŋ] adj. without caring whether to hurt or embarrass others 无情的；不屈不挠的
Unit 12

unrest [ʌnˈrest] n. 动荡；动乱；骚动
Unit 4

utensil [juːˈtensl] n. an implement for practical use (especially in a household) 器具；器皿；用具
Unit 10

utilize [ˈjuːtəlaɪz] v. put into service 使用；利用
Unit 3

V

vanish [ˈvænɪʃ] v. get lost, especially without warning or explanation; become invisible 突然不见
Unit 1

variation [ˌveərɪˈeɪʃn] n. an instance of change 变化；（生物）变异；变种
Unit 8

varieties of 各种各样的
Unit 10

venue [ˈvenjuː] n. the scene of any event or action 地点
Unit 7

versus [ˈvɜːsəs] prep. in the teeth of 与…相对；对抗
Unit 6

vertical [ˈvɜːtɪkəl] n. 垂直线；垂直面 adj. 垂直的；直立的
Unit 9

vertical looms 垂直织机
Unit 9

vicious [ˈvɪʃəs] adj. violent and cruel 凶猛的；残暴的
Unit 2

vocational [vəʊˈkɪʃənl] adj. 职业的；行业的
Unit 5

vogue [vəʊg] n. fashion 时尚；流行
Unit 7

volume [ˈvɒljuːm] n. 卷；大量；册
Unit 13

W

wheat [wi:t] n. 小麦；小麦色 　　　　　　　　　　　　　　Unit 10

whitish ['waɪtɪʃ] adj. resembling milk in color or cloudiness; not clear 带白色的；发白的 　　　　　　　　　　　　　　Unit 9

wilderness ['wɪldənəs] n. a wild and uninhabited area 荒野；荒漠 　Unit 2

with the exception of 除了 　　　　　　　　　　　　　　Unit 2

with regard to 关于；至于 　　　　　　　　　　　　　　Unit 3

with the support of 在…支持下；有了…的支持 　　　　　　Unit 1

wither ['wɪθə(r)] v. dry up, become weak and die 凋谢；衰弱；萎缩 　　　　　　　　　　　　　　Unit 4

Y

yield [ji:ld] vi. be the cause or source of 屈服；投降；给出，产出 Unit 9

图书在版编目（CIP）数据

神秘的阿拉伯＝Mysterious Arab Countries：英汉对照/姜克银，季春燕编．—北京：时事出版社，2019.6
ISBN 978-7-5195-0306-2

Ⅰ.①神⋯　Ⅱ.①姜⋯②季⋯　Ⅲ.①阿拉伯国家—概况—英、汉　Ⅳ.①K937.1

中国版本图书馆 CIP 数据核字（2019）第 054102 号

出 版 发 行：时事出版社
地　　　址：北京市海淀区万寿寺甲 2 号
邮　　　编：100081
发 行 热 线：（010）88547590　88547591
读者服务部：（010）88547595
传　　　真：（010）88547592
电 子 邮 箱：shishichubanshe@sina.com
网　　　址：www.shishishe.com
印　　　刷：北京旺都印务有限公司

开本：787×1092　1/16　印张：19　字数：321 千字
2019 年 6 月第 1 版　2019 年 6 月第 1 次印刷
定价：118.00 元

（如有印装质量问题，请与本社发行部联系调换）